How Social Movements (Sometimes) Matter

To Zena, Jean, and their generation, who will remake the world.

And to Bill Gamson, who always reminded me of that fact.

How Social Movements (Sometimes) Matter

DAVID S. MEYER

polity

First published in 2021 by Polity Press

Polity Press
65 Bridge Street
Cambridge CB2 1UR, UK

Polity Press
101 Station Landing
Suite 300
Medford, MA 02155, USA

ISBN-13: 978-0-7456-9684-3
ISBN-13: 978-0-7456-9685-0(pb)

A catalogue record for this book is available from the British Library.

Typeset in 11 on 14 Sabon
by Fakenham Prepress Solutions, Fakenham, Norfolk NR21 8NL
Printed and bound in Great Britain by TJ Books Ltd

The publisher has used its best endeavours to ensure that the URLs for external websites referred to in this book are correct and active at the time of going to press. However, the publisher has no responsibility for the websites and can make no guarantee that a site will remain live or that the content is or will remain appropriate.

Every effort has been made to trace all copyright holders, but if any have been overlooked the publisher will be pleased to include any necessary credits in any subsequent reprint or edition.

For further information on Polity, visit our website: politybooks.com

Contents

Acknowledgments

I have worked to understand the issues covered in this book over the years at the University of California, Irvine. I have had the good fortune to teach a graduate course on social movements, often with Dave Snow, who always helped me figure out when I was wrong in initial guesses – which was often. I also often taught an undergraduate course on protest politics, where I learned a lot from working with Kelsy Kretschmer, Erin Evans, and Megan Brooker, all creative and committed teachers. I am also very grateful for the good research assistance offered by Katelyn Malae.

I learned a great deal from collaborators on various research projects over the years, including Eitan Alimi, Vince Boudreau, Kaylin Bourdon, Steve Boutcher, Megan Brooker, Catherine Corrigall-Brown, Kris Coulter, Erin Evans, Kelsy Kretschmer, Eulalie Laschever, Lisa Leitz, Lindsey Lupo, Alex Maresca, Deb Minkoff, Nhu-Ngoc T. Ong, Christine Petit, Amanda Pullum, Ellen Reese, Daisy Verduzco Reyes, Rottem Sagi, Suzanne Staggenborg, Sid Tarrow, Nella van Dyke, and Nancy Whittier.

And I'm particularly grateful to my family, Margaret Coutts, Zena Meyer, and Jean Meyer, who continue to offer constant challenges wrapped in encouragement.

Introduction

People protest in all kinds of ways and for all sorts of reasons: they protest because they're disappointed or angry; they protest because they want to connect with others who share their views; they protest because someone invited them. Most importantly, they protest because they want to have an impact on the world around them. They want to make the world better – or at least stop it from getting worse. This book is about how and why protest *sometimes* works. These are questions of critical importance in modern life, and ones people who protest and those who watch them are asking more and more.

An example: On the January day that Donald Trump took the oath of office for the American presidency, thousands of frustrated protesters staged a wide variety of events. Gay and lesbian activists staged a Queer Dance party outside incoming Vice President Mike Pence's residence featuring a variety of music, costumes, flags, and a lot of glitter. More aggressively, hundreds of DisruptJ20 protesters launched unpermitted marches through the streets of Washington, DC, protesting US foreign policy, inequality, and discrimination. The demonstrators certainly had grievances with the incoming Trump administration, but importantly, planning for the demonstration had begun in July 2016, when it appeared that Hillary Clinton was sure to win.

As announced on an organizing site: "DisruptJ20 rejects

all forms of domination and oppression, particularly those based on racism, poverty, gender, and sexuality, organizes by consensus, and embraces a diversity of tactics."[1] Organizers emphasized urgency and tactics rather than issues, proclaiming their ideological and tactical diversity, while promising not to help law enforcement maintain public order. A few worked hard to disrupt public order, using bricks to break the windows of a limousine and several storefronts, including the entrances to a Starbuck's and a Bank of America. Police arrested more than 200 people for being in the streets amid the destruction, and the federal government lodged harsh felony charges for conspiracy to riot that could have resulted in decades in prison.[2]

The day after the inauguration and the DisruptJ20 events, much larger groups staged a Women's March in Washington, with hundreds of thousands filling the national mall, and a much larger number animating sister marches across the country and around the world. Millions protested, and although they expressed many grievances, there was a unified focus on the unsuitability of Donald Trump as president of the United States.

Protesters could take some comfort in their commitment, their solidarity, their numbers, and their acumen in organizing such a large set of events so quickly. But Donald Trump didn't resign, and immediately set about executing some of the policies that he campaigned on, policies that protesters found abhorrent. Does that mean that the various protests during the inaugural weekend were futile?

I start with an example from the United States because, as an American, I see them close up, sometimes in person, but more often in books and articles, and I hear stories told in classrooms. I see the impact of social movements in American history, and I understand the context in which they developed.

As we work through this book, there will be more stories about social movements in the United States than in other settings, but I will show how the processes that we see in play can be translated to understand the politics of protest elsewhere, providing examples from social movements in very different contexts.

Protests against authority are hardly limited to the United States. In just the last few years, organized protests against authorities have erupted around the world. In Turkey, Iran, and Russia, recurrent campaigns for democratic reforms have dogged authoritarian leaders. Activists deployed umbrellas as a symbol of their commitment to democracy in Hong Kong. Citizens filled the streets in Tunisia, protesting against the cost of living and the government's austerity policies – and this government had come to office in response to another set of protests in the Arab Spring movements just a few years earlier. Activists have lodged anti-austerity protests against left, right, and centrist governments in Greece since 2011, and Europe has been racked with disruptive protests targeting immigrants and immigration policy. Mass movements have surged in the capital cities of Thailand, Belarus, and Lebanon, in response to crises, political and otherwise. These protesters everywhere turn out because they see the failure or futility of more conventional political actions, and they think there's at least a chance that protests might work.

But protests haven't been limited to efforts to mount anti-systemic campaigns. Protesters routinely turn out to support or prevent changes in policy, sometimes in colorful and creative ways: Five scantily clad women representing People for the Ethical Treatment of Animals (PETA), and costumed as animals, marched outside a fashion show in Sydney, Australia, calling for animal rights.[3] Actress Lucy Lawless, best known inhabiting the title role in *Xena: Warrior Princess*, brought global attention to an international group of environmental activists determined to challenge Norway's efforts to search for new oil reserves in the Barents Sea. The activists boarded small rubber boats to block the path of much larger ships heading off on their exploration.[4] An estimated 50,000 people marched in London to protest the United Kingdom's planned exit from the European Union, a decision taken by referendum a year earlier.[5] All these protests are dramatic moments in larger sustained movements animated by people who want to change the world.

Social movements of all kinds and sizes campaign for an extremely diverse array of goals: against hikes in university tuition, austere budget policies, taxes, corruption, immigration, and carbon emissions – to name only a few recent issues. In much of the world, social movements have grown into a virtually permanent presence in mainstream politics, often supported by state subsidies or tax preferences. National and transnational groups concerned with the environment or human rights advocate for their visions of justice, sometimes engaging in mass politics.

These are only a sampling of relatively recent examples of mass movements attempting to step into the political fray, redress wrongs, and change the world. When you read this, you will be able to find stories of even more recent protests and campaigns that are just as odd, interesting, appalling, or inspiring. There's an excitement and a romance associated with regular people trying to step into history and change the world, but do their efforts matter? Would people turn out to protest if they thought they couldn't make a difference?

Sometimes, they do.

We tell stories about movements that seem to play a critical role in affecting change. Gandhi's Salt March is part of the Indian Independence movement's success story. Similarly,

Lech Walesa's leadership of the Solidarity movement in Poland during the Cold War is seen as a critical factor in the end of Communism, democratization of Poland, and the end of the Soviet Union. In the United States, schoolchildren learn to celebrate historic protest moments, including the Boston Tea Party and the 1963 March on Washington, and their impact on making the United States what it became. But those histories often pull the moments out of the context of the larger movements of which they were a part.

Politicians and political activists certainly act as if social movements might matter, and scholars have been trying, for the better part of at least four decades, to figure out why, when, and how. Although we know more than we did previously, discussions about the origins and influences of social movements frequently retreat into competitive assertions about what mattered and what was irrelevant. Obviously, people who talk about social movements in general, and even more so, about particular social movements, often have a strong stake in valorizing or vilifying them. People often react to movements by creating heroes or villains. And the question of potential effectiveness is generally the most important criterion in evaluating a movement. Courageous heroes broker sacrifices that could lead to political influence; misguided misanthropes act out when it doesn't matter.

Our histories show that protests can matter a great deal, but not by themselves, and often not in ways activists intend. When King George III learned that colonists had dressed as Indians to throw discounted tea into the Boston Harbor, one of many acts of resistance, he saw his empire unraveling and responded harshly. Repression spurred further protests – and ultimately, America. It wasn't the Tea Party by itself that made the American revolution successful; rather, the events one night at Boston Harbor were part of a much longer, larger, and more complicated process that included other protests, armed conflict, speeches and pamphlets, and more mainstream politics in the colonies and England. Although throwing crates of tea off a ship makes for a dramatic story, it is only by putting that protest in a larger context that we can understand how movements really matter.

In this book, we'll see how protest movements *sometimes* work to influence politics, policy, and culture, and show how a protest in the streets can translate into something more than an afternoon's entertainment. We will also see the numerous contingencies involved in movement politics, as well as the necessities of alliances within government and mainstream politics.

It's crucial to understand that protests can best be understood as part of a larger social and political process, and that mainstream politics provides obstacles for organizers to navigate and tools that they can use to increase their influence in a variety of ways. Social protests change the world, but they can't do it by themselves; they depend upon mobilizing others to act on their behalf, and activists have little control over the ultimate outcomes of their efforts.

Here's the argument: When people protest, they tell authorities that they're unhappy about something and, often implicitly, threaten to do more than protest: vote, contribute money, lobby, set up a picket, blockade a road, or try to blow up a building, in hopes of getting what they want. Opponents and allies in government make judgments about how strong and widely held demonstrators' grievances are, and respond, sometimes with concessions and reforms, sometimes with harsh repression, and sometimes with a mix of both. Social movement activists react to those responses, often starting a chain of events that produces something far different than anyone initially imagines.

We make a mistake when we imagine the outcomes of a social movement to be determined solely by the battle between organized activists and their opponents, focusing exclusively on the moral passion, organization, or tactics of the movement. It's critical to examine social movement activism in a larger context that includes more conventional political efforts that activists provoke or encourage.

Demonstrators can stiffen the spine of would-be allies in government, suggesting there might be advantages in pressing for new positions on climate change, abortion, or gay marriage. (Politicians and other leaders often use social movements to "force" them to do what they want anyway.) No savvy politician will admit to changing direction in response to demonstrations in the street, but of course, it happens all the time.

When activists make progress, it's always less than what they want. The antiwar movement in the Vietnam era ultimately ended the draft, but the war dragged on. Immigrant rights and anti-immigration demonstrators stopped their opponents in 2005, battling to a stalemate that frustrated everyone. (Across Europe, advocates of immigration rights and opponents of immigration have mobilized, linking with allies in government to both welcome and to prohibit new immigrants.) People don't generally take to the streets looking for smaller reforms, but often it's only by asking for more that they get anything at all.

Social movements work through a variety of means, changing the lives and values of those who participate in them, establishing or altering organizations that coordinate them, effecting policy reforms, and influencing norms and culture. Demonstrators also signal to other citizens who might share their views that they are not alone, that things could be otherwise, and that they might be able to do something about it. The large national event that receives coverage in the national papers reflects hundreds of smaller, less-visible actions and meetings in church basements and living rooms around the country, as people develop the temerity to think they can change the world. Sometimes they can.

Here's what's coming:

In chapter 1, we'll explore why movements emerge in the first place. Although saints and psychopaths may be so committed to a cause that they're ready to protest all the time, most people are concerned with the day-to-day business of managing their lives, their work, family, and friendships. Although activists are always trying to promote mobilization on the issues they care about, they only succeed sometimes, by convincing others that protest is possible, necessary, and potentially effective. Because large and powerful movements aren't a constant presence in most societies, we can't understand what works unless we make sense of why those movements only appear sometimes. In fact, the factors that invite or provoke movements also promote social change. Unlike the foolproof recipes offered in a cookbook, the success of different strategic and tactical recipes for action depends upon the context in which they're deployed.

Chapter 2 focuses on movements that attempt to launch revolutions, fighting not only particular policies, but the regime and rules that govern a state. There are far more revolutionary movements than revolutions that actually change a regime and try to overturn the basic rules and structures of power. But even when a movement succeeds in overthrowing and replacing a leader and imposing new structures of government, delivering on the promises of political change is extraordinarily difficult. Revolutionary movements, in which challengers seek to dislodge an oppressive regime through dramatic protest, create dramatic pictures and images that spur the imagination of other activists. Translating the often courageous and moralistic protests in the streets to democratization and ultimate governance, however, is no easy task.

In order to effect influence, activists must mobilize a community beyond themselves, often a community that extends beyond their borders. In this century, new communication technologies allow activists to spread news of their ideas and activities around the world without depending upon mainstream networks. Revolutionary movements depend upon the support – or at least the quiescence – of foreign powers. We'll examine how movements communicate their efforts and their cause beyond their borders. We'll also look at the difficult politics of establishing new regimes, and how the translation of democratic dreams into functioning regimes reflects the networks and efforts that preceded the drama emerging from revolutionary movements.

In chapter 3, we will focus on states with democratic processes in place and functioning political institutions; social movements in those settings generally make narrower claims, using mainstream tactics and allies as well as protest to get what they want. We'll see how grievances create the opportunity for savvy organizers to build broad political coalitions and lodge effective claims. The challenge is that every reform can make it harder to maintain, much less build, a broad and concerned constituency for further change. More generally, government policies set the terms on which activists will challenge governments, and their success in lodging those challenges can undermine their basis for mobilization.

Activists protest when they think it might help them get what they want – and when they think they can't get it any other way. Such decisions are sometimes strategic and well-considered, and sometimes just a matter of habit. Organizers successfully mobilize movements when they can convince people that the issue at hand is urgent, that positive outcomes are possible, and that their efforts could make a difference.

Democratic states are set up to channel discontent through the electoral process. Social movements face difficult choices in engaging in mainstream politics, because it always entails some degree of compromise. Depending upon the electoral structures in place, successful movements sometimes focus on particular candidates, while in other settings they can build protest parties. Social movements can use elections to influence policy by changing officials, that is, throwing the rascals out of office, and by changing minds, by threatening to throw the rascals out.

Social movements, by the popularity of their arguments, or more frequently, the strength of their support, can convince authorities to reexamine and possibly change their policy preferences. Movements can demand a litmus test for their support. Although movement activists promote specific policies – a nuclear freeze, an equal rights amendment, an end to legal abortion, or, more recently, a cap on malpractice awards – their demands are usually so absolute that they do not translate well into policy. (Placards and bumper stickers offer little space for nuanced debate.) Indeed, the clearest message that activists can generally send is NO. These absolutes rarely become policy, but by promoting their programs in stark moral terms, activists place the onus on others to offer alternative policies that are, depending on one's perspective, more moderate or complex. Politicians often use such alternatives to capture or at least defuse social movements.

Chapter 4 provides a closer look at the organizations that promote change in democratic states. Although the stories that we remember about important movements of the past emphasize events, the movements of which they're a part are the result of purposeful organizing. The size, structure, and number of groups vary over time and across different settings, but we need to look at those groups to understand how they launch challenges, and how those challenges affect the groups as well as the larger society. In democratic states, protest movements are coordinated by established organizations that must seek to support themselves as well as advance their claims. Sometimes support can come from the government or political parties; sometimes, it comes from interested parties with their own commitments and agendas. Formal organizations provide a foundation for continued protest and making claims, but they also produce drag on the peak moments of mobilization. The establishment and maintenance of such organizations are outcomes of social movements that define part of institutionalization. The other venue for institutionalization is government. Social movements can build inroads into both the bureaucracy and mainstream politics to continue advancing their interests, often less visibly and more incrementally. We will see how the organizations underpinning social movements reflect and create different institutional structures.

Social movements can alter not only the substance of policy, but also how policy is made. Governments often create new institutions such as departments and agencies in response to activists' demands. Governments grow as they create bureaus for arms control, women, the environment, refugees, or civil rights. These offices become permanent institutional venues for responding to a set of issues and constituencies, even as those issues or constituencies first became visible through protest in the streets. Although these offices do not always support activist goals, their very existence represents a permanent institutional concern and a venue for making demands.

Social movements also spawn dedicated organizations that generally survive well after a movement's moment has passed. The environmental movement, for example, firmly established a "big ten" group of national organizations, including the Sierra Club and the World Wildlife Fund, which survive primarily by raising money from self-defined environmentalists.[6] They cultivate donors by monitoring and publicizing government action and environmental conditions, lobbying elected officials and administrators, and occasionally mobilizing their supporters to do something more than mail in their annual membership renewals. Here too, the seemingly permanent establishment of nongovernmental organizations around the world, even if these groups often lose, has fundamentally changed the process of making policy. Salaried officers of the organizations routinely screen high-level appointees to the judiciary and government bureaucracy and testify before legislatures. Mindful of this process, policymakers seek to preempt their arguments by modifying policy – or at least, rhetoric.

In chapter 5, we see how protest movements can change the trajectory of the lives of people who participate in them. Life in a movement can change the way individuals think about themselves, the friends they choose, the work they do, the food they eat, and certainly the way they think about politics. Activists in one movement go on to engage again and again in subsequent movements.

Broader movements also change culture by producing new symbols and values. In addition to changing policies, movements make new cultural productions that affect others who may never have been interest in politics. We can see art, music, and even food reflect particular social movements. Changes in language can become artifacts of a movement, like the honorific "Ms.," created with the express intent of changing the way people think about women and work.

Social movements also change the people who participate in them, educating as well as mobilizing activists. They promote ongoing awareness and action that extends beyond the boundaries of one movement or campaign. Those who turn out at antiwar demonstrations today have often cut their activist teeth mobilizing against globalization, on behalf of labor, for animal rights or against welfare reform. By politicizing communities, connecting people, and promoting personal loyalties, social movements build the infrastructure not only of subsequent movements, but of a democratic civil society more generally.

In chapter 6, we'll look at how we understand the impact and influence of movements. Popular histories tell stories about movements (or omitting movements) that don't necessarily line up with broadly understood facts. We tend to tell event and leader-centered stories that abbreviate the historical process of social change. This is understandable: brave leaders and dramatic events make for a better story than the much more difficult and time-consuming processes of changing the world. Activists have to work to recognize their influence, and then claim credit for it. Because movements never get exactly what they seek, and depend upon a host of outside factors to be influential, it's easy to miss the impact of protest; moreover, the accuracy of a story isn't the only factor that affects the acceptance of a story. A compelling account matters, as does the position of the person telling it. We will look at how the accepted understandings of the movements of the past affect the movements and activist campaigns that emerge in the future.

CHAPTER I

Why Movements Emerge and How They Work

Contemporary visitors to Boston can tour the Boston Tea Party Ships and Museum, and follow a guided tour of "the event that started a Revolution"[1] through a museum of the revolution, educated and entertained by actors who recreate heroic figures from America's War of Independence. The tour ends with visitors mounting the deck of a replica of a colonial-era ship, throwing crates of tea over the side. Because the tour is pedagogical, rather than political, the crates, secured by ropes, don't quite reach the waters of Boston Harbor. The boxes can be quickly retrieved so that the next visitor can enjoy the revolutionary experience.

The event holds an iconic place in American history. In the winter of 1773, colonists opposed to a selectively administered tax on tea – and British rule more generally – assembled by the harbor to stage a political protest. In the midst of his rally speech, rebel organizer Sam Adams signaled his supporters to act. Perhaps a hundred men who came prepared, costumed as Indians, screamed as they boarded the ships and began to throw tea over the side; they were joined by another hundred or so volunteers who had come to watch, but were inspired by the moment. More than 1,000 others watched, cheering the protesters on. Even in the drama of the moment, protesters were careful not to hurt anyone, nor to damage the ships (Griswold 1972).

The Boston Tea Party affected more than the next morning's breakfast. Outraged and threatened, local police arrested and punished a few of the vandals they could find. And in London, Parliament instituted a series of "Coercive Acts," intended to punish the colonists, particularly in Massachusetts. Among other insults, Parliament shut down the Boston Harbor, until the colony could pay for the tea in the sea, imposed direct British rule on the colony, and provided for the quartering of British soldiers in Massachusetts. Patriots called the response "The Intolerable Acts."

In the short run, the Tea Party looked like a bad idea. Colonists had long opposed taxes on tea, and had found a way around them, buying untaxed smuggled tea, some of it shipped by John Hancock, who was already a major political figure in Massachusetts. The tea that ended up in the harbor, which was to be sold by the East India Company, would actually have been sold at discount, even cheaper than the smuggled tea. The tax break offered by the Crown represented Britain's attempt to boost the company's failing fortunes. The protest, which destroyed their goods, didn't help. Meanwhile, tea smugglers, whose businesses were threatened by the cheaper official tea, were among those supporting the Tea Party.

Over a slightly extended time frame, however, the Tea Party further polarized politics in the colonies, increasing pressure on people to take sides. Opposition to the Intolerable Acts created additional protests over the next year, and resistance led to the first Continental Congress, held in Philadelphia the following year. That Congress petitioned King George III to end the Intolerable Acts, declared a boycott of British goods, and scheduled a second Constitutional Congress – just in case the Crown didn't respond to the petition. It didn't. Resistance grew in the colonies, and armed conflict between the British military erupted in the Battles of Lexington and Concord in the

Spring of 1775. Shortly thereafter, the second Constitutional Congress convened, and that Congress eventually endorsed the Declaration of Independence and began to muster an armed resistance. Meanwhile, Thomas Paine (2019) published *Common Sense* in 1776, a series of pamphlets codifying and justifying the case for an independence movement. In this frame, the Tea Party was critical in setting into motion the events that culminated in American independence (Maier 1972).

So, we can tell a relatively coherent story in which the Tea Party was a catalyst for all that followed, including increased repression and provocation from the British, intensified organizing among the colonists both politically and militarily, and the cultivation of a liberal democratic ideology that supported an independence movement. But history didn't begin on that December night in Boston Harbor. The circumstances that give rise to dramatic protest events, and to social movements more generally, also contribute to the broader process of social change.

We might start by acknowledging that European colonization of the United States began more than 150 years before the Boston Tea Party, and the immigrants were mostly people who were unhappy with their lives under British rule. Generations grew up in America, with British governance only a distant force in the background most of the time. The colonists built local governments and businesses, and conducted their own commerce and conflicts with each other and with the Indigenous people already occupying the continent.

The conflicts that led to the Tea Party can be traced back nearly a decade before that dramatic confrontation. In seeking to finance both current wars and debt from previous wars, King George and Parliament sought to extract as much value from their colonies as possible, imposing taxes on virtually anything that might generate revenue, starting with sugar, then adding glass, lead, paints, and paper. Britain imposed taxes on printed materials and imports generally. It also sought to exercise greater control over governance in the colonies, and maintained a large military presence in the New World. Parliament demanded that the colonists build barracks for the British soldiers and, failing that, to house them in stables, inns, and ale houses and, ultimately, in any vacant space. Parliament also held the colonists responsible for providing the funds to feed and support the British troops.

An organized resistance preceded the Tea Party. Virtually every provocation from Parliament generated a response. Political activists like Samuel Adams produced pamphlets and letters arguing that Parliament could not impose taxes on the colonies without their input. The arguments and letters circulated around the colonies, deepening the ties among the colonists, while building sympathy for the cause of independence. Britain responded with increased force; its efforts to squeeze the colonies all met with resistance, leading to the revocation of some laws, but also intensified conflict. In 1770, protest against the quartering of troops in Boston led to armed confrontation in the streets. In response to the colonists' harassment of soldiers, British soldiers opened fire on a crowd, resulting in the death of five colonists. There was a level of conflict, often violent and disruptive, that preceded and followed the more theatrical Tea Party, but the better choreographed event has an iconic place in narratives of American history that often edit out more violent events (Schiff 2020).

The point is that a decade of disruption preceded the Tea Party and the Revolution; speeches and pamphlets, intensified by long discussions in parliaments and taverns, occupied a far larger part of the process of building support than the drama of a costumed attack on commerce – even though the Tea Party makes a better story in a history book. Over the period of growing resistance, support for British governance faded in the colonies, a response to both organizing in America and repeated incursions by the British. Efforts to deepen the ties among the colonies, which traced back at least 20 years before the Tea Party, gradually found greater support, as British policy gave the colonists a common enemy. To make sense of the growth of the independence movement and the Tea Party in particular, we need to understand the context in which it developed.

I don't mean here to provide a comprehensive account of the American Revolution; rather, I want to use this movement to point out the necessity of putting any movement effort in a broader historical and political context. From the example of the Tea Party, we can identify factors that are critical to the emergence, organization, and impact of any significant social movement.

We want to recognize that most people don't protest most of the time. Although a few committed organizers are virtually always trying to recruit others to their causes, most people think about their personal commitments and aspirations far more than they attend to larger issues of social change. Movements grow and gain the potential of influence when they engage large numbers of people who would otherwise be consumed with work, family and friends, and the pressures and possibilities of everyday life. Protest and political engagement come with some cost, and we have to pay attention to the circumstances under which people will take on the extra work of trying to change their world, rather than just live in it. Most people add social movement participation to their agendas only when they think that something's wrong, it's fixable, and that protest might matter.

Social Movements, Events, and Political Context

The world outside a movement is critical to how much that movement can grow, and we can think about that world as offering a set of *political opportunities* (McAdam 1982; Meyer 2004; Tarrow 2011; Tilly 1978). Potential participants in a social movement look at the world around them when they decide how to respond to an invitation to act. They need to believe that a cause is actionable, and that it's possible – or safe enough – to join with others (Gamson and Meyer 1996). No matter how good an organizer is, what's going on in the rest of the world makes it easier or harder to sell his or her message.

Back to the American Revolution: Separated from colonial rule by the Atlantic Ocean, colonists enjoyed the space to do more than a little self-governance. Over time, they built wealth, organizations, and identities that were not exactly "British." When England began to impose greater restrictions on the colonists' business and autonomy, it created shared grievances in America, and those grievances contributed to the development of a distinct American identity. Colonists aggrieved by new taxes or restrictions on participation in governance initially tried to resist them; essentially, the first efforts were conservative ones, trying to keep things as they were. When this proved increasingly difficult, support for independence grew as the most viable alternative.

Political opportunities also include the means available to try to advance one's political interests, and vary for different racial, professional, and class groups, over time, and across different contexts (Bracey 2015). Most people are unlikely to protest if they think they can get what they want by employing more modest means that entail less cost and less risk. Advocates experiment with different ways of getting what they want: writing letters, making speeches, organizing demonstrations, staging theatrical acts of vandalism, and ultimately, in this case, taking up arms and going to war. In the case of the American independence cause, there's an interaction between social movements and the authorities they challenge – as is always the case in protest movements. When Britain punished the colonists and excluded them from normal institutional politics, it could have crushed the cause altogether; instead, it drove them to war as the best available alternative.

Some of the most educated and affluent people in the colonies were already familiar with philosophical arguments against monarchy, and the beginnings of a liberal philosophy of limited government (Wills 1978), but then, as now, relatively few people find the time to work their way through books of philosophy. As the cause of independence grew, however, Patriots developed ways to translate and promote their ideas to a broader public. A free press circulated work from advocates of independence. Most notably, Thomas Paine, newly arrived in America in 1774, promoted ideas of independence and human rights as "Common Sense" in 1776. The coincidence of the right text with a critical time produced a national bestseller, and gave the Patriots a script to justify their organizing efforts.

Ultimately, the colonists won a war of independence, but the ideas and the organizations inspired citizens of the new nation to demand more. Even as the revolution moved the locus of governance from London to colony capitals, the United States allowed slavery, the continued expansion to Indian territories, and some states did little of consequence to advance the interests of most of their citizens. Farmers in western Massachusetts, seized with the revolutionary spirit, in 1786 armed themselves and occupied a courthouse to protest the difficulties they had in paying debt owed to creditors who mostly controlled the legislature. Shays' Rebellion helped provoke the Constitutional convention, which strengthened the federal government and made it even more difficult for farmers to get credit on the terms they wanted (Richards 2002). The Constitution also left some supporters of the revolution disappointed or angry. Farmers on the western edge of the early United States, accustomed to distilling their surplus grain for personal use and for sale, resisted a federal tax on domestically produced spirits. Beginning in 1791, recalling the principle of fighting "taxation without representation," the Whiskey Rebellion included tax evasion, mass meetings and demonstrations, and physical assaults on tax collectors (Slaughter 1986). President Washington led a militia of 13,000 men to put down the rebellion, buttressing the new republic at the expense of the vision of many of those who fought for it.

Telescoping out from the Boston Tea Party, we encounter the complications in making an assessment of the influence of social movements. Even a simple reading of the event must situate it in a larger independence movement that, over a period of years, produced a war and a new nation. Even then, evaluating that movement as a success means neglecting the lofty aspirations and concrete expectations of many of those who turned out for the effort. For these reasons, the Tea Party provides a good way to start examining how social movements matter. The Tea Party and the larger American Revolution of which it was a part was a distinct series of events, whose outcomes were defined by context and contingency. Nonetheless, we can use it to establish and define concepts that will be helpful in understanding a wide range of other campaigns in a broad variety of contexts.

Elements of Political Protest

"Social movement" is something of a catch-all term, designating organized and sustained challenges to some kind of authority. Movements are comprised of groups and individuals who share some common aims, but also differ on issues of ultimate goals, as well as the best ways to achieve them. Movements include ideas and actions, which generally play out both in mainstream politics and outside the mainstream. A movement links discrete events, like demonstrations, meetings, and speeches, over an extended period of time. Using movements, organizers aspire to change both the world outside them and the ways in which participants live their lives (Meyer 2014). Inherently unstable, movements can grow into revolutionary campaigns, where insurgents seek to control territory and displace a governing regime. They may also develop into more routine political organizations and practices, in which organizers make accommodations with authorities and pursue their interests in less disruptive ways.

A *grievance* is a source of dissatisfaction that activists view to be actionable. Unpleasant cold temperatures on a winter's day may be frustrating, but people don't see collective action as a route to redress. Individuals can bundle up, go inside, or just shiver. In contrast, growing belief that a practice or policy could be fixed leads people to unite with others and take purposeful action. The grievance can be one that potential recruits already know, but don't view as either wrong or changeable, like female genital mutilation, wages, work conditions, or racial or religious segregation. In such cases, organizers have the job of suggesting alternatives, and giving their would-be supporters a sense that change is possible. Part of the process involves showing people that the issues they face aren't peculiar to them; that a problem is collective, not personal.

Alternatively, a grievance can be constructed around a distant threat, like nuclear weapons or climate change, issues about which most people think and know very little. Here too, organizers have the task of providing education, albeit with the difficult task of helping people to define their interests more broadly than they normally do. In all cases, identifying a grievance and alternatives is a step toward bringing people into a movement and into action of some sort. Organizers turn grievances into claims, that is, demands upon those in authority.

Mobilization means engaging people and getting them to take directed action in the service of some set of goals. Organizers recruit and direct supporters by convincing them that something is wrong, changeable, and that their actions might make a difference (Gamson and Meyer 1996; Rosenstone and Hansen 1993). They use the raw material of social problems and conditions, and offer directed plans for action (Snow and Benford 1992). But recognizing a problem and accepting a cause are only steps toward concerted action. Engaging people in a movement is hard work. In seeking to mobilize others, organizers can craft direct appeals, through conversations and meetings, or retail efforts to publicize the cause and their efforts, through newspapers and broadcast media. The modes of communication change over time, of course, and social media provide more accessible ways to reach people directly and wholesale (Bennett and Segerberg 2014; Earl and Kimport 2011; Rohlinger 2015, 2019; Tufekci 2017). Similarly, recruitment often comes one individual at a time, building new organizations, but the most efficient way to build a movement is to recruit and engage the already organized. Speaking at a meeting at a church or sports team or professional association allows an organizer to reach people who are already able to do something beyond the work of maintaining their lives, and people who already share some kind of connection.

Social movements arise only after governance structures are in operation, and those structures or governments come with strategies to contain discontent, which also comprise a set of political opportunities. These opportunities constrain what issues can be contested, who can engage in making claims, and how they can try to advance their beliefs. Authoritarian leaders, for example, claim infallibility and legitimacy by default. If God had wanted someone else to be king or pope, someone else would be doing it. In joining in a challenging movement, individuals have to confront their own beliefs about the vulnerability of a government to their claims. What's more, authoritarians usually also enjoy the capacity to inflict severe punishment on dissenters. Challengers risk fines, imprisonment, isolation, and even their lives. It's not that there are no people with grievances in authoritarian states like North Korea, for example; it's just that there's no available space for organizing or expression. With few dissenters and no qualms about respecting due process or civil liberties, authoritarian states can brutally repress incipient movements, eliminating the challenge and demonstrating a cautionary example for other would-be dissidents.

Take, for example, the abbreviated White Rose campaign in Nazi Germany. Domestic resistance to Hitler evaporated relatively quickly, but in the summer of 1942, a handful of Christian students at the University of Munich drafted and distributed six leaflets, sometimes through the mail, sometimes by hand delivery, and sometimes just leaving the papers where someone might pick them up. The papers criticized Hitler and the Nazis and called for "passive resistance." Later, they escalated to posting political graffiti near the university (Nuborn and Dumbach 2007 [1986]). Once identified and reported by a custodian, the members of the collective were arrested, interrogated, summarily tried, and executed.[2] A moral exemplar perhaps, the tragic story was a deterrent to others who might criticize the regime from within. The key to understanding the extremely limited influence of the White Rose campaign lay not in its integrity or its strategies, tactics, or ideas, but in the larger political context.

At the other end of the spectrum, democracies invite and channel participation in politics to less threatening means of engagement. The minority that loses an election will always hear that they can organize and compete more effectively ... next time. Campaigning for office entails accepting the rules and restrictions of governance, and managing conflicts with an idea toward winning elections, in which the identification of a person or a party can trump any connection to issues. It can also entail an acceptance of unfavorable policies in the moments in between. Learning to live with losses is somewhat easier if you believe that they are temporary and reversible through your efforts.

The rules of political engagement vary greatly across democratic polities, and those rules also shape available opportunities for activists pushing a cause. Some governments strictly regulate the funding and conduct of electoral campaigns, whereas others allow longer and more expensive efforts. In systems that offer single member district representation, we'll generally see two dominant political parties, and specialized concerns that attract a smaller share of the electorate, say workers or the environment, have to make their peace with one of the major parties (Duverger 1954). In contrast, in states that host proportional representation systems, starting a new political party based around particular constituents – like Israeli Arabs or German Greens – is always a possibility.

Some elements of opportunity, like the electoral system or the nature of government institutions, tend to be pretty stable over time. Others, however, like the positions of people in power and their coalitions of support, are far more dynamic. The savvy organizer pays attention to all of this. Her job is to find the most effective route to political influence, after assessing both available opportunities and the resource of her supporters.

Resources are the tools and assets that a movement can deploy in support of its ideas, and they vary tremendously across movements and contexts (McCarthy and Zald 1977). It's inspiring to talk about "people power," for example, but it depends upon large numbers willing to take on risks in collective action. What's more, all people don't count equally in a political system. Individuals with disproportionate wealth, status, or knowledge can generate more attention, and potentially exercise greater influence, than far larger numbers of less elite people.

Such resources are not stagnant, and skillful deployment of assets can leverage other assets. A movement with a great deal of money can start with paid advertising and paid supporters, which, carefully deployed, might recruit more volunteers. A movement that starts with a committed few can take dramatic action to generate political attention to its issues of concern and its actions, thus leading to more public support. A movement with broad support at the grassroots can mobilize that support effectively to demonstrate the capacity to affect elections, and thereby recruit institutional allies. None of this, of course, is automatic, and organizers' success in leveraging resources effectively depends not only on skill and context, but also tactics.

A *tactic* is a way to send a message. Organizers can send a message clearly and directly by holding a press conference or sending a letter. Enlisting others to send the same message in letters or phone calls represents an effort to increase its visibility. Organizers can amplify their message with larger numbers by holding a demonstration, march, or rally. They can demonstrate the depth of their commitment by taking more dramatic action, ranging from nonviolent and symbolic civil disobedience to vandalism and violence against property and persons. In choosing a message, organizers generally draw from a familiar "play list" of tactics, familiar to both supporters and authorities. In choosing tactics, movement organizers need to be cognizant of at least three distinct audiences: authorities, supporters, and potential supporters. To make sense of the range of possible approaches to strategic action, Tilly (1978) suggested that a tactic is a performance that sends a message to all about activists' *worthiness, unity, numbers,* and *commitment.* Costumes, like the faux Indian disguises donned by the Boston Tea Partiers, the animal costumes worn by animal rights activists, or the naked displays of crusaders against gender violence, are a frequent tactical addition. Importantly, although organizers enjoy direct means of communicating with all of their audiences, larger numbers can be reached through mediated communication, when mass media choose to cover and define an event. The ideal tactic affirms supporters, attracts bystanders, and gets authorities to worry about what else these protesters might do (Rochon 1998). A savvy organizer is mindful of developing approaches that are likely to engage all potential audiences, and to be attractive enough to mass media to extend beyond the movement's network.

Protest movements are organized. Although events, a crystallized combination of tactics, constituencies, and claims, often include elements of spontaneity, like the bystanders who decided to join the patriots clambering on the tea ships, there is always an element of planning underneath. Organizers try to engage supporters, pick places, promote particular grievances and alternatives, and try to figure out what happens next. The continuing relationship among people committed to a particular vision of social change can broadly be thought of as an *organization*.

Here too, there is an enormous range of organizational forms and commitments. A small group that meets regularly in a church basement or around a kitchen table, where no one is paid, and participants get to know each other very well, can be the basis of an ongoing campaign for massive political change. At the other end of the organizational spectrum, social movements are often staged by well-established and well-resourced groups whose efforts span long periods of time and decades of engagement. Such organizations develop complicated bureaucratic structures for governance, and division of labor to execute plans. Some organizations develop in the service of one narrow objective, planning a particular protest or demonstration; they start with no commitment beyond the event. Others develop with longer-term goals that contain a range of events, activities, and even services (Blee 2012; Kretschmer 2019; Levy and Murphy 2006). All groups must manage the struggle of supporting their efforts, but those with a shorter-term, more limited focus, can often depend upon volunteer labor and low overheads. A group dependent upon volunteer efforts will have a difficult time sustaining presence over an extended campaign, because most people have to balance commitments beyond politics.

In contrast, organizations with broader or much longer-term objectives must develop systems to ensure that they have the money and expertise to continue. They need to rent offices, buy computers, maintain telephone lines and websites, and pay staff. Many different sources can provide that support, but each comes with different obligations and constraints. A group dependent upon funding from the government, for example, must follow the rules and restrictions of that government. A group dependent upon a few wealthy funders can't risk offending or alienating those supporters, and can be subject to the whims of the funders. A group dependent upon large numbers of small donors must invest a great deal of time in soliciting that money, and is vulnerable to changes in the political environment.

Even as maintaining a stable presence in politics is costly, it also comes with some advantages. Professionals engaged in movement work may be reasonably well-paid and enjoy routine access to media or authorities. They can develop expertise in policy or politics, and they can pay close attention to events and policies, and act opportunistically (Staggenborg 1988). And a group that knows its efforts will be sustained can think about longer-term efforts. Organizations plan, and well-funded, stable, and professionalized groups should be able to plan better.

Strategy is a coherent plan of claims and tactics targeted at particular audiences that is intended to promote social change (Maney et al. 2012). Sometimes plans for social change are well-developed and articulated, based in informed understanding of the workings of government. At the same time, everyone engaged in a piece of the effort is unlikely to be aware of some master plan, or even a longer-term plan altogether. Sometimes, participants just know that they have to do *something* to express their own concerns, trusting that well-intentioned and morally grounded action will somehow contribute to the change they seek to promote. At the same time, some organizers will have a vision of how social change takes place, and the influence of a set of actions they can coordinate can trigger further action. Strategy involves choices about which grievances to emphasize, who to focus on recruiting, and what to have adherents do. Importantly, however, purposeful strategists operate in a larger universe they can't control, with both supporters and opponents making their own initiatives.

Challenging and Entering Political Institutions

Social movements are not unitary actors. Because a movement contains a diversity of organizations and individuals, often including people with at least one foot in governance or mainstream politics, the politics of coordination and cooperation within a movement is critical to its development and its ultimate impact. Allied organizations argue about which issues are most pressing or promising, and how to address them most effectively. They argue about which political leaders to trust, and which ones to target. They argue about who will represent their efforts and who will be kept off the podium. And they argue about how to get things done. All of this matters.

Perhaps more significantly, movement activists are not the only ones who decide what they want, who their leaders are, and what constitutes acceptable progress. All of these issues are contested in public, with authorities, media, and supporters playing a role in advantaging some ideas and people at the expense of others. To take an example, while the organizers of a rally can decide who will appear on their speakers' roster and when, outside coverage of those speeches need not follow the organizers' preferences. Similarly, when social movements advance broad calls for social change, media outlets choose which to cover most extensively and which to ignore.

In democratic states, media generally follow public attention, and are likely to give the most attention to the most dramatic events, that is, actions that involve conflict and/or celebrities and/or theatricality (Rohlinger 2015, 2019). Organizers compete with the range of other events in life, as well as other contingents of activists, to capture the attention of mainstream media. Mainstream media are also likely to follow public interest in identifying spokespeople, which means gravitating toward celebrity, novelty, and clarity. Organizers who are media savvy know how to promote themselves and their cause, how to return inquiries quickly, and how to provide media outlets with the sort of quotes or appearances that will draw audiences. Thus, a movement that, like most, contains multiple factions, may see itself portrayed as offering a more radical or more modest set of claims than most at the grassroots support. Actually, media outlets face a clear choice: they can promote and cover radical or outlandish aspects of a social movement – and every movement has some – thus contributing to discrediting or marginalizing that movement. Alternatively, they can promote the most mainstream and least contentious elements of a movement, reducing the claims of those in the streets to those which are not too threatening. The nuclear freeze campaign, for example, a movement for nuclear disarmament and a reconfiguration of foreign policy, started in the 1970s and gained little political traction. In the early 1980s, however, it won widespread public support as politicians redefined it as a return to a superpower arms control process that accepted large standing nuclear arsenals as a reality of modern life (Meyer 1990).

Government officials also make choices about which people and proposals to legitimate by discussion and which to marginalize through neglect or ridicule. Like media, they face similar choices in emphasizing the outlandishness of a particular movement, or its utter reasonability and pragmatism. Those officials can also choose to recognize some individuals as spokespersons for a movement, ignoring others. There is an inherent difficulty in finding spokespeople who have sufficient credibility with the grassroots to still political protest, yet are willing to negotiate moderate policy reforms with authorities. For example, the minority white government in Rhodesia, facing domestic pressure, a guerrilla war, and international sanctions, sought to respond by designating Black leaders of moderate groups that it could negotiate with. The eventual negotiated agreement, however, did nothing to still either the guerrilla war launched by other Black leaders or even international pressure. The attractive negotiating partners couldn't deliver the peace the white government wanted. Eventually, the government had to deal with the opponents who commanded armies (Matthews 1990).

In much of the world, activists launch effective movements without guerrilla armies, but the same sorts of dilemmas remain for authorities. Seeking to maintain a governing majority and reduce disruptive protest, they want to find opposition leaders who aren't too oppositional, yet retain sufficient credibility with activists to be able to reduce disruptive protest. At the same time, movements at the grassroots struggle to hold their own leadership accountable to the ideas that motivated them in the first place.

Taken together, the elements of a movement suggest a stylized process through which a movement cycles. The prospect for potential impact is everywhere in that cycle, but it's critical to recognize that movements don't work in a vacuum, and that their influence is determined by their relations with other actors, inside and outside of government.

We might begin by acknowledging that there are always people who are trying to convince others that something in their society is drastically wrong, and to recruit those people into purposeful action to change it. The range of issues is virtually infinite: individuals can be upset about moral failures in the larger society; economic injustice; the prevalence of male circumcision; the persistence of female circumcision; the lack of civil liberties; the availability of guns; the use of public lands; the degree of civil liberties afforded most citizens; foreign policies; wars and preparations for wars; taxation; or the distribution of food. Discontent with a set of issues is normal. In any polity, some of those who are dissatisfied will be working through normal political channels – whatever they are – to secure their interests; others will be located well outside normal political actions, confined to the margins of mainstream discourse. Visibility is low, and there is little contact with a public that isn't normally concerned with those issues. It's not that everyone involved is happy or satisfied with the status quo, but rather that most people concerned with a set of issues view the established politics of the issue to be relatively stable, with changes on matters of policy taking place in increments. Political stability tends to reflect stalemate rather than satisfaction (Baumgartner and Jones 1993).

Social movements commence when institutional actors look to develop an outside strategy to pursue their aims – or those on the margins suddenly see greater success in reaching a broader audience – or both. This is usually a function of what's going on in mainstream politics. They have to be convinced that additional means of politics are necessary and potentially effective. Those who are normally on the margins suddenly seem more relevant and potentially influential. Most interesting, those on the margins now can see common cause with those normally confined to mainstream politics.

When does this happen? Usually these moments are a reaction to regular politics and policy. When new leaders come to power and develop different coalitions of support, pushing some previously used to ostensibly meaningful political access out of political institutions, and welcoming those normally excluded in, the calculus of would-be activists changes. When political leaders offer new policies that depart from previous practices, partisans can sense a possibility of influence or the threat of severe losses. Most people take to the streets when they think their efforts are both necessary and potentially effective.

We can see reciprocal processes of mobilization coming from the mainstream and the margins. The public events of dissidents get larger, and generate more interest. Those who operate within more mainstream politics generally now take more time and effort to expand their audiences and explain their concerns to public groups they can normally ignore. As Schattschneider (1960) noted long ago, the important actors in a fight are usually the bystanders, who have the potential of taking sides. Successful social mobilization means engaging the crowd. Under normal circumstances, those at the margin have great difficulty doing so, and risk having the largest part of the public join on the side of the opposition. Under normal circumstances, those comfortable in mainstream institutional politics have no interest in doing so.

Like any overnight sensation, the sudden emergence of a social movement marks a long period of less immediately successful attempts to effect change and to reach a public. In authoritarian polities, those efforts might be secret, played out around kitchen tables and around the edges of work, with a *samizdat* literature circulation used to spread information. In democratic states, efforts to change the world can be extremely public, reflected by activists handing out leaflets, then making phone calls, and later, posting information on websites. When circumstances allow, that small core will extend to reach broader constituencies, convincing new people that organizing and taking positions is necessary and/or potentially effective.

Through literature, conversation, and through other events and products, organizers develop ideas. The work develops not only the ideas, but also commitment to them. People trying to recruit others to the cause use ideas, slogans, and symbols to do so (Rochon 1998). Even as ideas or demands expand, the depth of commitment or understanding needed to join in diminishes. Short-hand descriptions stand in for elaborated understanding.

The growth in support feeds the growth in support, creating a kind of bandwagon effect (Oliver et al. 1985). The presence of greater numbers of people engaged on the same set of issues serves to draw attention to both the issues and the activities of movement organizers. Visibility legitimates their efforts and their issues. More organization and more people mean more events, and more opportunities for potential supporters to join in, and make it far more likely that a prospective activist will already know people who are engaged. The movement seems to be more urgent, demonstrate a greater chance of making a difference, and thus more attractive to engage. It's easy to walk past a single leafletter on the streets, and hard to imagine that this effort will make a difference. As the crowds grow, and as they generate attention, they are harder to ignore and easier to join. Bystanders join in as risks diminish, and as movements can offer more incentives for others to join. Importantly, one does not have to sign on to all elements of a movement's campaign in order to join, particularly as it grows. Indeed, life within a social movement provides a basis for transmitting values and beliefs (Munson 2009).

The growth of a movement also feeds the supply of resources available to it. More people can do more. More money allows hiring full-time organizers, opening additional offices or outposts, producing more media, and creating more events. All of this aids visibility, aiding recruitment, and driving legitimacy. And the larger a movement becomes, the more imperative it becomes for authorities to respond, and the more visible those responses are. Growth makes subsequent growth easier.

As a movement grows, of course, diversity within it increases. Although successful campaigns may be able to coalesce around a central demand, the contours of their claims and the nature of their ultimate goals are going to be increasingly contested. As more diverse factions join, they come with different ultimate goals and different sets of commitments to ultimate aims. Importantly, people are more likely to sign on to a movement as a vehicle for sending a message, when that movement appears capable of conveying a message. Others, who may start with no commitment to the cause, may sign on simply because the movement appears as the strongest expression of any kind of political alternative.

Authorities' responses become increasingly critical to a movement's future. When a campaign succeeds, those in authority are forced to answer questions about it, and about the issues activists press. Institutional political opponents of the government will adopt the concerns of a movement for their own purposes, and mainstream journalists will continually demand that government officials explain what they're doing. Even when authorities justify the policies activists protest, the role of social movements in setting the agenda for institutional politics is the place where influence can take place.

Authorities respond to both the actions and the ideas of social movements. Those responses matter, and they are not necessarily seamlessly connected.

In response to the actions of activists, authorities typically draw lines that separate permissible or accepted modes of dissent from those that they will not tolerate. In liberal democracies, governments give most causes ready access to the tools of protest. Democracies allow participation in all sorts of other ways as well. Organizations can develop permanent and visible offices, raise money, contribute to campaigns, and lobby elected officials. Demonstrations, marches, and rallies have become routine for all concerned in liberal democratic polities. Organizers generally negotiate with authorities before an event on parade routes, likely crowd sizes, and the amount of sound produced, and the number of portable bathroom facilities needed. Police monitor the boundaries of the demonstration, often keeping distance between protesters and their opponents, and arresting people who would violate whatever the negotiated protocol might be. Even civil disobedience can be managed through elaborately choreographed, ritualized performances, in which the time, place, and manner of arrests can be negotiated in advance (Earl et al. 2003).

Liberal democracies generally claim to allow a broad spectrum of protest tactics, regardless of the causes they are meant to advance. But governments don't always live up to the content-free ideal. European democracies sometimes ban the symbols and rhetoric or Nazism, or other hate speech. In the United States, the protest actions of groups with radical ideas – on the left and right – are policed more aggressively, and with far less tolerance. State authorities manage policing differentially, targeting protesters they view as the most threatening with particularly harsh treatment. But the level of threat is assessed not only by a protest campaign's tactics, but also its claims and its constituencies. Violence and arrests are also more likely when the protesters represent minority groups (Davenport 2007; Davenport et al. 2011; Reynolds-Stenson 2017).

Authorities also make decisions about how to respond

to the ideas expressed by social movement activists. In any polity, there is a spectrum of legitimate discourse and policy proposals, although that spectrum can shift over time. Authorities are generally not compelled to respond seriously to claims that fall outside that spectrum. Thus, the British parliament would not have to respond to the calls for ending the National Health Service, and – until relatively recently – American leaders haven't had to respond to claims to create an American version of that service.

Social movements set an agenda for discussion, but institutional political figures choose which elements of that agenda to respond to and with how much seriousness. Political leaders can embrace aspects of a movement's claims, redefining them in the process, or reject them outright. Their responses provoke challenges within a social movement coalition, as factions that win acceptance have to calculate whether it's worthwhile to ditch their social movement connections to try to enhance their access to people with power (Amenta 1998; Amenta et al. 1994).

Harsh state responses to protest in the streets can crush the public expression of social movement ideas. Thus, in 1989, when democracy demonstrators filled Tiananmen Square in Beijing, everyone carefully watched the response of the state and of the police. The national government, run by the Chinese Communist Party, had supported policies of economic liberalization without concomitant political openings. In response to the death of former leader, Hu Yaobang, young activists filled the square to mourn, and to support policies that promoted democracy and freedom, which they said reflected Hu's ideals. Protesters moved in and out of the public square over weeks, receiving mixed signals from authorities about how their protests were being received. In May, a group of students commenced a hunger strike, which generated both international and national attention. When the protests began to spread across China, authorities cracked down harshly, mobilizing hundreds of thousands of troops, including mobilized military units based in the countryside, and aggressively dispersed the crowd, leading to hundreds of deaths, and dramatic pictures of unarmed activists standing up to military tanks (Zhao 2001).

The crushing of the Tiananmen protests essentially stifled protest in China for years, and economic liberalization proceeded apace.

But sometimes harsh repression spurs activists to do more. When governments crack down on protest violently, they challenge their own military forces to engage in conduct they may find deplorable. They also expose themselves to international scrutiny and, generally, approbation. The harsh repression of the Iranian government under the Shah served largely to undermine public support for the regime, helped build dissident networks, and essentially encouraged opponents of the regime to organize more effectively. Philippine president Ferdinand Marcos, faced with a domestic insurgency, found that he could not count on the support of his own military. Rather than repress the protesters, the military joined them. Robbed of his support within the military, Marcos was essentially forced to cede power and leave the country with as much wealth as he could carry (Boudreau 2004).

There is, then, a paradox, in which harsh repression can still dissent, or it can stoke it, depending upon the effectiveness of the repression, the solidity of governance, and the resources the opposition has. Similarly, in democratic polities, reform efforts can encourage further mobilization and broader goals, or they can undermine the organization of a protest movement.

The key to unpacking these apparent contradictions lies in the nature of the challenging coalition. When authorities respond to protesters, their prime strategic goal must be to split their challengers. Because movements are comprised of diverse factions with a range of concerns and commitments to different sorts of tactics, government moves provide the chance to reconsider alliances. Government repression challenges those who are less committed or have more to lose to ask whether it makes sense to continue to tie their fate to others less popular. Government concessions, in terms of policy reforms or political inclusion, challenge coalitions in exactly the same way, but with opportunities for change rather than the threat of repression. In both cases, those on the radical edge of a movement and those in its more moderate wing, constantly have the opportunity to rethink how loyal they should be to each other, particularly in the context of potential risks and potential gains. Strong protest is polarizing, pushing bystanders to take sides, and the nature of the schism, particularly how extensive and how large and powerful the forces on each side of the divide are, determines the likely outcome.

Social movements, although ubiquitous, represent commitments and levels of engagement that are, for most participants, unusual. The stalwarts continue mobilizing even when there's some kind of accommodation with power, but for most people, there is a process of coming to terms with partial solutions, and moving onto other issues or other elements of life (see Hirschman 1982). We can think about that process as *institutionalization*, that is, setting up a set of relationships with other people, with authorities, and with a cause, that becomes routine, where the costs are limited and predictable (Jepperson 1991).

At peak mobilization, social movements are defined by ongoing engagement with mainstream political life. That moment is always limited, and the outcomes of movements are described by the character of mobilization. One component of institutionalization is entering the political system in some organized way, such as a political party, a stable interest association, or the bureaucracy. Another is marginalization, when those in power are no longer compelled to pay attention to what activists want or what they do. In liberal polities, the decline of social movements is generally defined by both processes. When the margins and the mainstream become more distant from each other, there is a decline in visibility, and the imagination of broad goals and extensive engagement diminishes as well (Meyer 1993).

Summing Up

We can outline a schematic process to map the trajectory of a social movement cycle. We begin with the recognition of a political, social, or policy person. Such recognition could come from government, citizen action, or the confluence of events, like an accident, a war, or new information. The development of a problem may reflect a change in objective conditions, or simply the perception of those conditions. Step two entails the development of a schism among political elites. The divide may come over the recognition of the problem itself, or about the range of possible remedies that can be considered legitimate. The divide within governance leads to a third stage, greater public attention, facilitated by the relevant media of the moment. With divides and political attention, a fourth stage opens when groups concerned with citizen mobilization grow, with new groups developing and established ones taking on new activists, and generating more activity – and visibility. These groups offer criticism of current policies or realities and offer alternatives. Activist groups grow around a particular set of claims and potential resolutions. This is a particularly unstable moment, and liberal democratic governments respond in a variety of ways, often accepting some portion of activist goals or rhetoric while rejecting others. Social movements end with a sixth stage, when a new institutional accommodation is reached, and unusual mobilization no longer takes place (Meyer 1993).

Like any stage framework, this model is a heuristic that offers a map for understanding any movement, but not a very good description of any particular movement. Action is taking place in all the stages at once, and in the contemporary era, movements don't really end so neatly, but continue on in more modest and less visible ways – although not necessarily with less impact (Meyer and Tarrow 1998).

We need to sum up some of what all this means. Most significantly, social movements are themselves the product of political dynamics, as well as contributors to those dynamics. Social movements surely play a role in creating history, but they are not completely insulated from the history that gives rise to their emergence (Amenta et al. 2010; Giugni 1998). The forces that create the impetus for social protest also create the pressure for political change. In this context, the efficacy of social movements involves maximizing the impact of the waves that they are on, but movements have limited impact on creating those waves.

To make sense of the influence of movements, that is, how movements matter, we need to develop a good understanding of the factors that give rise to them, that is, the conditions that allow movements to emerge in the first place. In this regard, the influence of social movements is a function of the ability of organizers and activists to get the most out of the waves they ride.

Here's the surfing analogy: Surfing is an extremely difficult sport. A surfer needs to paddle out through current, ducking under or paddling over waves, and then position herself in the ocean ready to catch waves when they come by. As the waves appear in sets, the skillful surfer starts paddling purposefully when a promising wave appears, but there are generally missteps, and there are moments of competition and courtesy with other surfers seeking to ride the same wave. Often, a surfer is wiped out immediately, or unable to catch the wave. The most skillful, however, time their paddling carefully, stand at the right time, and can not only navigate survival upright, but also pose moves up and down the face of the wave. A great surfer can maximize the length of his ride, and pull off when what the wave offers is no longer interesting, paddling out once more to be in position for the next opportunity.

What's not quite right about this metaphor is that social movements, unlike surfers, can help kick up the waves as well as ride them.

CHAPTER 2

Protest, Revolution, and Regime Change

On December 17, 2010, Mohamed Bouazizi, a street vendor who sold vegetables from a cart in Tunis, set himself on fire. Police had confiscated his cart and its contents, and beat and humiliated him when he tried to pay a fine and recover his goods. It's not clear whether he was staging a protest against harassment by the police and the corrupt government, or was simply and overwhelmingly frustrated about his life, but his desperate efforts sparked a wave of protests across the Middle East and North Africa (Hasan 2018). People in Tunisia took to the streets in response, and translated their frustration to protests directed against the regime of Zine el Abidine Ben Ali, who had ruled a one-party state for more than 30 years. Well before Bouazizi took his life, widespread frustration had grown throughout the country, beleaguered by government repression, high inflation, particularly on food, and general corruption.

The first sympathy protests appeared at regional government offices, and were directed at Bouazizi's mistreatment; they were met with tear gas and beatings. Protests continued, along with a few additional suicides, and spread to different sectors of society. Trade unions organized demonstrations in several cities, and a few hundred lawyers staged a rally in front of a palace in Tunis. Labor and lawyer protests continued in different sites, almost always ending with violent confrontations with the police. By early January, most of Tunisia's lawyers had declared their own strike, in protest against the brutality of the police.

Ben Ali tried to respond to the protests with a combination of broad repression and selectively dispensed benefits, to calm the storms around him. He reshuffled his Cabinet, promised reforms and jobs, and simultaneously vilified the demonstrators and the threats they represented which, he said, were promoted by foreign agents who had mobilized mercenaries and malcontents. Police selectively arrested a few bloggers and organizers, while Ben Ali called for new elections months in the future. In fairly short order, the leadership of the army turned against Ben Ali, who declared a state of emergency and fled the country for asylum in Saudi Arabia – less than a month after Bouazizi's suicide.

Violence and civil unrest continued, as political and military leaders jostled for control of the government, negotiating and renegotiating alliances and seeking to restore – or create – civil order. Secularist and fundamentalist factions competed for power, both in subsequent elections and in battles with police in the streets. The already weak economy suffered, and refugees fled the country (Alexander 2016; Macdonald and Waggoner 2018).

The immediate reaction to a vigorous and sometimes violent uprising against an authoritarian government was a spate of other uprisings. Inspired and encouraged by the rapidity and the apparently relative ease of the Tunisian revolution, dissidents in Jordan, Egypt, Algeria, Yemen, Bahrain, Libya, Syria, and other Middle Eastern states took to the streets to try to topple their own autocratic rulers in what came to be known as the Arab Spring (Alimi and Meyer 2011). But nothing turned out to be quite so easy or so quick as Tunisia's Jasmine Revolution initially seemed. The contrasts between the breathless accounts of democratic revitalization and the actual outcomes of these rebellions is instructive.

Inspiring and Cautionary Examples

People unhappy with authoritarian regimes poured into the streets, sometimes with arms. Some were looking for some version of democracy, but others wanted to install explicitly religious regimes. Demonstrators battled police and the military, and each other. In some countries, authorities were able to repress the revolutionary movements, tightening their control of the economy and social life. In others, insurgent factions staged revolutionary armies, controlling territory and administering governance in distinct areas while they waged civil wars.

Initially, Egypt provided the most encouraging case for partisans of democracy elsewhere, and the most dramatic story over the short term, and it reflected grievances that had been brewing for decades. The Egyptian state has always had to balance different pressures from within and without, severely constraining the development of democratic politics. In 1978, Egyptian President Anwar Sadat had negotiated a peace with Israel that entailed Israel's return of the Sinai Peninsula. The Camp David Accords brought Egypt some security on its borders and the regular infusion of money and weapons from the United States. It also marked Sadat as a provocative target for domestic dissidents, including factions within the military and religious fundamentalists. Sadat maintained power by increasing domestic security and repression.

After a radical imam had issued a fatwa authorizing Sadat's assassination, members of Islamic Jihad staged an assault on Sadat and the government in October 1981. The dramatic attack killed the president and 10 other officials, and injured another 28 people, including Hosni Mubarak, his vice president. Mubarak, who enjoyed strong support within the military, assumed the presidency, and held the office for nearly 30 years. He did so by maintaining an authoritarian state that worked hard to stop dissident groups from growing, becoming politically visible, or affecting public discourse and public policy. The repression was justified by a ruling under an emergency law adopted more than a decade before Mubarak took office, and in constant effect since the moment he took office.

While the Tunisian Jasmine Revolution was still in its earliest phases, dissident groups flooded social media to call for the end of Mubarak's reign and the institutionalization of civil liberties and basic freedoms in Egypt (Del Panta 2020). Young people advocating political liberalism were the most visible, but opposition to Mubarak's presidency united people across a wide ideological spectrum, including Islamic fundamentalists. The Muslim Brotherhood, for example, was a group with a large following at the grassroots, was deeply opposed to Mubarak's government, and had absolutely no interest in political liberalism.

Large protests in the streets started dramatically on October 25, scheduled to be a day to recognize and celebrate the police. Organizers focused their efforts on police brutality, calling for demonstrations across the country to protest the state of emergency and call for free and fair elections, as well as a campaign to end official corruption. Using both social media and old-fashioned leafleting, organizers focused on turning out in the streets to bring about a revolution. Tens of thousands turned out in Cairo, massing in Tahrir Square, thousands of others appeared in other cities. Most of the protest was explicitly nonviolent, but it included some civil disobedience actions, and some confrontation with police.

As protests spread, Mubarak tried to offer some ostensibly moderate concessions while simultaneously working to
make it harder for the insurgents to organize. In short order,
the Egyptian government shut down major Internet service
providers, in hopes of interrupting the communication and
coordination among the activists. Paradoxically, this effort
drove more people out into the streets, as it was the only way
they could get reliable information about what was happening.
The largest and most visible demonstration was the ongoing
occupation of Cairo's Tahrir Square, where estimates of crowds
from established news sources ranged from hundreds of
thousands to more than a million people. Mohamed ElBaradei,
formerly head of the International Atomic Energy Agency and
an establishment critic of the Mubarak government, returned
from a self-imposed exile to Egypt to offer an alternative, and
more democratic, government.[1]

The Mubarak administration worked frantically and unsuccessfully to find a way to drive the protesters out of the
Square, but a declared curfew proved to be unenforceable.
The regime then tried first the police, then the military, then
released prisoners, and even armed counterprotesters riding
camels into the Square. None were successful, and members
of the military resisted a call to attack the protesters with live
ammunition. At the same time, Mubarak announced dramatic
and frantic efforts at reform, appointing a vice president, firing
his entire Cabinet, announcing new elections ... months in the
future ... then pledging not to run in them, and only to govern
a transition. He delegated the power to rule to his new vice
president, but asserted that he would remain as head of state.

This resolution didn't stop the demonstrations, and the army
refused to repress them, forcing Mubarak to tender his resig-
nation to his new vice president. The apparent influence of the
protest movement, where mass protests forced the removal

of an authoritarian leader who had been in power for nearly 30 years, seemed to confirm that power in people power, and the potential for extraordinary change from below. But the larger issues of poor economic performance, corruption, and political freedom remained. Indeed, in the aftermath of this revolution, everything got worse.

Although Mubarak had been forced from office, the main coalition supporting him continued to rule Egypt. The military, in particular, continued to exercise ultimate influence on virtually every meaningful decision in foreign and domestic policy (Springborg 2017). A Supreme Council of the military governed Egypt, while promising a transition. Politics remained contested, and protests, along with violent suppression of those protests, continued, through the adoption of a new Constitution, and rounds of parliamentary elections. More than a year after Mubarak's ouster, Mohamed Morsi, representing the Muslim Brotherhood, won the presidency, and set about implementing policies to establish Islamic rule. An already mobilized Egyptian populace went back to the streets, including Tahrir Square, less than a year after Morsi had assumed the presidency, this time bringing tents. This round of protests included liberals, Christians, and secularists, but not Islamic fundamentalists, who supported the new president. In July of 2013, the military removed its second president from office in less than two years, again imposing a state of emergency, as Morsi's supporters took to the streets. An interim government was headed by civilians, but essentially run by the military, and the former defense minister, Abdel Fattah el-Sisi, assumed the presidency a year later, while all the grievances that had originally led to Mubarak's ouster remained largely in place.

The promise and inspiration of the Tunisian and Egyptian revolutions, and indeed, all of the Arab Spring protests, spread around the world, suggesting the prospects for widespread, nonviolent, democratic change. The results, at least thus far after a decade, haven't lived up to that promise. The leader at the top of the Egyptian state appears very much like Mubarak or Sadat, the long-tenured Egyptian presidents he's succeeded.

A Theory of Revolution

Throughout human history, new leaders have cycled through governments, and states outlast those who run them. Kings die and are replaced by their heirs, but the monarchy survives. Leaders are ousted through wars, and sometimes through organized efforts by internal opposition, as ministers or the military impose leaders they find more congenial. Commonly, this is called a *coup d'état*. Leaders also change through a process of elections, either within a governing party, or in a competition between individuals or parties. None of these efforts depend upon social movements or revolutions, and none of these promise change beyond the particular person who sits atop the state. Such efforts rarely mobilize large sectors of the citizenry, and are mostly outside the scope of our concern in looking at social movements and revolutions.

The revolutionary idea is far more ambitious, promising more than a change in personnel, but instead, a broad change in the processes and positions of virtually everyone in society. It's far more difficult to pull off than a coup, and far more consequential. But the idea of a revolution precedes the idea of a social movement. The first notable revolutions, in France and the United States, date to the eighteenth century, but the first major theorist of revolutions is Karl Marx, who wrote in the nineteenth century (Tucker 1978).

The shadow that Marx casts on both the politics of the nineteenth and twentieth centuries, and on the development of theories about how social change takes place, mean that his ideas are inescapable. At the same time, we need to recognize that most of what he predicted turned out to be wrong, and his notions of revolution would have little useful to say about the development of efforts like the Arab Spring, much less the revolutionary efforts that preceded them in Europe or Asia.

Marxist theory starts with an assumption about interests, that is, the factors that affect the development of someone's life. Marx envisioned a wholesale upheaval in social relations that would result from the mobilization and political engagement of large sectors of the population. A simplified version of Marx's template predictions about revolutions helps here. For Marx, interests are objective and determined by an individual's relation to "the means of production," that is, the source of the creation of wealth. Marx claims that history is a process and product of class struggles, that is, battles between those who own property and those who work for wages to sustain themselves. This basic schism is at the root of all history, and a series of battles over governance and policy.

Capitalism itself was the motor for bourgeois revolutions, in which property owners worked to throw off the restrictions of tradition, offering a clear-eyed vision of the world of commerce, and demanding that it be applied to the political world around them. Marx himself was a better analyst of capitalism than of what might follow. In *The Communist Manifesto*, he is almost breathless in his admiration of the power of the emerging economic system, as new merchants and manufacturers worked to build a world around themselves that aided commerce. He and Engels wrote

> The bourgeoisie, wherever it has got the upper hand, has put an end to all feudal, patriarchal, idyllic relations. It has pitilessly torn asunder the motley feudal ties that bound man

to his "natural superiors", and has left remaining no other nexus between man and man than naked self-interest, than callous "cash payment" ... The bourgeoisie has stripped of its halo every occupation hitherto honoured and looked up to with reverent awe. It has converted the physician, the lawyer, the priest, the poet, the man of science, into its paid wage labourers ... It has been the first to show what man's activity can bring about. It has accomplished wonders far surpassing Egyptian pyramids, Roman aqueducts, and Gothic cathedrals; it has conducted expeditions that put in the shade all former Exoduses of nations and crusades.

The bourgeoisie cannot exist without constantly revolution-ising the instruments of production, and thereby the relations of production, and with them the whole relations of society ... Constant revolutionising of production, uninterrupted distur-bance of all social conditions, everlasting uncertainty and agitation distinguish the bourgeois epoch from all earlier ones. All fixed, fast-frozen relations, with their train of ancient and venerable prejudices and opinions, are swept away, all new-formed ones become antiquated before they can ossify. All that is solid melts into air, all that is holy is profaned, and man is at last compelled to face with sober senses his real conditions of life, and his relations with his kind (Tucker 1978: 475–6).

When the capitalists, or bourgeoisie, were the ascendant class, they were the forces behind Enlightenment revolutions and reforms, most notably in the United States, and later France. Although the revolutionaries made claims about the power of reason and the primacy of the people in forging governance, they had difficulties in living up to the promises they made. In the United States, slavery continued for more than 70 years after the colonists asserted the unalienable rights of man; in France, passionate reformers overreached, creating terror and counterrevolutions.

But Marx was looking at the next revolutions, those he imagined dominating the nineteenth century and executed by the workers. For Marx, capitalism created the basis for widespread social movements that would produce revolutions. He argued that among capitalism's extraordinary contributions to human history was the creation of the proletarian. The competitive environment of capitalism would have owners constantly under pressure to revise and improve the means of production, squeezing more value out of labor, and paying people to work as long and earn as little as possible – just enough so that they could come in to work the next day. As agriculture grew more efficient, large numbers of people would be forced off the land and turned into wage laborers, working to produce in factories and enrich those who owned the factories. The creation of major cities and large-scale workplaces would put regular people in touch with each other and make organizing opposition possible in a way that had never been possible before. The drive for profit would turn professionals, like doctors or attorneys, into wage laborers, who would ultimately find their best interests advanced by unity with industrial workers. Coupled with greatly expanded communications and easier travel, workers could unite across local and national barriers, building a series of large movements that would, he claimed, usher in a new epoch of history.

The extraordinary accomplishments of capitalism would provide a foundation for the resistance that would end the privation and despair that it also created. Capitalism's achievements made it possible for states led for and by workers to provide adequate livelihoods for all that would limit the amount of work and provide for fuller lives for all. Importantly, socialist revolution depended upon an earlier bourgeois revolution which created the wealth and infrastructure necessary to build a revolutionary movement and to administer an economy and a polity that provided for its citizens. Of course, such revolutions would occur in countries that had developed the groundwork for workers' movements and socialist states.

And the nineteenth century was filled with organized efforts in the richest countries to promote increased democracy and advance the interests of working people, none of which resulted in a socialist revolution, as Marx imagined it, and none of which resulted in a Communist state. The Communist revolutions that occurred in the twentieth century, particularly in Russia and China, emerged and toppled ruling governments in the countries Marx had thought were *least likely* to generate meaningful revolutions. The new regimes in those countries then set about, rather ruthlessly, forcing the economic and social development that Marx expected capitalism to provide. Forced industrialization, mandated relocation of workers or farmers to areas deemed of need, and state-governed development and construction produced some achievements, to be sure, but at tremendous costs. Both countries were able to industrialize relatively quickly, but did not develop the infrastructure of civil society that democratic theorists take for granted. Meanwhile, the failure of capitalism to produce the revolutions Marx envisioned is a critical one for understanding the development of social movements in advanced industrial states, and to make sense of the process of reform.

The Bible story of Jonah provides a good metaphor for understanding why revolutions didn't take place, and why social movements did. The simple story: God came to Noah and told him to go to the city of Nineveh and announce that its destruction was imminent, a punishment earned by the ongoing sins of the population. Jonah was unwilling to take on the task because he thought that the Nineveheans would make a show of repentance and God would postpone the city's destruction, leaving the prophet humiliated when his predictions did not come to pass. Jonah fled, rather than take on the task, and was swallowed by a great fish – the part of the story that is most remembered. Ultimately, however, he had to go and deliver the news. As the prophet had predicted, the people of Nineveh made a great show of their regrets and repented, demonstrating the visible signs of their regret: covering themselves with ashes and tearing their clothes. And, as Jonah had also predicted, divine retribution never came. Jonah left the city disgusted.

An easy read of the story is that Jonah's warning (from God) worked. Nineveh was no longer a residuum of evil and sin. The people recognized their misdeeds, and committed to living more reverent lives; fire and brimstone weren't required.

The story of the absent revolutions in advanced economies bears some similarities here. Workers movements spurred reforms such that the capitalist futures Marx described didn't exactly pan out. And at least some of the benefits of the Communist states he imagined came from capitalist economies. To see what happened, take a look at the goals Marx and Engels announced in *The Communist Manifesto*. Acknowledging that the demands would differ across countries, the pamphleteers described core concerns that would be consistent:

1. Abolition of property in land and application of all rents of land to public purposes.
2. A heavy progressive or graduated income tax.
3. Abolition of all rights of inheritance.
4. Confiscation of the property of all emigrants and rebels.
5. Centralisation of credit in the hands of the state, by means of a national bank with State capital and an exclusive monopoly.

6. Centralisation of the means of communication and transport in the hands of the State.

7. Extension of factories and instruments of production owned by the State; the bringing into cultivation of waste-lands, and the improvement of the soil generally in accordance with a common plan.

8. Equal liability of all to work. Establishment of industrial armies, especially for agriculture.

9. Combination of agriculture with manufacturing industries; gradual abolition of all the distinction between town and country by a more equable distribution of the populace over the country.

10. Free education for all children in public schools. Abolition of children's factory labour in its present form. Combination of education with industrial production, &c, &c. (Tucker 1978: 490).

When we look through Marx's expression of Communist demands from 1848 and compare them to the policies and politics of advanced industrialized nations, we get a somewhat different perspective on the influence of revolutionary social movements. There are defeats: private property (#1) remains a stable feature of liberal capitalism, and democracies are loath to confiscate the property of dissidents (#4). Some demands seem odd or confusing to a contemporary eye, particularly the "combination of agriculture with manufacturing," which is hard to make sense of, as is the notion of equally spreading a population across the country (#8). But some seem like partial victories or concessions by liberal capitalism. Private property can be passed on to heirs (#3), but in most places is subject to substantial taxation. Industrial armies might be seen in times of national crisis or war, and jobs are not guaranteed, but in most liberal democracies, a basic standard of living is (#8). States provide a great deal in the way of banking and transportation. In some countries, national banks do not have a monopoly on credit, but they make a substantial impact on the economy. Private banks are regulated and insured by government (#5, #6). Large transportation systems, including railways, highways, and air traffic, may be held by regulated private companies or state companies, or a combination of both. And still others seem like total concessions: child labor is banned, and working hours are regulated everywhere; free public education is a foundation of liberal democracies (#10).

Looking at the laundry list of demands from 1848 is instructive in many ways. In putting forward such a broad and ambitious agenda, Marx, Engels, and the Communist Party they promoted served multiple goals. To be sure, it makes sense to think they wanted the policies they highlighted. But those demands also reflected an attempt to market the cause and the party to an audience of workers who might join in their efforts. Although some of those demands didn't translate into policy, it's a drastic mistake to focus exclusively on the shortfalls.

Similarly, in contemporary politics, climate change advocates have advanced a vision of change anchored in a "Green New Deal."[2] The idea was that a massive government investment program, targeted to appropriate economic and social goals, could link diverse constituencies in a comprehensive effort to protect the earth from environmental threats – and more. The proposal, which appeared in a scant 14-page resolution in the United States House of Representatives, included aspirational goals about reducing carbon in the atmosphere, providing stable high-wage jobs with guaranteed medical leave, developing high-speed rail systems, and providing national health insurance. More a political program than a developed policy agenda, winning victories on some of the proposals would reflect great influence for the movement.

Similarly, it's a mistake to dismiss Marx and Engels's aspirations because the Communist revolution in advanced industrialized nations didn't happen, just as Jonah's prophesized destruction of Nineveh didn't occur. But, like the city of Nineveh, the warning spurred reforms that made the necessity of destruction less obvious and far more difficult to achieve. Liberal capitalist democracies responded to insurgent revolutionary and labor movements in a variety of ways, including repression, but importantly also including incorporation and policy reforms. Marx, who saw the liberal state as a vehicle for protecting the interests of big capital and sorting out their disputes, missed the possibility that the state might develop its own interests and capacities, and respond to more diverse interests and constituencies. By bending, adapting, and incorporating, capitalist democracies survived, but in a form that Marx would not have imagined. By the 1880s, Germany's conservative chancellor, Otto von Bismarck had begun to establish the foundation of the modern welfare state. Perhaps his efforts were the product of deeply felt moral convictions, but we must recognize that incorporating reforms were an effective means to still and channel the demands of insurgent labor, and to ensure the survival of his government (Hicks 1999). While explicitly limiting the freedom of the Socialist Party to organize, Bismarck simultaneously introduced reforms designed to undermine its appeal, including health, accident, and old age insurance. The capitalist state he managed was one that proved a more elusive target than the ones that Marx imagined overthrowing.

Adopting, Adapting, and Spreading a Model

Communist revolutions took root in countries that were economic laggards, with governance that was incapable of defending itself either militarily or through reform. Communism proved to be a banner to fly for insurgents seeking power, but once in power those governing set about centralizing production and distribution in ways that crushed personal liberties and failed to provide the comfort and autonomy that Marx promised.

So, Marx was a powerful writer and analyst, but he got a great deal wrong. For our purposes, what he got wrong is instructive for our understanding of the influence of social movements.

First, Marx saw the essential grievance animating social change as one about the ownership and disposition of property. To be sure, the cleavage between the haves and the have-nots continues to animate social movements and conflict around the world. But people don't always recognize the same vision of their economic interests and they develop additional concerns as well. Marx viewed concern with something other than cultivating the ownership of the means of production as a "false consciousness," this is to say, a distraction from the fundamental issues that really matter. Attention to race, religion, and nationalism served to stop people from recognizing the need to unite around their true interests and mobilize effectively. Marx assumed that belief that such things mattered would simply disappear. Grievances about gender, sexual orientation, or values were certainly not on his analytical radar. But those grievances have all served as the basis of strong social movements, and sometimes revolutionary campaigns – some of which toppled governments.

Second, Marx drew a sharp line between those who controlled the means of production and those who worked for wages. Using the factory as his model, he saw globalization and automation as continuing pressures that would force wages down and concentrate ownership in fewer and fewer hands. The story that emerged over nearly 200 years is somewhat more complicated. Although economic inequality has increased over the past decades in advanced industrialized countries, some wage earners have been very well compensated. It's not just professional athletes or entertainers who negotiate multi-million-dollar contracts for their services, but also attorneys, financial managers, and computer coders who are not remotely close to immiserated. The orthopedic surgeon who works at a hospital won't see an obvious shared interest with the janitor who cleans the building. Although each sells his labor to an employer, the surgeon enjoys considerably more leverage. What's more, through the expansion of finance markets, substantial populations own some portion of the means of production. Although the shares for many are quite small, the identification with the well-being of the markets is a far more powerful force than Marx predicted.

Third, Marx did not imagine the capitalist states that could incorporate and accommodate unrest, brokering policies that constrained – to varying degrees – the autonomy of large owners, or provide some kind of social safety net for the less affluent, as described in the example of Bismarck above. States regulate businesses, to varying degrees, as well as social benefits and labor conditions.

Fourth, the importance of the international political and security order in facilitating or stifling revolutionary movements far exceeded what anyone could have seen in the middle of the nineteenth century. Both the Russian and Chinese revolutions occurred at moments when the existing regimes faced severe international military challenges. Distracted or disabled by those challenges, tightly organized insurgencies could overthrow faltering regimes and impose new political orders. During World War II, and more dramatically afterward, with the onset of the Cold War, the competition between two rival military and political blocs spilled over into the rest of the world through proxy battles.

Organized Communist movements tried to recruit and compete for state power across Europe, but were successful in East Europe, and not the West, largely because of the efforts of the Soviet Union, an outside sponsor. The division of Europe more or less formalized at Yalta, allowed the Soviet Union to provide strong military and economic support for Communist revolutionaries in the East, and to deter Western allies from overt military action. Simultaneously, it afforded the West, particularly the United States, the cause and the legitimacy to help combat insurgencies in Western allies, even if it meant propping up authoritarian ones.

Revolutionary movements that emerged in the Global South had incentives to align with one or another bloc, which would funnel in financial and military resources that allowed campaigns to continue, and sometimes to win control of the state. Thus, nationalist movements in Vietnam or Cuba, for example, claimed Communist identities in order to garner international support. The Communist threat Western leaders saw led them to support unpopular and authoritarian governments that faced their own challengers in places like Iran or Guatemala. Nationalism was a more powerful force for organizing and motivating insurgent armies than class struggle, although insurgents could claim class struggle as a way to try to leverage Soviet financial and military aid.[3] And, of course, espousing "anti-Communism" was a way to get military and financial aid from the United States. The result was that nationalist revolutionary movements became part of a larger Cold War landscape in which those independence aims were at least partly redefined, and their intent potentially compromised.

Although revolutionary movements depended upon local

support, it's hard to overstate the importance of the international context, as the Cold War rivalry played out across the Global South. For the most part, the United States effectively staved off Communist movements in the Western hemisphere, and the Soviet Union and China effectively supported some revolutionary movements in Asia. In the Middle East and North Africa, each superpower supported client states, propping up dictators whose regimes would be challenged decades later.

What was the impact? Both Communist and anti-Communist revolutionaries imposed authoritarian states, severely limiting individual liberties, human rights, and opposing political organizations. Strict authoritarian control allowed leaders to impose policies that had attractive elements: Castro's Cuba dramatically increased access to both literacy and health care, for example. The Shah of Iran, installed by an American coup in the 1950s, instituted a White Revolution that promoted economic modernization, land reform, women's rights, and secularization. But such authoritarian governments also engendered revolutionary opposition.

While the Castro regime was able to maintain power well past the end of the Cold War, it did so partly by expelling dissidents or allowing them to emigrate. Other regimes were not so stable. Leftists and Islamists supported a revolutionary movement in Iran that was unified in opposition not only to the Shah's harsh repression, but also the imperial strictures imposed by US support. After toppling the Shah in 1979, the revolutionary coalition quickly unraveled, and the secular and leftist supporters of the movement were forced into exile. Since that time, Iran's government has been formally regulated by a council of religious leaders, who have been effective in maintaining power, but not delivering on economic growth as they have adamantly opposed some kinds of secularization and modernization.

There is a temptation to find the ultimate fate of revolutionary movements embedded in their organization and their tactics. An impressive research stream focuses on the outcomes of nonviolent revolutionary movements in comparison with armed campaigns (Chenoweth and Stephan 2011; Schock 2004). Diving into extensive case studies and large-scale comparisons of many campaigns, rigorous scholars typically find that the nonviolent campaigns are far more likely to succeed, and far less likely to result in mass killings than armed rebellions (Perkoski and Chenoweth 2018). There is even the bold claim that the key predictor of successful revolutionary movements is the participation of 3.5 percent of the population in a nonviolent campaign (Chenoweth and Belgioioso 2019).

The findings about the effectiveness of nonviolent action, at least when sufficiently widespread, are provocative and inspiring. We would all like to believe that there is a connection between the means and the ends of politics. But the focus on tactics, while minimizing the influence of contextual factors, can mislead us into thinking there is a calculable and replicable recipe for social change (Meyer 2019a). The circumstances under which a revolutionary campaign can mobilize large numbers in the streets are unusual, dependent upon an admixture of provocation, grievance, and tolerance. It's never really clear if the conditions that permit the development of such a movement are really what makes it possible for a revolutionary campaign to succeed. When we look at the long and complicated process of promoting revolutionary change, we see the importance of contextual factors, the simultaneous presence of different kinds of approaches to organizing protest, and the importance of outside actors, beyond the

struggle between protesting challengers and governing authorities. In order to make sense of what works, why movements
sometimes matter, we need to look at the context in which
they emerge, the challenges they face, and the ways they
change over time.

The South African Story

The importance of the international system in supporting
or stalling revolutionary movements in the Third World can
clearly be seen in the story of the South African government
and a decades-long movement against institutional racial
discrimination. Discrimination on the basis of race was an
essential part of politics in South Africa, which intensified
when the country declared independence from Britain in 1910.
Segregation by race was the law of the land, and became firmly
institutionalized when the Nationalist Party won elections
in 1948 and established a formal system of *apartheid*, or
separation. Race, as identified by observation and on formal
papers, restricted where anyone could live, what schools they
might attend, and with whom they might associate. Blacks
were further formally allowed to live in only certain areas, and
were blocked from political participation.[4]

Organizing against racial discrimination in South Africa
preceded the formal institution of the system. Indeed, Mohandas
Gandhi, who led a successful independence movement in India
decades later, spent more than a decade in South Africa organizing a nonviolent campaign against racial discrimination. But
Gandhi left South Africa in 1914, with little in the way of
political accomplishments.[5]

Opposition to racial discrimination and white dominance
in South Africa began in an organized way long before the
establishment of the National Party's formal apartheid regime,

starting about when South Africa declared independence very early in the twentieth century. From the start, the ANC, along with precursors and allies, organized resistance campaigns against racially defined passbooks and residential segregation.

After the National Party came to power and began strengthening and formalizing discrimination, the ANC stepped up its own opposition, resisting the implementation of new laws with tactics that now evoke the style and strategies of protest in America for civil rights and against war. Activists burned passbooks that identified race, purposefully and openly entered designated white areas, and staged demonstrations, beginning with a Day of Protest, on June 26, 1950. To build on these efforts, in 1952, the ANC announced a Defiance Campaign, which would start on its anniversary, which included civil disobedience and large demonstrations.

The government responded with repression that was at least as harsh as civil rights activists in the United States faced at roughly the same time. Employing harsh repression and mass arrests, the National Party government arrested and incarcerated thousands of nonviolent ANC demonstrators. Refusing to cooperate with the government by defending themselves in court or accepting alternative sentences such as probation, activists filled the jails, intending to heighten pressure on the government. The government responded to the pressure with more aggressive policing, stricter laws, and harsher punishments. While the Civil Rights movement in the American South was able to pressure the federal government to offer some degree of protection, the ANC found no such allies in the national government. Without restraint, the government was able to pass laws prohibiting protest against the apartheid laws, which the police enforced aggressively.

Racial politics in South Africa became increasingly polarized, and attending demonstrations grew to be extremely risky for participants. New organizations developed to promote and stimulate opposition to the regime, which led to more pressure on the government, and even harsher repression. On March 21, 1960, thousands of demonstrators appeared at the Sharpeville police station to offer themselves up for arrest for not carrying passbooks with racial identification. Police attempts to intimidate the crowds that grew in support led to confrontation with the demonstrators, and an escalation in violence. Police opened fire on the demonstrators, killing 69 protesters and wounding nearly 200 others. The Sharpeville Massacre occasioned even more repression and even more opposition.

Social protest raised the cost and difficulty of maintaining order for the national government. As it tightened its grip, activists intensified their own campaigns. A new leadership within the ANC pushed for more aggressive action, including sabotage. Among these new leaders was Nelson Mandela, who formed *Umkhonto we Sizwe* (The "Spear of the Nation") to coordinate an armed struggle against apartheid. Of course, this provoked additional repression.

The Rivonia trial of 1963–4, in which 10 anti-apartheid activists were charged with accepting help from foreign agents – including Communists – and conspiring to plot sabotage, offers a window through which we can see how the revolutionary campaign advanced.[6] Ostensibly defending himself, militant leader Nelson Mandela spoke for five hours, targeting his comments less at the judge than at a broader international audience.[7] Mandela outlined his grievances with the apartheid regime and his own political history. He emphasized that the turn to sabotage was occasioned by a rational assessment that it provided the only reasonable prospect of political influence against the regime:

I must deal immediately and at some length with the question of violence ... I do not, however, deny that I planned sabotage. I did not plan it in a spirit of recklessness, nor because I have any love of violence. I planned it as a result of a calm and sober assessment of the political situation that had arisen after many years of tyranny, exploitation, and oppression of my people by the Whites ...

Firstly, we believed that as a result of Government policy, violence by the African people had become inevitable, and that unless responsible leadership was given to canalize and control the feelings of our people, there would be outbreaks of terrorism which would produce an intensity of bitterness and hostility between the various races of this country which is not produced even by war. Secondly, we felt that without violence there would be no way open to the African people to succeed in their struggle against the principle of white supremacy. All lawful modes of expressing opposition to this principle had been closed by legislation, and we were placed in a position in which we had either to accept a permanent state of inferiority, or to defy the Government. We chose to defy the law ...

We had no doubt that we had to continue the fight ... Our problem was not whether to fight, but was how to continue the fight. We of the ANC had always stood for a non-racial democracy, and we shrank from any action which might drive the races further apart than they already were. But the hard facts were that fifty years of non-violence had brought the African people nothing but more and more repressive legislation, and fewer and fewer rights ...

At the beginning of June 1961, after a long and anxious assessment of the South African situation, I, and some colleagues, came to the conclusion that as violence in this country was inevitable, it would be unrealistic and wrong for African leaders to continue preaching peace and non-violence at a time when the Government met our peaceful demands with force ...

The lack of human dignity experienced by Africans is the direct result of the policy of white supremacy. White supremacy implies black inferiority. Legislation designed to preserve white supremacy entrenches this notion ...

During my lifetime I have dedicated myself to this struggle of the African people. I have fought against white domination, and I have fought against black domination. I have cherished the ideal of a democratic and free society in which all persons live together in harmony and with equal opportunities. It is an ideal which I hope to live for and to achieve. But if needs be, it is an ideal for which I am prepared to die.

The court convicted Mandela and nine other ANC leaders of sabotage, sentencing them to life in prison. For nearly three decades, the leaders were blocked not only from normal life, but from public visibility; Mandela, for example, could not be photographed.

While the ANC moved to include armed struggle in its efforts to end apartheid, it also sought to mobilize allies outside the country to pressure the National Party government. The strategy of calling in outside help when you are on the losing side of a political battle is a well-established one (Schattschneider 1960). The crowd can change the balance of power, constraining those who are advantaged and providing support to those on the losing side of the battle. In South Africa, the allies came largely from outside of the country, demonstrating a "boomerang effect," where appeals targeted to international audiences are meant to rebound back to activists in the country that launched them (Keck and Sikkink 1988). Such an approach is often the best bet that activists in repressive countries have in effecting progress.

The injustice of racial segregation was a claim that was easily accepted in most of the world, but agreeing on ways to get the South African government to go along was extremely difficult and time-consuming. In 1962, before the Rivonia trial, the United Nations passed a non-binding resolution that expressed the body's opposition to apartheid and calling for sanctions on the South African government, both to signal the values of the body, and to pressure the government. The following year, the Security Council passed a resolution that called for a voluntary embargo on the sale of armaments to South Africa. Activists began holding conferences in the ensuing years to highlight both injustice in South Africa, and their own moral and political commitments. Some countries began embargoing the sale of weapons to the South African government, but the National Party had established reliable partnerships with enough outside allies to maintain a steady supply of sophisticated weaponry.

In 1977, the United Nations Security Council codified a weapons embargo, but enforcement was still erratic, and the South African government found ways around it, including stepping up domestic production of weapons. In another decade, the Council would pass subsequent resolutions to tighten the loopholes in the ban. Leaders of some Western governments also criticized the morality of apartheid, describing it as a crime against humanity. Such charges dated back to the early 1960s, but increased throughout the 1970s.

In 1986, large trading partners, including Japan and the European Community, imposed economic sanctions on limited elements of the economy, and also stopped trade in certain products, including oil – although the regime could always find ways to circumvent such embargos. Although the economic costs to the government were limited, they did slow the rate of growth, stir unrest, and undermine the government's capacity to buy peace with its own dissidents.

Political and cultural sanctions may have been more meaningful, and they developed slowly. Because apartheid prohibited integrated participation in sports, international sporting associations began to block the country from participating in international competition, beginning with table tennis, but soon extending to other sports. In 1962, the Olympics banned South Africa from participation. In 1961, South Africa withdrew from the British Commonwealth, as its leaders knew they would have to begin to dismantle apartheid in order to remain in it. The United Nations banned South Africa from participation in its General Assembly in 1974, making foreign relations more difficult. International travel also became more difficult for those with a South African passport; artists and entertainers began to take South Africa off the list of places they might work. The South African government had to work harder and harder to project itself as a normal country and ensure cultural, political, and economic relations with the outside world.

When some governments, including the United States and Switzerland, were particularly reluctant to promote economic sanctions, activists globally turned their attention to individual companies. Seeking to stave off sanctions, some Americans promoted only certain kinds of economic engagement with South Africa, that is, business investment that would not promote apartheid and would promote political change. Beginning in 1984, activists, including members of Congress, staged civil disobedience actions outside the White House, subjecting themselves to arrest. College students in the United States protested apartheid in South Africa, staging demonstrations and building shanty towns to pressure their campuses to divest from companies that did any business in South Africa (Soule 1997). Some cities and towns embraced the same strategy of divestment.

Activism spilled into the cultural realm as well. In addition to entertainment boycotts of South Africa, activist artists tried to go further and organize. Inspired by "Do They Know it's Christmas," a recording featuring a few dozen popular musicians coordinated to raise money for famine victims in Ethiopia, Harry Belafonte decided to organize a similar effort. Belafonte, an actor and singer who had his own long history as a civil rights activist, commissioned Michael Jackson and Lionel Richie, then among the most popular singers in the United States, to write a song that could include dozens of musicians representing different styles. "We Are the World" featured about 50 famous musicians singing together and in solos, and representing a broad range of genres. The release of the single recording, accompanied by a video and an album, drew nationwide attention and raised more than $10 million in a few months, money that was donated to hunger relief efforts. The effort was coordinated by a new organization, USA for Africa, which continued its efforts in the following decades.

The anti-hunger records offered a kind of consensual politics, emphasizing charity rather than political change, but they inspired other musicians to try to do more. Steve van Zandt, now better known as an actor than a musician, worked to take the collective song in a more pointed direction, focusing on the cultural boycott of South Africa. A few dozen artists representing a range of genres – including punk, folk, hip-hop, and rock, appeared on the recording, which was released in 1985 with a provocative video. The "Sun City" video included clips of police beating black Africans demonstrating against apartheid, and offered glimpses of extreme poverty in the townships. It also offered direct criticism not only of apartheid, but also US president Ronald Reagan's expressed strategy of "constructive engagement," describing "quiet diplomacy" as "nothing but a joke." Although the song was considerably less popular than the charity-oriented records that preceded it, it accelerated the process of identifying South Africa as a pariah state (Goldberg 2016).

Social, economic, and political pressure increased incrementally on the National Party government in South Africa, gradually weakening the commitment of its leaders to maintaining the apartheid system that had grown increasingly costly. The National Party government began secret negotiations with Nelson Mandela on the politics of a transition in 1985, while the ANC leader was still in prison. Public negotiations between lower-level members of the government took place at international meetings to both test and shape public opinion on the politics of ending apartheid.

In 1989, F.W. DeKlerk became president of South Africa, and continued the negotiations, at first informally. At a major speech early in 1990, DeKlerk announced the unbanning of the ANC and other political organizations, as well as the release of Mandela and other political prisoners. Negotiations between DeKlerk, Mandela, and other leaders extended over years, and through periods of intensified tension. In September 1994, South Africa held its first multiracial elections, in which Mandela was elected president. The transitional agreement afforded DeKlerk a position as deputy, and the National Party joined the ANC in a national unity government.

When we think about the outcomes of social movements, the South African case provides a useful reminder about the extraordinary difficulty of promoting revolutionary change. Apartheid lasted for nearly 46 years, and the campaign for a multiracial democracy organized and mobilized through most of that time. The long life of the movement depended upon the stalwart commitment of people who were organizing under extremely difficult circumstances and taking great risks. It also took the active engagement of supporters around the world. Governments and citizens funneled financial and moral support to the ANC and the anti-apartheid movement. Activists pressured their own governments to pressure South Africa, partly by publicizing the horrors of the apartheid system. In South Africa, the struggle included nonviolent demonstrations, often at the funerals of activists, sabotage, and moral argument. Outside the country, the repertoire of action was perhaps even broader, including extensive efforts to draw additional players into the conflict. The world's governments exerted political, social, and economic pressure on the South African state.

In this broad context, it's impossible to pinpoint the relative weight of different tactics employed by different groups at different times on promoting the end of apartheid. It is clear, however, that social movement organizing had a cumulative effect. ANC officials benefited from support from outside, and their efforts spurred more support. Activists in the North took comfort from the support of entertainers as well as politicians. And all of the pressures made maintaining control of the country increasingly unattractive, and ultimately untenable, for the National Party.

Nelson Mandela served as South Africa's president for five years, and presided over the implementation of a Truth and Reconciliation process in which the details of misdeeds of previous decades were heard – and formally forgiven. He also set out to redress the gross inequality that the apartheid state had supported without alienating white supporters. Unsurprisingly, the results were extraordinarily wide-ranging and nonetheless disappointing to the activists who had taken to the streets.

South Africa's struggle to implement a multiracial democracy continued over the two decades since Mandela's presidency ended, underscoring the difficulty for outsiders to recognize the impact of movements and evaluate their success. Efforts to end apartheid were complicated by the gross inequality of wealth and property in the country, and the cumulative impact of other inequalities. The work has to continue over a very long period of time, crossing several generations.

We started this chapter with the Arab Spring of 2011, whose results are disappointing to advocates of democracy – thus far. We then saw how long a real revolutionary struggle takes to enjoy substantial influence. Let's close by looking at the comparative outcomes of revolutionary movements across six Eastern European states that toppled Communist governments in 1989.

The Revolutions of 1989

The end of World War II ushered in a period of Cold War competition, in which the United States and the Soviet Union supported governments that their leaders believed advanced their international interests, often at the expense of concerns about domestic performance. The Western bloc, anchored by the United States, proclaimed the advantages of democracy and open markets, but generally prioritized anti-Communism. The Soviet Union, of course, supported its version of Communism, which generally also emphasized reliable agreement on foreign policy.

Immediately after the war, the Soviet Union helped establish Communist governments across Eastern Europe, and buttressed those governments against domestic and foreign opposition with financial resources and the constant threat of military intervention. Communist governments in East Germany, Czechoslovakia, Poland, Hungary, Romania, and Bulgaria varied considerably in terms of their openness and their domestic policies, but not in their deference to Soviet wishes. Dissent developed in Eastern Europe, but varied in terms of size and tactics in each country. After Soviet leader Joseph Stalin's death in 1952, reformers in Eastern Europe began to imagine the possibility of independence from the bloc (e.g., Djilas 1957).

Hungarian reformers, led by student protesters, took to the streets in 1956, quickly followed by protesters from different sectors in the society, and the government called for Soviet military help against its own citizenry (Gati 2006). Reformers within the Hungarian Communist Party replaced the leadership with people who would commit to modest reforms that, they hoped, the Soviet Union would tolerate; they were wrong. Soviet tanks invaded and the Hungarian army fought against a far better armed Soviet military. Within days, the temporary leader was purged and members of the Hungarian Communist Party imposed a new government with the explicit support of the Soviet Union.

A revolutionary movement in Czechoslovakia took a somewhat different form, as a reformer, Alexander Dubček, came to lead the Communist Party there before there was any kind of mobilization in the streets (Tismaneanu 2011). In 1968 Dubček promised "socialism with a human face"; while the Communist Party would retain primacy, there would be increased civil liberties and freedom of the press, and better access to consumer goods. In this period of liberalization, known as the Prague Spring, citizens demanded quick progress on delivering those reforms, and felt more free to criticize the Soviet Union than the leaders of the regime did. The Soviet Union negotiated with the Dubček government to limit the reforms, but ultimately decided to intervene militarily, ousting Dubček and installing a more compliant regime.

Revolutionary resistance emerged once more in Poland in 1980. In the face of a stalled Polish economy, ship workers in Gdansk organized the first independent trade union in the Communist country, Solidarity (Ost 1990). Lech Wałęsa extended the labor movement to include activists within the Catholic Church, building a broad anti-Soviet campaign that was determinedly nonviolent. After initially meeting with Wałęsa and promising negotiations and limited reforms, Polish leader General Wojciech Jaruzelski imposed martial law, claiming that the move was an effort to avoid a Soviet invasion. Although Jaruzelski implemented harsh political and economic strictures, Solidarity survived two years of martial law and more than five years of Jaruzelski's Communist regime.

The point is that efforts to spur democratic reforms in Eastern Europe were recurrent, but were severely constrained by the shadow – and sometimes presence – of the Soviet Union. The most visible revolutionary activity was promoted by dissidents, who offered opposition to Communism and the Soviet Union mostly through a war of ideas, and through writing. In essays, drama, and poetry, dissidents clarified their grievances and defined their longer-term goals as clearly as they could. They often enjoyed a larger audience outside of their own countries than within. Reformers outside government had to navigate their paths toward reform mindful of the threat of military intervention, and Communist leaders, no matter what their own personal intent, worked to find ways to maintain order and keep the Soviets out.

Dramatic changes unfolded in 1989, but they began developing years earlier. When Mikhail Gorbachev won the leadership of the Soviet Communist Party in 1985, he began pushing for economic and political reforms that, he hoped, would save the country. The two pillars of the program were *glasnost*, or political liberalization, and *perestroika*, or economic restructuring. Gorbachev displayed no interest in ending the dominance of the Communist Party, but believed that market-based economic reforms and some degree of political openness would make for a more resilient economy and a more resilient regime (Mason 1988). He urged his Communist allies in Eastern Europe to adopt similar policies.

Partly in response to this opening, Polish workers staged a series of strikes in 1988 that led to negotiations between Wałęsa and Jaruzelski about the recognition of Solidarity. These talks resulted in an agreement to legalize the trade union and stage multiparty elections in which it could participate. In June of 1989, Solidarity won overwhelming political victories in those elections, and the Communist Party coalition collapsed. Solidarity formed a coalition that produced a new president who was both a devout Catholic and a committed anti-Communist. Within the next year, the Polish Communist Party had dissolved itself and Wałęsa himself became president. With government support, activists began dismantling the visible signs of Communist rule, including the statues of Communist heroes.

Anti-Communist revolutions followed across Eastern Europe (Garton Ash 1990; Kaldor 1998). Mass demonstrations in Hungary, which had already implemented some economic liberalization, led to negotiations between the governing party and a range of democratic reformers. The government began taking down fences separating Hungary from Austria, which allowed Czechoslovakians and East Germans to migrate West, further destabilizing their own governments. In the fall, multiparty negotiations led to a series of Constitutional reforms that created the infrastructure for multiparty governance and liberal democracy.

Massive popular demonstrations in East Germany and Czechoslovakia pressed governments to respond. When it became clear that the Soviet Union would not offer military support to prop up unpopular governments, Communist leaders sought to find ways out of the unrest that surrounded them. In both cases, reform-oriented Communists replaced more repressive leaders and then negotiated transitions to free elections and liberal democratic political structures. Bulgaria followed, as its long-term leader was ousted by a coalition of reform-minded Communists, who then developed a Constitution and instituted multiparty elections. All of these transitions were extraordinarily nonviolent, as the Communist governments found that they could no longer depend on their capacity to repress civil opposition.

The revolutionary dynamic played out most disruptively in Romania, which had been led by Nicolae Ceauşescu for nearly 25 years (Siani-Davies 2007). Unlike his counterparts in other East European states, Ceauşescu expressed his clear intent to use any means necessary to ensure the survival of his rule; he ordered the military to suppress peaceful demonstrators violently, as such efforts had worked in the past. In December of 1989, however, the army refused to fire on the demonstrators, and turned on Ceauşescu instead. They captured Ceauşescu and his wife, held quick trials for treason, and executed the ousted rulers. An interim government announced new elections the following year.

Much like the Arab Spring, the East European revolutions captured the political imagination of reformers around the world, and everything seemed possible. Over 30 years later, we're in a position to evaluate the different progress each country has made toward stable liberal democracy, assessing the outcomes of different sorts of revolutions which started in different places. The Communist parties in Hungary and Poland had included reformers, and both had made moves to incorporate market-based reforms into their economies. Czechoslovakia and East Germany had relatively advanced economies, but very strict limits on political freedom.

Opposition was, however, well developed in each state. More tightly controlled governments and societies in Bulgaria and Romania, led by autocrats more than parties, had not afforded the dissidents the space to build opposition movements.

The more developed opposition movements provided a base of support for the new governments that would have to be set up. Lech Wałęsa, for example, became president of Poland in 1990, and although he was new to government, he came into office with a party infrastructure capable of making and implementing policies. When a revolutionary movement succeeds in ousting and replacing a regime, it assumes the burdens of managing all of the functions of the government it replaced. Poor performance by the previous rulers in no way relieves the new government of the same responsibilities. The day after the revolution, someone has to pick up trash. Within a relatively brief amount of time, roads need to be managed, maintained, and likely extended. Trains need to run, children need schools to attend, taxes need to be collected, and pensions distributed. Militaries need to be managed and soldiers paid. All of the mundane elements of government provide the base for the more complicated tasks of managing foreign and military relations.

Additionally, new governments in revolutionary situations have to confront the damage inflicted by those they've overthrown, as well as the accumulated grievances. Soviet dominance repressed or marginalized both democratic movements as well as old and ugly rivalries and campaigns, including racist nationalism. All of these movements reemerged with the end of state Communism. Even the freshest beginning is built upon the achievements and detritus of what came before. We would think that the movements that were most successful in building their own infrastructure and governance would be best equipped to usher in new changes. The six

Eastern European cases give us a chance to examine these premises.

Hungary

In stark contrast to the failed revolution of 1956, the 1989 Hungarian transition was perhaps the least disruptive in all of Eastern Europe, and it initially appeared in the best position to develop some form of liberal democracy. The Hungarian Communist Party had been comparatively open to different visions of governance and the country was better developed than its Eastern European neighbors and more engaged with the West in trade and cultural exchange; its economic infrastructure was also stronger. The record, as it developed, however, is more mixed.

Because the social democratic left had come out of the Communist Party, it carried with it electoral liabilities. In the first free elections, center-right parties were able to win substantial victories. Those governments rather quickly moved toward a Western orientation, joining NATO, but had more difficulty in managing the economy. Rapid privatization produced economic dislocation, governance challenges, and broad public dissatisfaction. The center-left government that followed was equally unsuccessful and unpopular. Populist nationalism proved to be a domestic political solution to the problems of governance and legitimacy. Viktor Orban, leader of a conservative party for more than a decade, has slowly pushed that party toward a more nationalist posture, blaming immigrants and outsiders for the political and economic difficulties Hungary has faced. First serving as prime minister at the turn of the century, he won support internationally from conservatives for his expressed commitment to a limited state and free markets. The conservatives then spent nearly a decade in opposition, turning increasingly toward a populist nationalism to criticize the government and build electoral support. Taking office again in 2010, Orban has been openly skeptical of a liberal democratic state, European integration, international agreements, and minority groups, committing to create an "illiberal" state based on Hungarian identity instead. At the same time, he has implemented restrictions on a free press and the autonomy of the judiciary. Thirty years on, Hungary's transition story is not particularly encouraging.[8]

Poland

The Polish transition was based in a broadly organized labor union, Solidarity, and the Polish Catholic Church. In opposition, often underground, Solidarity and its leader, Lech Wałęsa, had developed a strong organizational infrastructure and a popular legitimacy that was unlike opposition organizations elsewhere in Eastern Europe. The labor union developed the capacity to mobilize substantial protests in short order. But popular support was dependent upon papering over differences within the union over governance, economic objectives, and the role of the Catholic Church. Additionally, rival factions battled for control of the union.

Solidarity, led by Wałęsa, took office in 1990, leading a party and a country ill-prepared for the responsibilities of governance, but committed to opening to the West. Poland moved to join NATO and increase its economic integration with the West. The new Polish government sought Western guidance in moving toward a more market-oriented economy. Leaders chose to implement a rapid transition, dramatically reducing state control of economic enterprises and state support of individuals. This "shock therapy" was extremely disruptive, but also encouraged the development of entrepreneurship in Polish industry.[9] Politically, Wałęsa's union government was oddly responsible for implementing very conservative economic policies. Solidarity transformed itself into an electoral alliance, and then through subsequent reforms, into a party of the right, and ultimately one that disappeared. Meanwhile, Wałęsa failed to get reelected in 1995 following a challenge on his own left, a sort of social-democratic alliance (Ost 2006). Ten years of governance from a left that was bedeviled by its own internal rivalries and governing challenges produced the return of right-wing governments that had committed to a stronger nationalist political profile. The dominant coalition in Polish politics organized around neoliberal economic policies and Christian conservative social policies, heavily influenced by the Catholic Church. The governments that coalition led have faced their own governance challenges, and a democratic Polish state remains a project.

Czechoslovakia
The Velvet Revolution that swept across the country in roughly a month in 1989 seemed to appear with even less visible precedent than its counterparts elsewhere in Eastern Europe. Since the failed revolution of 1968, the Czechoslovakian government had opened its economy to the West, but sharply restricted political freedom within its borders. Notably, critical playwright Václav Havel was banned from the official theater, and increasingly turned his efforts from producing theater in Czechoslovakia to promoting political change. Czechoslovakian dissidents were active in producing a particularly fertile *samizdat* literature that often leaked to the West, and to frame their grievances in terms of universal human rights and democracy. Havel was one of the organizers of an international movement, Charter 77, which called for the Soviet Union to live up to human rights standards to which it had committed. Havel (1985) advocated "living in truth"

as a political strategy, which meant describing accurately the world that East Europeans found themselves in. He spent years in and out of prison and under political surveillance.

By the time citizens took to the streets in 1989, staging strikes and demonstrations across the country, the government enjoyed little political support and was quickly prepared to surrender power. In Prague, activists from Charter 77 organized a new group, the Civic Forum, to coordinate the extremely wide spectrum of dissent and ease a nonviolent transition to democracy. Artists, intellectuals, and students were most visible at the forefront of the movement, which grew quickly. Capable of coordinating a general strike across the country, within a few dramatic days it induced the leadership of the government to resign, turning the politics of the transition over to more sympathetic members of the Communist Party. Members of the party and the media defected to the opposition, which included a spectrum that ranged from free market fundamentalists to cultural critics like Havel who were more committed to some kind of liberal democracy. Havel was appointed president of a transitional government, with free elections scheduled for the following year. In June of 1990, Havel's Civic Forum, in alliance with a Slovak counterpart group, won a majority of parliamentary delegates, and Havel was elected president.

Havel offered a distinct and attractive profile of revolutionary governance,[10] rejecting the most formal trappings of office, dressing informally, and promoting cultural diversity and moral clarity. His first official visitor in January 1990 was the avant-garde musician, Frank Zappa, whom he appointed "Special Ambassador to the West on Trade, Culture and Tourism." He visited the United States in February 1990, delivering a philosophical address to the US Congress, describing his vision of the end of an international system of strategic blocs, adding, "Consciousness precedes being, and not the other way around, as the Marxists claim."[11] The members of Congress, likely unaccustomed to hearing discussion of "being" in their chamber, stood and applauded wildly.

But governing was more complicated than toppling a government, of course, and the new president exercised less political and economic influence than the parliament. The first major challenge was figuring out what to do with people who worked in the now discredited Communist government. On one hand, working with the state party was hardly avoidable for many people, and its veterans were experienced and often expert at the technical aspects of administration. On the other hand, antipathy toward Communist oppression was widespread, and many people harbored a great deal of resentment. Parliament pushed to create some kind of restorative justice for the victims of the Communist state, and passed a *lustration* law that would bar those who collabo-rated with the government from high-level jobs. Over his own declared opposition, Havel signed the law. Strategic political actors used the law to harass their enemies.[12]

Tensions within the Civic Forum grew with the challenges of governing. Some of Havel's putative allies were committed to harsh market-based reforms in the economy. Neoliberal reforms produced civil dislocations, as people lost jobs and factories were no longer supported by government subsidies. The Civic Forum split and Havel's own base of support was rooted in his personal popularity rather than any clear political agenda. The reforms were particularly difficult for the Eastern part of the country, Slovakia. The Czech part of the country was far wealthier, and in early 1991 Parliament declared the end of support payments to Slovakia. In 1992, the new prime minister, Václav Klaus, demanded tighter central national control, while Slovakian leaders sought some kind of confederation that would allow them more autonomy. Although opposed by most Slovaks and most Czechs – including Havel – this dispute led to the dissolution of Czechoslovakia into two new countries. Both the Czech Republic and Slovakia have maintained parliamentary democracies and good relations with the West, but both have also been subject to populist nationalist movements focused on the dangers of immigrants.

Bulgaria

When street protests started in Sofia in November 1989, the Bulgarian Communist Party was quick to jettison Todor Zhivkov, who had led the party and run the country for 35 years. The Communist Party renamed itself and won the first parliamentary elections in 1990, but quickly lost power to a free market fundamentalist party. When privatization of industry and the institution of strictures on the secret police led to massive social dislocations, the reformed Communists regained power – but only briefly. Frequent elections have produced dramatically shifting policies toward the market and the West more generally, and corruption has been a recurrent problem. Thirty years on, Bulgaria is a member of NATO and of the European Union, and has recently experienced a government toppled by street protests. Although civil liberties have improved dramatically in comparison to Communist rule, the country is still bedeviled by corruption and organized crime.

Romania

The transition to democracy begun in 1989 was more disruptive and violent in Romania than in its neighbors. Opposition to Nicolae Ceaușescu clustered in a new political party that welcomed dissident Communists. Establishing civil order was an ongoing problem, but multiple parties formed and competed for power, with control of governance changing fairly frequently. Economic reforms were disruptive, as they were everywhere, but Romania instituted and largely maintained democratic governance – often challenged by protests – and civil liberties.

East Germany

The Communist Party ousted its longtime leader, Erich Honecker, in opposition to his use of the military to suppress the first demonstrations of 1989. The government soon collapsed under both political and economic pressure; by 1990, West Germany offered financial bailouts to stabilize the economy and facilitate a democratic transition. East Germans emigrated in large numbers to West Germany for both economic and political reasons. In 1990, the two Germanies negotiated reunification. Although the former East Germany remains poorer than the rest of the country, it has become a stable part of the larger Germany, with a generous social welfare state and guarantees of basic civil liberties.

Thirty years after the dramatic and extremely hopeful moments of revolution in Eastern Europe, the outcomes of those movements are best described as mixed. Transitions to free markets and to popular governance were difficult, and mostly remain incomplete. Communist dominance had stilled civil liberties and human freedom, but it had also silenced nationalist and xenophobic movements, which have returned to challenge democratic governance. Notably, the countries that seemed best prepared for transition, Hungary and Poland, have struggled to respond to strong illiberal movements which have gained power through parliamentary means. The optimism about apocalyptic change was confronted with the difficult and often mundane business of running an economy. To be sure, the end of state Communist rule was a step forward, but many more steps need to be taken.

We have to view revolutionary campaigns with some skepticism. While dislodging a leader is extremely hard, reconstructing a political and economic system is orders of magnitude more difficult. The translation of democratic dreams into the reality of governance reflects the networks, politics, and problems of previous regimes. Evaluating the success of any campaign requires sorting out the short- and longer-term achievements, and setting them against activists' original intentions. The enthusiasm that greets initial waves of reform is hard to maintain, and delivering on the hopes that animate revolutionary movements is best thought of as aspirational.

Groups espousing revolutionary change can sustain themselves in more stable political environments, but rarely offer a credible threat to take power; we might add, they also rarely demonstrate the capacity to govern. Social movements organize to promote smaller changes in the institutions of governance, and far more frequently, changes in policy. But they depend upon the existing structures of government to maintain stability and to implement their policy preferences.

CHAPTER 3

Protest and Policy

On Friday, March 9, 2018, Florida governor Rick Scott signed into law a bill that makes it a little more difficult to buy a gun legally in the state. The new law raises the age for legal purchase of a rifle from 18 to 21, the same age required to buy a handgun, and institutes a three-day waiting period for most gun buyers. It also prohibits the sale of "bump stocks," which allow a semi-automatic weapon to function more like an automatic weapon and fire multiple rounds more quickly. In addition, the bill provides funding for public schools to use in instituting tougher security measures and posting armed "resource officers." Finally, the bill provides access to funding for school districts to train qualified teachers to carry firearms at school to protect their students.[1]

Even by the comparatively lax standards of the United States, Florida has historically offered very easy legal access to guns. Local governments are prohibited from regulating the purchase or carrying of firearms. Licensed people can carry concealed weapons almost anywhere, and can show those weapons as long as it's not threatening. And a "stand your ground" law allows people who feel threatened to defend themselves with firearms. In many ways, the state has been the most successful outlet for the preferred policies of the National Rifle Association (NRA).[2]

In 2018, however, Florida's legislators responded to the pressure from high-school student activists, some of whom were present at Governor Scott's signing ceremony. Just weeks before, a 19-year-old man had entered the Mary Stoneman Douglas High School in Parkland, Florida, carrying a semi-automatic rifle, which he used to kill 17 people and wound 17 others. One of the best high schools in Florida, it is filled with sophisticated and opinionated young people from relatively affluent backgrounds. In short order, the survivors became activists.

It started on social media, with a hashtag, #NeverAgain, describing the student survivors' determination to make sure other high-school students didn't have to endure a similar tragedy. They also devised a strategy: stigmatize and isolate the NRA, a powerful lobby group representing gun manufacturers and owners, which promotes easy access to firearms. The Parkland kids organized a rally in their hometown, and a bus trip to the state capital in Tallahassee to lobby for gun control. A few appeared on television and in newspaper and magazine stories. The president of the United States staged a "listening session" in the White House to hear from survivors of mass shootings about their pain and their suggestions for reform. CNN organized a televised "town meeting" in which the students would meet with elected officials and a representative of the NRA to discuss the threat of violence in the schools. The NRA had previously offered a strategy of making schools "hard targets," installing thick glass and providing armed school defenders. The kids rejected that remedy; they wanted to limit access to guns.

Mass shootings have become a disturbingly familiar occurrence in the United States, including attacks in schools, and a familiar response pattern had developed. In the days after a tragedy, the victims' relatives and survivors would demonstrate their grief and call for tighter regulation of weapons, while political leaders expressed sympathy, offering "thoughts and prayers." The NRA would remain silent, and then the moment would pass, mostly, with reform efforts stalled in the complicated politics of legislation (Laschever and Meyer 2021). Nothing happened nationally; some states would pass modest reforms that made access to guns more difficult, while others would pass modest reforms that made it easier to get guns. Florida was in the latter category.

But the horror of the Stoneman Douglas shooting, emphasized forcefully and repeatedly by the Parkland kids and the allies they recruited, made this time a little different. Partly, it was a function of the cumulated impact of repeated tragic shootings that had helped gun control activists build ongoing organizations and some public visibility. If it weren't for the activism, however, it would have been harder for public recognition of repeated mass shootings to develop; activism made each successive horror more visible than it otherwise would have been. Beyond this, the Parkland kids' success was also a product of their strategy: rather than get lost in the details of debates about particular legislative reforms or specific weapons, the kids emphasized the malevolent influence of the NRA, demanding that politicians stop accepting its money for their campaign efforts.

The visible pressure offered by articulate teens and their supporters led the Florida legislature to respond when it hadn't before, and the legislative responses mattered. But there was much that the first response didn't do. Florida did not enact a ban on assault weapons like the semi-automatic rifle the school shooter used, nor did it ban the specific weapon, the AR-15. The state didn't institute regulations on high-capacity magazines, nor did it tighten background checks on potential buyers. (Licensed gun dealers are required to conduct such a check, but private sales are exempt from such scrutiny.) The legislative response was a compromise that, for the first time, recruited state legislators supported by the NRA to support some modest reforms – while emphasizing that their efforts would allow trained and armed personnel to protect the schools. Far less than what the Parkland kids wanted, it was also a greater concession than gun rights supporters imagined they would have to make. Meanwhile, the student activists continued plans for a national school walk-out day and a large rally in Washington, DC. They also repeated their commitment to voting as soon as they were able, remembering who had supported them – and who hadn't.

This episode of an ongoing battle about the regulation of guns in America provides a useful window through which to look at social movement influence and the policy process. The student activists from Parkland were part of a larger process of changing policy on firearms in the United States, a political battle that has spread over decades and includes engaged activists on both sides of the issue. We can make an inroad into this complicated political process by asking just how the Florida legislature, dominated by conservative Republicans opposed to gun control, might come to depart from the previous consensus on guns, and how and why members of the Florida legislature might have changed their minds about the regulation of guns.

Policy Reform and Democracy

Democratic polities are structured to respond to popular interests – at least when those interests are mobilized and, as a result, major changes in policy are rarely routine. Organized groups and constituencies grow up invested in a particular way of doing things, and any kind of change risks antagonizing those who have found ways to manage with things as they are. Oddly, democratic practices tend to have an institutionally conservative influence on politics. It's more difficult to promote change when the preferences of all stakeholders are taken into account. This is not to say that most people or groups are satisfied with current policies, but rather that those policies represent that balance of mobilized forces, and policy change can't happen without threatening that balance (Baumgartner and Jones 1993).

Social movements are an inefficient, but sometimes effective, way to promote change. They work by upsetting the stalemate of existing forces, bringing in or crowding out particular actors and interests, and changing the incentives of those who are already in the policymaking arena.

Every elected official manages a set of objectives and constraints that each may weigh differently. Some enter politics primarily to serve, some to advance a set of preferred policies, some to gain status and power. In order to do anything, however, the official must be able to maintain his or her job, satisfying some sort of electorate. A position on a particular issue is a means to achieving one end, although it may threaten another. The safest and easiest thing to do is almost always to maintain things as they are. (This is one reason why movements that seek to forestall some kind of change generally have an easier road to success than those that want to promote something new.)

This is not to say that policymakers don't want to design and implement wise policies; rather, I mean to emphasize that successful politicians need to consider more than the wisdom and effectiveness of any policy change. Social movements can influence the consideration of alternatives and the costs and risks of particular alternatives. We can begin to understand how the Parkland kids – and for that matter, virtually any other social movement or advocacy group – exercise influence, by thinking generally about the process of change in democratic polities.

Social movements represent the interests of those who are losing – or are concerned that they might lose. Those who turn out in the streets to protest are not generally those in a position to make policy. Movements make institutional inroads in a variety of different ways, but understanding those inroads requires thinking about effecting influence within the mainstream institutions of politics. We can start by identifying at least four different *mechanisms* through which movements change policy, that is, the stuff government does or doesn't do (Meyer 2014).

First, democratic governments are based on the notion that elected officials respond to the mobilized concerns of their constituencies. If they don't, the voters can throw them out of office, *replacing* them with someone more responsive. In democracies, this happens most often through elections, although social movements have also attempted to promote impeachment or pressured resignations as well. The direct influence of movements in electoral campaigns is generally on the margins, setting agendas, raising money, mobilizing voters, but margins can matter. Elections in functioning democracies are rarely landslides. Effectively competing political parties work to win, fighting to claim political space and constituencies. Movements can tip that balance between competing parties, and for movements to replace an opponent with elected officials who might meet with them and consider their claims makes for radically different possibilities for influence.

Second, the threat of that marginal influence is one factor that can lead to *conversion*, that is, getting an official to change his or her position on a matter of policy. Exposing a recalcitrant legislator or administrator to the power of a movement's ideas – or, alternatively, the power of its supporters – means altering the composition of a policy network without changing the identity of the players. It's not really all that important to determine whether conversions, such as George H. W. Bush's decision to oppose abortion rights in 1980 or Jesse Jackson's decision to adopt a pro-choice position in 1983, come from opportunistic calculus or reflective soul-searching. Each man recognized that he had to change his position in order to be a viable candidate for his party's presidential nomination. Of course, this doesn't mean the change wasn't sincere. Indeed, someone who has callously calculated a policy change for partisan advantage may be more likely to display the zeal of the newly converted and perhaps to operate more effectively and strategically in institutional politics.

More subtly, and far more common than the explicit shift in policy preferences, elected officials can alter their priorities, moving an issue receiving a great deal of attention from the bottom of a to-do list to the top. Like everyone else, legislative time is limited, and a more subtle shift in priorities can move the environment or guns or health care to the front of their attention and the legislative agenda. This is very much like a shift in the allocation of legislative time (Hall and Wayman 1990).

Third, activists working within a movement can pressure government to *create a new policy arena*, institutional setting, or network. This can dramatically alter the composition of the network of people and institutions responsible for making decisions. Creating new agencies or habitats, such as the Arms Control and Disarmament Agency, the Environmental Protection Agency, or the Department of Agriculture, ensures the ongoing and formal presence of concerns that would previously be represented only idiosyncratically, dependent upon the shifting preferences, constituencies, and skills of elected officials. When government creates a space for a particular set of concerns or views, there is always the possibility for political action on those issues. Policymakers create these habitats in response not only to policy problems and new issues, but also the purposeful efforts of mobilized constituencies through social movements. Once established, these habitats develop lives, constituencies, and concerns of their own. We see this dramatically with the creation of cabinet-level agencies directed to education, under Jimmy Carter, and veterans' affairs, under George H. W. Bush. President Lyndon Johnson established the cabinet-level Department of Housing and Urban Development as a cornerstone of his Great Society programs. The department was a response to the civil rights movement and to urban riots in the earlier part of the decade and provided an institutional setting for ongoing social welfare and urban development programs. Importantly, the institutions generally outlast by a long stretch the moments of commitment that created them.

The reallocation of bureaucratic resources represents movement influence. Early in the twentieth century, several democratic countries, including New Zealand and Australia, established government ministries dedicated to combatting climate change.[3] These new bureaus added to government profiles that already included agencies dedicated to environmental protection and natural resources more generally. The climate change ministries offered high-profile appointments to ambitious politicians, who could build careers by working on this global issue. They also afforded activists and social movements an institutional target and a resource to encourage, direct, amplify, and respond to their efforts.

Finally, social movements can *reconfigure* an existing policy monopoly by placing new personnel and procedures in it. Weed's (1995) tale of the victims' rights movement shows how the newly institutionalized presence of actors who were formerly spectators in the courtroom changes what happens not only in the courtroom, but also in the legislatures. Activists promoted the idea that victims of crimes had a direct stake in the process of legal actions, and in their ultimate outcomes. This gives judges an incentive to bring those victims into the courtroom. This matters, not only in the court proceeding at hand, but also in promoting the ideas of the movement more generally. After sports medicine physician Larry Nassar pleaded guilty to seven instances of sexual misconduct, Judge Rosemarie Aquilina required Nassar to listen to the testimony of his victims, including those whose accusations were not subject to the plea. Over several days, Nassar sat while 156 women described sexual assaults they suffered on his examination table, as well as the impact that the abuse had on their well-being. Judge Aquilina castigated Nassar before pronouncing a sentence that would keep him in jail for the rest of his life.[4] But the testimony was important for more than informing her jurisprudence or therapeutic catharsis for the women. Projected across the country in mainstream media, days of testimony provided a social sanction and a warning against sexual abuse more generally.

Similarly, Nancy Matthews's (1994) analysis of the feminist antirape movement shows how political mobilization by feminists against rape altered the content and implementation of policy and established new institutions: Rape Crisis Centers (see also Gornick and Meyer 1998). The Rape Crisis Centers provided direct service to victims of sexual assault, but also – at least initially – organized institutions for policy advocacy and politicization that didn't previously exist. Organized movements train and promote activists who march through institutions, changing them in the process. Lee Ann Banaszak (2010) identifies the influence of the feminist movement in the 1970s, executed by training activists who took positions within mainstream governmental institutions and thereby changed what those institutions did. Essentially, activists in these cases expanded the scope of a political conflict to alter the bias in the arena.

Competing For Attention: Agenda Setting

When the student activists from Parkland, Florida, used the murder of their classmates to bring attention to gun violence, they made it harder, but certainly not impossible, for their representatives to leave things as they are. The **first thing** the students did was make their elected officials acknowledge the problem.

Winning attention is no small matter (Hilgartner and Bosk 1988). Attention, like every other resource, is limited in political institutions, in mainstream media, on organizational agendas, and in individual lives. The student activists had less time to study calculus, play music, or read novels when they devoted their time to gun politics. As they learned about gun policy and school safety, their efforts crowded out other things they might otherwise be doing. They intended their efforts to encourage others to make the same choice of priorities that they had made, and not just students. They demanded that mainstream media pay renewed attention to the issue of gun violence, and that legislators consider the problem. This is called "agenda setting." Social movements reset priorities and make time. As the students reorganized their own personal priorities, they encouraged legislators to change the way they and their institution organized their time.

As the students made inroads in social media, they made demands on the time of readers. They worked to take advantage of the moment of attention the shooting had created, and to extend that moment. When mainstream media like television and newspapers picked up the story, the student activists commanded time previously devoted to other issues. And when they reached the Florida legislature, they would see that time is in extremely short supply. The Florida legislature's annual session is limited to 40 days, during which politicians can address the full range of issues in a large and diverse state. The student activists competed for a scarce resource, public attention to their concerns.

Although there are likely to be a few members of the legislature who are completely committed to gun issues, for most the issue was something that got in the way of their doing anything else. All things being equal, the general tendency would be to find a way to do something to stop the disruption that the shooting and the students caused. And generally, they will want to take steps as small as possible to try to restore the precarious balance of many different issues and pressures. The resulting legislation was a big departure for Florida politicians, but contained only modest steps to control the dangers of gun violence. It was far less than what the activists wanted, but it was far more than what seemed possible before the students protested. And it's important to note that what the student activists proposed was not particularly innovative or new; rather, they were promoting policy reforms that gun safety activists had worked on for years.

So, how did politicians convert, that is, change their minds about devoting attention to regulating guns? More than the shooting, the student activists upset the balance of forces acting upon the legislators. When the students came to the capital in Tallahassee, they brought attention with them. When they met with legislators, news cameras followed them, and when legislators could not find time to meet with the students, the activists found the cameras and reported on that as well. Their efforts forced politicians to discuss issues and policies that, under normal circumstances, were easy to avoid addressing.

Social movement protests push citizens, media, and politicians to address their issues. In doing so, they bring attention not only to the problem, but to their definition of that problem. **Second**, social movements can propose alternatives. In the case of the Parkland kids in Florida, those policies revolved around restrictions on access to weapons; the students wanted a ban on assault weapons and restrictions on individuals who seem dangerous getting access to weapons altogether. Effective protest strategies shine a light on those alternative policies and set up public debates on their wisdom and efficacy. In rejecting them, political opponents have to explain why, and offer their own alternatives.

Third, underscoring a social problem provokes or inspires others, including other advocates and academics, to find alternatives policies to address that problem. Importantly, even if policymakers reject the demands of protesters, they will accept the problem they are addressing, and search to find alternatives to support. In this case, some of the alternatives were more modest steps than what the students demanded, banning assault weapons or gun ownership by 18–20-year-olds, for example. Others, like the funds to arm teachers, are antithetical to their demands. Even when movements matter, activists don't always get what they want.

Fourth, by mobilizing attention to a social problem and highlighting legislative resistance to reform, social movements give their supporters in government an incentive to do more. The Florida state legislator concerned about taxes, health care, and the environment, will see that his constituents care about guns. Those who show they care certainly seem more likely to vote in the next election, to contribute money to campaigns, and maybe even work in future campaigns. The legislator also sees that mainstream media are going to pay attention to the issue. This isn't changing a politician's mind so much as adjusting her priorities and the intensity of her commitments.

Fifth, opponents put on alert that their opposition might produce adverse consequences. Gun control advocates might run against the supporter, contribute money, dig into other controversial issues, or just call and visit incessantly. The gun rights supporter, recognizing the potential costs of his stance, is going to seek cover. This might be through softening his opposition, which happened for some in Florida, or through offering alternatives. Conversely, it might entail digging in and defending the gun rights stance. These defenses also matter, continuing the process of framing a public debate, effectively reinforcing the importance of the issue.

Sixth, effective protest changes the image and urgency of all those involved in the debate. The Parkland protesters targeted the NRA, demanding that the politicians stop accepting money from a large and powerful interest group. Even if no legislators accede to this demand, which is quite likely, those who continue to accept NRA support could also receive additional scrutiny, effectively a cost to charge against whatever benefit NRA money conveyed. Likewise, every proposal offered by the NRA will also be subject to more thorough examination. By targeting their opponents, even if protesters win nothing in the moment, they make it more difficult for those opponents to pursue their own initiatives. Indeed, when the Parkland kids started their protest, one house of the US Congress had already passed a bill, supported by the NRA, that provides for a nationwide law that would allow anyone with a license to carry a concealed weapon from any state to use that license anywhere else. The odds against that proposal got significantly worse when protests reached national news. The bill never received consideration from the US Senate, a sort of victory for the gun safety activists, albeit one that would appear as a stalemate – if recognized at all. Successful protest influences not only current policy debates, but also subsequent ones.

In a stylized way, we can look back at the fundamentals of democratic politics. Legislators are elected to represent the interests and preferences of their constituents. Effective protest mobilizes citizens to do more than protest, changing their opponents in government. This may be by replacing the legislators directly, electing representatives; but it may also be by converting the opponents, softening opposition.

Political figures, of course, are unlikely to credit their passions or positions to the entreaties or threats of organized movements. It's hard to imagine a successful politician explain publicly that while he thinks ready access to guns is a good policy, he will not pursue the policy because he is scared of a social movement. But it's easy to envision the same politician explaining that he changed his mind in response to new events and information, and careful consideration. We need not doubt the sincerity of such conversions. Movements align political incentives with the moral choices activists want officials to make.

As noted, policy is generally defined by stalemate rather than consensus. In most areas, a limited set of political figures, including legislators, bureaucrats, and advocates, are routinely involved in most debates. To simplify and streamline the political process, political figures and bureaucrats alike behave in predictable ways, largely confining themselves to a narrow part of the possible agenda. In order to affect political reforms, social movement activists need to find ways to disrupt politics as usual. They need to find ways to extend the political agenda, the range of political alternatives considered, and bring attention to the things they care about.

Social movements can affect policy in three distinct, but

interrelated ways. First, they can affect the agenda, that is, the things that are discussed as problems and the range of possible solutions. Second, they can affect the composition of the domain making decisions. This may mean redefining a problem so that different policymakers are involved in decisions. Campaigners for drug law reform, for example, may work to define drug decriminalization as an economic policy rather than a crime control policy. If they are successful, a different group of policymakers are responsible for making decisions, and a new group of experts have something relevant to say about the issue. Third, they can change the identity of policymakers involved in relevant decisions. The most obvious way to do so, in a representative democracy, is to replace those who make policy. The standard way to do so is through elections, using elections to remove opponents and install allies. Less frequently, social movements can convince political allies to oust their opponents. But the threat to do so also matters. Social movements, by dint of demonstrating their power of persuasion and the mobilization of incentives, can change the minds of those in office. Sometimes, this means convincing an opponent to flip a position on a policy issue. More frequently, however, the power of protest can alter the intensity of commitment a politician has to a position or an issue, stiffening the spine of allies and weakening the passionate commitments of opponents.

Policy Arenas

The potential influence of social movements, and the pathways through which they can influence policy, vary across policy areas. The rules, routines, and routes for influence vary, as do the prospects for organized citizen influence. Policies are what institutions do – or don't do. Mostly, when we discuss social movements, we think about government institutions, including national and subnational bodies. Governments make decisions about all kinds of things, producing rules and offering incentives (goodies) and sanctions (punishments). Vigorous debates surround the question of what issues to regulate and which ones to leave alone. European countries, for example, typically impose far stricter regulations on labor practices and food than those imposed in the United States. In both European countries and the United States, activists battle for or against current regulations, but also about whether such issues should be regulated at all. Activists make claims about what areas are in desperate need of oversight and which are best left to individual people or the broad market to make decisions about.

Government policies are also made in different venues through different processes. In democracies, those who implement policies, like police, food inspectors, or teachers, enjoy some discretion in making decisions (Lipsky 1980), but broad directions of policy are made quite far from the implementation of policy – either by bureaucrats and administrators who set rules, or by legislators of executives who oversee them. Elected policymakers are also constrained, not only by the rules of the institutions they work within, but also by the mobilized opinions of those whom they represent. On occasion, outside actors, like courts, can intervene to further constrain those policymakers.

Social movements can intervene in any part of the policy process to promote – or resist – policy change. This means, they can attempt to convince or intimidate bureaucrats, persuade legislators and executives, and mobilize citizen opinion.

Policy change operates somewhat differently outside democratic governance, as the incentives to which policymakers respond might be different. For example, American companies offer benefits and salaries to recruit and retain workers. Nicole Raeburn (2004) found that technology-intensive companies dependent upon highly skilled workers were quicker to respond to calls for same-sex health and welfare benefits. The story is relatively simple: companies that needed skills in relatively short supply were ready to respond to organized efforts for a new standardized benefit. These decisions were not made by democratic processes like elections, but by executives responsible for their companies' success. Those executives may have been disposed to treat all workers the same regardless of the worker's sexual orientation, but more critical was the pressure of responding to a competitive marketplace for labor. Responsible for maintaining the company's profitability, they enjoyed the latitude to make decisions about how to treat their workers, knowing that their decisions would be supported by employees and boards of directors as long as the company remained profitable. Organized employees were most effective when they recognized the levers of influence they could pull, specifically, the threat to leave and the arguments about profitability they could make.

Trade unions are another form of social movement organization that advocate for workers to improve benefits, wages, and working conditions. Although the unions themselves are subject to democratic pressures, the private companies they seek to influence are not. Executives make decisions about how to treat their workers, and although these decisions might be influenced by moral or political biases, they are ultimately most responsive to the perceived pressures of business and employment markets.

Democratic theory is premised on the notion that the people will choose leaders who will make decisions on their behalf. If convinced that the politicians are either unable or unwilling to protect their interests, supporters will defect from their support and turn elsewhere for representation, augmenting participation in conventional political action with more disruptive or confrontational means of claims making. Voting is supplementing by phone calls and demonstrations. Pleas for action are superseded by threats. Successful politicians have an interest in managing their opposition, and stopping this kind of escalation from taking place. They offer reforms, rhetorical concessions, or new policies at least partly to forestall disruptive collective action and preserve their own power. Democratic responsiveness is predicated on elected officials watching the people they are supposed to represent or to lead, and making affirmative efforts to stay connected with them.

It is not only politicians, of course, who need to be responsive to the efforts of social movements and protesters. Importantly, actually significant responses may be delayed, but still traceable to the efforts of activists. The theater provides a salient example. In 1991, producers brought *Miss Saigon*, a musical based on *Madame Butterfly*, to Broadway. The show had already begun a successful run in London, and the producers had secured the original leads to open the Broadway production, including Jonathan Pryce in the role of The Engineer. To play the role, Pryce donned prosthetics and yellow makeup to appear theatrically Asian.

Asian American communities in New York City were not sanguine about the casting of white actors in the roles of Asian characters, and particularly with the performance in *yellowface*. The Actors Equity Association rejected Pryce's right to play the role. Activists staged protests, wrote editorials, and picketed the performances. The producers stood behind Pryce, and invoking Pryce's star status, pressed the Actors Equity Association to change its position and allow the star to reclaim the role. Pryce stayed in the role for a year, and won a Tony award for his performance. But no white actor has been cast in the role in any major production since then (Paulson 2017). Although the protests had largely disappeared by the time Pryce left the role, their impact on the production and on Broadway more generally extended over many years. Finding the influence of social movement protest on something normally insulated from such pressures, like a casting decision, requires us to use an extended timeline and recognize a long and often complicated process of social change. We see the different dynamics of influence and decision-making outside of government, as well as the long timeline for finding political influence.

Business and Movements

Governments are not the only institutions that make policy, creating social wrongs and rights. Activists have also pressured companies to adopt policies that are friendlier to labor or the environment, and businesses are responsive to somewhat different sets of pressures than governments. Here, the moral argument is made most effectively when coupled with economic pressures. The place of moral and political considerations in the business world is one that has been controversial for a very long time. On the one hand, an ideal type version of the company in a free market economy operates to deliver profits to those who own it. Market forces will ensure that companies deliver on the claims they promise and charge competitive prices to do so. Regulation from government will assure compliance with labor and environmental strictures that may not otherwise affect the market. Since all companies need to adhere to those strictures, such as paying a minimum wage, offering distinct benefits, and refraining from pollution, no company will enjoy a competitive advantage.

But the legal pursuit of profit may still offend moral sensibilities. Quakers came to recognize the immorality of slavery and the slave trade by the middle of the seventeenth century, but devising effective strategies for opposing it took a much longer time (Marable 1974). It was more profitable to employ slaves in the plantation economies of the American colonies, and investment in the Atlantic slave trade was particularly lucrative – and legal. Individuals carved out different responses to an obvious moral dilemma. Some determined to treat their slaves humanely, providing education and the prospect of moral uplift. Others profited from the slave trade, but advocated for a change in the law. Over time, slave-owning grew to be stigmatized in the Quaker communities, and groups advocated changes in laws and practices. They divested their investments in the slave trade not so much because of the impact on slavery directly but to avoid undermining their commitments for political advocacy. In other words, divestment from business was part of the process of becoming a more effective campaigner against slavery.

This idea followed through to the development of social investing in the United States and elsewhere, where investors tried to keep their money from supporting even legal businesses that violated their moral sensibilities (Hill et al. 2007). It's not clear that the business decisions themselves played much of a role in the end of slavery, but the idea of making one's investments consonant with one's values continued to grow. By the turn of the twentieth century, other religious groups programmatically eschewed investment in companies that derived profits from tobacco or alcohol. Again, the political impact was limited, as other investors were available to provide capital for these vices.

The idea of relieving moral culpability extended to actually trying to change the economy and the behavior of businesses in the 1950s and beyond. More contemporary social movements start with the idea of moral clarity and philosophical or political persuasion, but move to social and economic pressure. In the 1950s, civil rights activists in the United States and in South Africa called for boycotts of companies that profited from racial discrimination. Rosa Parks' famed defiance of racial segregation on Montgomery city buses was followed by a year-long boycott of the bus lines. The effort built a strong organization that coordinated alternative transport, including rides in the city, while also putting economic pressure on the bus line. Subsequent civil rights demonstrations linked economic pressure with moral and political pressure; the lunch counter sit-ins, for example, shut down businesses. In a thoughtful study of business concessions to civil rights protests, Joseph Luders (2010) explored why some businesses were quicker to respond to civil rights protests than others. He found that businesses that served retail markets that could be disrupted by civil rights protesters, like downtown restaurants and retail stores, were far quicker to respond to protesters than producers of wholesale products that were somewhat protected from retail pressures. The message to take from this is that moral pressures are far more likely to effect change when coupled with social and economic pressure.

Of course, none of those businesses now explicitly discriminate against people of color. Each victory contributed to the social pressure on the next company to follow. Each concession implicitly gave support to the activist claims about racial justice, and made it easier for activists to prevail upon government to pass legislation.

The process worked a little differently in South Africa, as outlined in the previous chapter. Divestment made it more difficult for companies to gain investment and do business profitably, in addition to creating social isolation. The activity helped organizers build a movement, and contemporary organizers have followed suit by organizing politically motivated boycotts of companies that make weapons or extract fossil fuels.

In the 1980s, efforts to ensure good corporate behavior grew into campaigns targeted at environmental and labor practices. Brayden King and colleagues (King 2011; King and Soule 2007; McDonnell and King 2013; McDonnell et al. 2015) have studied so-called shareholder campaigns to reform corporate policy. Battling to force corporate leaders to consider seriously factors other than profitability is a difficult task, but they find that when campaigners are able to produce a credible threat to share prices, companies are more likely to concede on some demands. They are aided in this regard when demonstrators outside the annual meeting of shareholders have their messages amplified by allies within those meetings.

Similarly, movements able to install an ally in a position of power are more likely to get a sympathetic hearing for their claims. For example, climate change activists have pushed a demand that their campuses divest their holdings in companies that produce fossil fuels. Generally, divestment campaigns are most likely to succeed when the economic stakes are small. But Stanford University, an extremely wealthy school, was one of the first universities to announce a partial divestment, of coal stocks, in 2016, facilitated by the presence of Tom Steyer, a billionaire climate activist, on its Board of Trustees.[5]

The big story in policy impact is that movement activists seek to marshal cumulative pressures from multiple sources, ideally incorporating both insiders and outsiders. The story of the long animal rights campaign against SeaWorld is instructive. Established in 1964, SeaWorld is a chain of marine-themed amusement parks. For years, the core of the SeaWorld visit was a marine mammal show highlighted by tricks from Shamu (the stage name of all the performing orcas), who became an iconic figure in advertising.

Animal rights activists targeted SeaWorld for years, in the context of campaigns against cruelty and mistreatment of performing animals, and this was a great focal point for a movement. Orcas are large, smart, social mammals (up to 26 feet long and weighing 12,000 lbs.), who live shorter, constrained lives in captivity. Because they spend more time at the surface in captivity, their distinctive dorsal fins droop, which is easy for people to interpret as sadness rather than the absence of water pressure. In 2011, People for the Ethical Treatment of Animals (PETA) filed a federal lawsuit arguing that orcas were entitled, as non-human persons, to 13th amendment protections against involuntary servitude. The lawsuit was dismissed in fairly short order, with the judge finding that the 13th amendment was intended to guarantee rights only to people (Miller 2012). But the lawsuit got attention. Activists picketed outside of SeaWorld and produced advertisements urging tourists to spend their entertainment dollars elsewhere.

In 2013, film maker Gabriela Cowperthwaite released *Blackfish*, a documentary focused on the sad story of Tillikum, an orca captured by SeaWorld, who was involved in the deaths of three people (Catsoulis 2013). The documentary amplified and focused the bad publicity the deaths of trainers had already produced. SeaWorld refused to cooperate with the making of the film, filed a complaint with the Department of Labor protesting that some of its employees did, and published its own factsheet online disputing the film. But just by making SeaWorld answer its objections – over and over again – PETA was shifting the battle, generating attention, and promoting action.

State legislators in California and New York proposed new

laws that would prohibit orca performances or keeping killer whales in captivity altogether; even when nothing had passed, SeaWorld was forced to continue its public relations battle. Even though the new laws stalled and the lawsuit failed, the campaign demonstrated that apparent defeats can contribute to larger victories. Attendance dropped at SeaWorld; at least some parents planning vacations didn't want to answer questions about the droopy fins. The company's stock price collapsed. Prominent musicians canceled performance dates at the theme park, and other businesses, like Southwest Air, severed their ties with the theme park. Credit rating agencies lowered SeaWorld's bond rating, making it more costly for the company to borrow money.

SeaWorld's executives sought to do as little as possible to manage the damage the activists were doing. They needed to rebuild the company's reputation and recapture its market share. First, it announced that it would provide larger pens for the orcas, without crediting PETA or protests for this decision, and emphasized how the care of the whales was always a top priority. Of course, the activists wanted much more than larger pens, and they didn't stop.

When the pen size and associated publicity campaign didn't work, SeaWorld announced a search for new corporate leadership. This wasn't explicitly about countering the activists; rather, the Board of Directors wanted their company to become more profitable and sustainable as a business enterprise. The public relations nightmare that Shamu became was one of the new CEO's challenges (Parsons and Rose 2018).

The new president and Chief Executive Officer of SeaWorld, Joel Manby, announced in 2016 that SeaWorld would no longer breed orcas, and that the parks would stop performing their signature Shamu shows. Manby also announced a new partnership with the Humane Society of the United

States, formerly a SeaWorld nemesis, to develop educational programs and take care of the animals still at the park, who would be unable to survive in the wild. This is a clear win for animal rights activists, but not necessarily because its protests convinced Manby or SeaWorld's shareholders of the justice of their claims. Rather, SeaWorld made a business decision. The parks' image had taken a beating over the past few years from protests at the site, the death of a trainer, a powerful documentary (*Blackfish*), and local government. Attendance, revenue, and share prices had all faltered as a result. The corporate rebooting of SeaWorld was an effort to respond to opponents successfully and salvage the business.

Importantly, SeaWorld gave in only after trying numerous other strategies that failed, in this case, relatively quickly. Remember, SeaWorld had launched a public relations campaign to dispute the charges made in *Blackfish*, planted paid provocateurs within the animal rights protests, announced reforms in the handling and husbandry of its orcas, and filed a lawsuit to challenge the California Coastal Commission's decision to ban captive whale breeding in San Diego. The protests continued, as did the decline in park visitors. The corporation replaced its leadership team, and the new CEO responded to the real facts on the ground, facts that animal rights activists had helped create.

Public Policy and Governance

Activists who seek to change government policy – or fend off change – have multiple routes to try to pursue their ends, and those routes reflect the nature of political opportunities in each country. To take an obvious example, and offering a striking contrast to the example at the outset of this chapter, just days after a horrific shooting in Christchurch, New Zealand,

Prime Minister Jacinda Ardern announced that the country would reform its gun laws; shortly thereafter, the government announced a policy banning the sorts of weapons involved in the mass shooting.[6] It wasn't the magnitude of the shooting or the prevalence of gun ownership that explained the difference. Rather, a parliament that enjoys the capacity to govern, unencumbered by checks and balances or a Bill of Rights, can implement policy. Gun safety advocates didn't have to build and sustain large organizations engaged in politics and public education, nor develop a strong infrastructure. Rather, by floating concerns and suggesting alternatives, they could effect change. This is very different than the world their counterparts in the United States faced. The rules, institutions, and politics that develop constrain what movements can do, and shape the tactics and claims they are likely to deploy.

Broadly speaking, the strength and autonomy of the legislature is one element in the "structure of political opportunities" activists face, critical to the emergence, impact, and development of a social movement campaign (Meyer 2004). Because most people are unlikely to protest when they have easier and less risky ways of getting what they want, the institutional routes for political influence are critical to the emergence, development and ultimate impact of a social movement. It's also another reason why activists seeking policy change nearly always face an uphill struggle.

Democratic institutions survive by providing most people with greater incentives to participate in mainstream politics than to desert it. In democracies, social movements don't represent a departure from institutional politics so much as an additional source of leverage, one often closely connected to mainstream political institutions. To see how movements exercise influence, we need to assess the available levers of political influence in the mainstream.

Although the United States offers a relatively distinct model of democratic governance, it also provides a useful comparison point with other democratic systems. US institutions invite social movements to engage, but make it very difficult for them to push affirmative change; the rules advantage the defense, that is, those seeking to forestall reforms (Meyer 2014). In the United States, policymaking power is divided among a variety of institutions that all offer distinct routes for political impact. The first division is between national governance and subgovernments at state and local levels. Although some issues are explicitly the province or jurisdiction of the national government, like military policy, many others, like education or the environment, are divided across different levels of government.

At the national level – and replicated at the state level, formulating and implementing policy is divided among different sorts of institutions: a legislature makes laws; an executive oversees a somewhat independent bureaucracy that implements and evaluates policies; and a judiciary passes on the legality or constitutionality of those laws, and can push other branches of government to change policy. Each institution offers distinct ways for social movements to try to effect influence.

Legislators are elected by citizens, and those legislators represent, more or less directly, political parties. Changing the people who sit in positions of power is one way to effect changes in policy. Engagement in electoral politics is one way to change the decision-makers, and social movements are frequently engaged in the electoral process, supporting friendly candidates through campaign efforts. But you don't have to change the people to change policies. Democratic governance is based on the premise that elected officials want to keep their jobs. They articulate policy positions based on beliefs about what is wise policy and what makes for good politics. Social movement activists can do a lot of work to change political and policy calculations.

Through conducting research and presenting information, activists can affect the perceptions of wise policies. By publicizing the dangers of climate change, the burdens of taxation, or the social costs of segregation, they can offer policy alternatives and convince policymakers of alternatives. By turning out large numbers of people in support of their ideas, social movement activists can convince legislators that it is a smart move to respond to activist concerns seriously. Obviously, these calculations overlap. A movement with a large and engaged following is more likely to get a hearing; a movement with wise alternative policies is more likely to generate a large following and engaged support.

Social movements do best when they align incentives, when preferred policies make for good politics. Legislators offer both direct and less direct routes to influence. Directly, activists can campaign for preferred candidates and lobby to support preferred policies. Either route can be highly professionalized or more informal. Professionalized movements endorse candidates, and advocate within political parties. They send experts armed with studies to talk to legislators and may emphasize their commitment with campaign contributions or favorable publicity. Movements can also unleash the grassroots to talk with their legislators, wearing political T-shirts and bringing their own experiences. Of course, broad and diverse social movements generally deploy several of these approaches at the same time.

Social movements can also try to affect politics and policy less directly, by staging performances or protests that dramatize their concerns and their support. After all, a *demonstration is a show* of strength, support, and commitment. Politicians are in the business of paying attention to engaged citizens, and large turnouts at demonstrations and expressions of intense commitment are ways to bring attention to an issue. An ambitious politician has every incentive to address issues that are of concern to her constituents, and to find ways to craft policies that will appeal to an engaged politics. Activists don't have to speak personally to a policymaker in order to get their message across.

Every democratic government provides multiple routes to political influence to its citizenry, which revolve around influencing or replacing those who make and implement policy. Social movements, when effective, generally fill those established routes of influence, and offer additional means of influence as well, in efforts to promote their issues of concern, their preferred policy responses, and their commitment to continued activism. Policymakers may be convinced of the wisdom of those policies and/or the political benefits of adopting movement positions.

It's useful to think of a continuum of activities designed to influence policy by how direct those efforts are. Most directly, activists can speak to, call, or write to a policymaker and explain the wisdom of their policy preferences. No matter how polite and deferential such a communication is, there is an implicit threat that if the target ignores or resists the proffered wisdom, or simply fails to respond with sufficient vigor, there could be electoral consequences. Such efforts at influence are likely to do best when they extend beyond an individual communication to include larger numbers of people with some capacity to affect the political fortunes of its target.

People who have lost the battle of policymaking can then turn to resisting the implementation of a policy. Organized groups enjoy some latitude in interfering with the implementation of policy, blocking the construction of a new pipeline or homeless shelter, for example, in the streets or through a lawsuit. Influencing members of the bureaucracy or the courts requires slightly different strategies. Arguments in courts required licensed and skilled advocates, and need to be made through established laws and disciplined arguments. Similarly, appeals through the bureaucracy are dependent on detailed attention to laws and institutional procedures. While such efforts don't routinely succeed, they often raise the costs and visibility of the issue, suggesting that the issue at hand is a matter of contestation. Indeed, filing an appeal, testifying at an informational meeting, and asking repeated questions, can prove to be effective in bringing more information to the public debate.

Alternatively, social movements can resist compliance with laws and procedures they find faulty. American antiwar activists in the 1960s made compliance with draft laws, and the draft card in particular, a site of contestation that used the draft to make claims about American participation in the war (Thorne 1975). Publicly displaying and destroying draft cards, for example, was a clear violation of the law, and one that risked severe punishment. Nonetheless, burning the draft card became a familiar form of resistance, inviting prosecution, trials, and overall, a great deal of attention. By itself, such an effort is extremely unlikely to achieve the stated aim of ending the war, but it does generate attention, provides activists with a vehicle for expression, and extends attention to both the act (through a trial and potential punishment) and the larger issue.

The more familiar social movement forms, including direct action and mass demonstrations, are generally less narrowly targeted at legislators. Instead, they play to a larger and more diffuse audience, signaling other citizens about the importance of an issue and the prospects for potentially effective political action. In obvious ways, the familiar demonstration is a means of communication. Although speakers from a platform may articulate extensively elaborated arguments and detailed policy proposals, the message that comes from an event as a whole is usually much simpler: the issue is important, as is focused action on it.

When movements are in the public eye, they gain coverage from mainstream media, and the attention of politicians. Between constituents and journalists, politicians are repeatedly asked to defend their positions. If they hold fast to a position challenged by a movement, they will need to come up with reasons, and repeatedly announce and explain those positions. Often, they will pose alternatives. Every bit of attention, however, is helpful to the movement.

Social movements arise to support new pieces of legislation and to stop the advances of their opponents, inside or outside of government, and to affect the development of particular aspects of a policy. In this regard, we can offer a broadly stylized version of certain kinds of goals: First, there is outright rejection, which can be broad. Activists can agree to oppose a particular tax bill, the development of nuclear power, or the entry of their country into a war. Second, there is a more localized desire to prevent a particular local outrage, without much explicit attention to the larger policy initiatives it represents. Local organizers can unite to oppose a pipeline, a particular nuclear plant, a change in zoning regulations, the institutions (or end) of rent control, or the creation of a homeless shelter. Third, social movements can unify around affirmative policies that promote new initiatives: extended insurance, regulation of environmental threats, policies toward immigrants, or access to higher education.

Generally, it's easier to organize around stopping something than making something happen. This is simply because diverse groups who can agree to oppose some policy are less likely to find easy agreement on what – if anything – to do instead. In democracies, it's also easier to stop something form happening than to initiate something. This is because democratic governance systems are filled with trip wires and veto points that make political change more difficult. Importantly, even initial defeats on matters of policy can have longer-term consequences, as the examples cited below will show.

In tracing these stories, we will note that social movements employed a variety of means to pursue their ends, spilling across conventional boundaries between conventional politics and movement politics. Protest has dovetailed with political organizing, lobbying, and elections. Importantly, even in response to very clear demands, authorities often offer alternatives that are consequential, but still not remotely a direct response to the articulated concerns of movements. Also importantly, the influence that social movements can exercise varies not only across national contexts, but also across issues and over time. Temporary defeats can wind up being important in building a larger movement and making substantial gains, and momentary gains can evaporate and give way to undesired political consequences.

War and the Draft

Conscription has as long a history as war does, and it has always been contested. Young men are often understandably reluctant to leave their homes and risk their lives to go into battle abroad. Their families have also been understandably reluctant to send their sons, and now daughters, off to foreign shores with the possibility of never returning.

Opposition to military service sometimes intersects with opposition to war in general or opposition to particular wars, although someone doesn't have to oppose war to want to avoid participating in it. And resisting a personal commitment to war can develop into a collective resistance to war. As a result, opposition to the draft is often the sharp edge of broader antiwar movements, and it has a very long history.

In the United States, notable opposition to conscription emerged strongly during the Civil War. When the United States set about replenishing its troops through a lottery in New York City, young men who did not want to serve staged a riot, as opposition to the draft spilled over into opposition to the Civil War altogether (Bernstein 1990). Protesters led by Irish immigrants destroyed the lottery wheel, tore up trolley tracks, broke store windows, and lynched Black men to halt the implementation of the draft. There's no indication that the protesters were particularly concerned with the wisdom or merits of the war, but they were clearly very concerned about the burden that taxes and military service might impose upon their lives. They were also visibly offended that wealthy men could buy their way out of service by paying $300 for a replacement. Violent and very disruptive, the riots did not develop into a sustained movement. As a result, the government responded by temporarily halting the call-ups. The riots exercised some influence, stalling the replenishment of Union soldiers to the battlefield, and providing yet another pressure on President Lincoln to press the war so that victory would be in sight before his own reelection campaign. The draft continued, Lincoln was reelected, and the South surrendered early in 1865, with the draft riots consigned to a small portion of the history of the Civil War.

Opposition to the military draft during the Vietnam era was quite another matter. Draft registration and conscription raised the salience of the Vietnam War for young American men, and gave them – and those who cared about them – far more reason to pay attention to international events and policies. The long war gave the movement the time to develop and exercise influence.

The military draft had been reestablished in the United States in 1940, in anticipation of participation in the war in Europe. At a relatively low level, conscription continued through the 1950s (including during the Korean War) and early 1960s giving one group of Americans, young men, special reason to join with those who already opposed the war.[7] Initially, conscription offered many loopholes for savvy and advantaged young men to slip through. Supportive doctors wrote letters recommending medical exemptions; some draft boards offered renewable deferments for college attendance and family obligations; and some local boards were extremely sympathetic. Local boards were also responsible for approving appeals for "conscientious objector" status, through which young men could avoid military service based on principled objections to the war, and provide alternative service in a hospital or school instead. The point is that the implementation of the draft in the early days of intensified military engagement in Vietnam reeked of the unfairness of the Civil War substitutes.

Conscription became a provisional target for the antiwar movement ("Stop the Draft, End the War"). Even as antiwar activists focused on the draft, opponents of the draft also learned about the war and developed opposition to it, digging into the relevant issues with passionate and personal motivation. The two movements initially supported each other and overlapped significantly. The draft provided organizers a series of sites or targets at which to launch protests (draft boards), as well as a set of tactics (burning draft cards, defacing files, providing draft counseling) that gave activists something to do. Both opposition to the draft in general and concern about one's individual fate pushed people into the full range of American political institutions, including the Selective Service bureaucracy, local draft boards, the courts, and electoral campaigns.

In conjunction with the broader movement against the Vietnam War, the antidraft movement has affected all sorts of policies since. President Richard Nixon oversaw the end to most deferments from service and the substitution of a lottery system in 1969, which seemed to put a larger number of men at risk for conscription. By making conscription more random, if not necessarily more fair, the new system had the effect of spreading opposition to the war and the draft (Erikson and Stoker 2011). As the war wound down, however, Nixon ultimately implemented the end of the military draft in 1973 – even as US participation in the war dragged on, if at a more limited level of engagement. The effects of ending the draft, in conjunction with winding down the war, diminished the scope and intensity of the antiwar movements.

On his first day in office, President Jimmy Carter encountered tremendous controversy when he issued a pardon to all the young men who had resisted the draft by failing to register or leaving the country, affecting an estimated group of more than 100,000 people. It was Carter, however, who restored draft registration of young men in 1980. Unlike the previous policy, however, the new registration process involved no physical or mental health examination, and no scrutiny by a local draft board, only completing a simple form providing a name, address, birthdate, and social security number. The registration was supposed to convey US resolve in response to the Soviet Union's invasion of Afghanistan, but the government never came close to proceeding to actual conscription.

Instead, the United States has relied on a volunteer military force since Vietnam, at least partly because of the antiwar movement, although the technological advances in modern weaponry have made this possible. More generally, the political fallout of the antiwar movement constrained US foreign policy for nearly 30 years. Congress asserted its prerogatives for policymaking by passing the War Powers Act in 1973. The Act formally limited the tenure of military forces abroad without the explicit authorization from Congress. Later, the so-called "Vietnam Syndrome" led to a reluctance to commit ground troops abroad unless the United States deployed overwhelming force and could reasonably expect to win and exit within a reasonably short time period. First articulated by Defense Secretary Caspar Weinberger (1990), it was embraced by his assistant, future Secretary of State Colin Powell, and defined policy for nearly 20 years – until finally repudiated directly by President George W. Bush's initiation of war in Iraq.

When we assess the outcomes of the antiwar and antidraft movements, we have to engage in a counterfactual exercise, and imagine the set of things that *might have happened*, if those movements had not. Even before the official era of Weinberger/Powell, the United States demonstrated a greater reluctance to send forces into combat abroad for extended periods. It's critical to realize that there were opportunities to do so. In 1978, Senator George McGovern, who based his extremely unsuccessful presidential campaign on opposition to the Vietnam War, pressed Congress and President Carter to coordinate an international force to intervene in the country next door to Vietnam, Cambodia, which had been taken over by foreign forces that implemented a harsh regime that executed a genocide. Not long afterward, President Carter refused to send troops to prop up authoritarian, but allied, regimes in Iran and Nicaragua, when they were threatened by political insurgencies.[8] Neither Carter nor his successor would send substantial American military forces to support indigenous forces battling the Soviet-backed government there, although they did send weapons. American intervention in Central America during the 1980s was largely clandestine, and frequently executed by proxy forces. President Reagan quickly withdrew deployed armed forces from Lebanon in response to the first casualties from a terrorist attack in 1983, although he was willing to topple a new government in Grenada in eight days during the same year. President Clinton refused to consider engagement of American forces in response to an ongoing genocide in Rwanda in 1994, and was only reluctantly drawn into an international intervention to stop a horrific war in Bosnia in 1995 (Power 2002). It's impossible to know with certainty what might have happened absent the powerful movements of the 1960s and 1970s, but it's not hard given knowledge of US military history to imagine ongoing commitments of US forces. The peace activists of the Vietnam era were not generally attentive to potential interventions not even on the horizon, and some, like Senator McGovern, may have wanted different choices. The point is, however, that movements can exert influence through stopping things from happening, as well as pushing initiatives forward, and sometimes exercise influence on policies that aren't even their explicit concern. Ending the draft also changed personnel practices within the US military, which now had to manage employees who had the option of quitting. Absent a draft, policymakers and administrators paid more attention to the quality of life for military personnel, devoting far more attention and money to recruiting, as well as to issues of compensation, housing, child care, and career advancement for service people. America grew more dependent upon contracting service and support from private companies rather than conscripts, driving up costs and reducing control. Service in the military, formerly a nearly universal experience for young American men, became an experience confined to a relatively small portion of Americans. Paradoxically, this may make it easier for contemporary presidents to send troops, now all volunteers, into combat abroad without broad popular support and for extended periods of time. The extended engagement of US forces in Iraq (2003–2011) seems to support this claim. Even more striking, the conduct of Operation Enduring Freedom, a response to the attacks on the World Trade Center in 2001, has itself endured as the United States invaded Afghanistan shortly thereafter, and maintained a large military presence and engaged in combat there since that time.

The movement and influence story here focus on the fact that a diverse set of activists and organizations engaged in protest against both a specific war and the draft. They represented a very broad range of concerns, from individuals who sought to evade military service to others who offered a wholesale analysis and critique of American foreign and economic policies. And the activists did not get to define the responses to their efforts. Rather, it was policymakers who faced proximate pressures and sought to find ways to respond to them. The antiwar and antidraft movement had made it most costly and more difficult to support conscription. Coming up with alternatives for staffing the armed forces didn't require rethinking either the Vietnam War or American foreign policy more generally. Protest mattered, but not necessarily in the ways that most activists or the organizations they animated hoped for. And the government response, putting into effect a volunteer military, took on a weight of its own, and through its own momentum affected a range of other policies, some not even imagined by activists who were protesting against the war or the draft.

The point is that social movements affect policy, although

not by themselves, and not in ways that are always predictable. The Vietnam era movements succeeded in changing the calculus of elected officials, and the lessons learned extended long after the fall of Saigon. And the reforms executed had longer-term impact on the nature of a set of related policies. Moreover, the extent of policy influence that social movements are able to exercise is contingent upon a range of other factors, including support from within political institutions and the exigencies of a particular policy area. The complications associated with the policymaking process make it hard for social movements to claim credit for their influence, particularly when impact means stopping political opponents from getting what they want.

We should add that foreign policy is the area in which social movements are going to face the most difficult challenges in effecting influence. Particularly absent a draft, most citizens are only occasionally engaged in foreign and military policy, and the nature of the policies are better insulated from popular influence than virtually any other area of governance. Influence on matters of smaller policy issues is easier to see and easier to execute.

Humane Food Production: Did the Eggs Come First?

It may be somewhat easier to effect influence on issues that are closer to the lives of most citizens, issues regulated by local rather than national governments, and issues on which international concerns are less salient. Take, for example, the case of eggs. Although California provides a massive share of the United States' produce, Californians eat eggs mostly raised elsewhere in America. Producing large quantities of eggs that can be sold cheaply isn't much like anyone's pastoral fantasy about farming. Laying hens spend their short lives in houses that look more like factories than farms, their beaks clipped, and crowded into small cages, with lighting, food, and medication manipulated to maximize egg production.

Animal rights activists intervened in California politics to ameliorate these conditions, winning a small policy reform through a statewide referendum. The state has a reform tradition which provides for relatively easy access for citizen groups to put propositions to a state-wide vote through the referendum process. Activists who initially focused on rules that would lead to the more humane production of eggs were committed to the belief that humane production of eggs was largely impossible, particularly on a large scale. The animal rights movement, more or less subtly through its most visible organizations, generally promoted vegan diets, that is, avoiding the consumption of animal products altogether. Mindful of the lack of broad public support for such a position, however, organizers chose to focus on relatively modest strictures on farming. The Prevention of Farm Animal Cruelty referendum, placed on the California ballot in 2008, mandated minimum amounts of space for sows, calves bred for veal, and chickens. The farm animals would still live severely limited lives, and farmers who violated the new standards would face rather modest misdemeanor penalties.

Framed as a modest solution to a large provocation, the measure won support from nearly two-thirds of California voters. In the wake of the election, Wayne Pacelle, director of the Humane Society, claimed a watershed victory, announcing that activists had "brought forth a new, more compassionate age."[9] Animal rights activists were quick to note the limits of their own efforts, and the rather modest improvements to the lives of farm animals.[10] The cost of eggs spiked, but briefly, and the California eggs became slightly more expensive than eggs elsewhere in the United States. Over time, however, the difference between eggs consumed in California and those consumed elsewhere diminished, as egg producers generally acceded to the new California standards for all of their product – because of the sheer size of the California market.[11] Activist impact radiated beyond the boundaries of the state of California.

So, we can tell the story of eggs in California as one in which a social movement affected influence in the ways in which millions of people constructed their diets. Capitalist enterprise is remarkably adaptable, and farmers in California and elsewhere adapted, adhering to the letter of the law; the market for eggs also adapted. At the same time, the activists who pushed for the referendum recognized that they had effectively helped to promote a notion of more humane cultivation of animal products, institutionalizing their consumption. It would be hard to find animal rights activists who believed that affording hens a few extra inches and a whiff of fresh air during their short lives was actually humane. At the same time, the referendum succeeded at least partly because its advocates convinced voters that it represented a real, and relatively low cost, solution to an important moral problem. Whether these modest reforms provide a barrier to future reforms or a foundation for them, is contingent upon a number of factors far beyond activist control. Humane food production, with or without animals, remains an issue that will be contested in much of the world.

Earth Day and the Politics of Commemoration

Public policy includes all of the things that government does (and doesn't do). When we discuss meaningful changes in policy, we usually focus on laws, programs, and budgets. But governments – and movements – also make symbolic gestures that can affect the way people think about social change, and the opportunities for mobilization. A particularly notable example is the May 1 (May Day) commemoration that takes place virtually everywhere in the richer part of the world, celebrating and asserting the importance of organized labor, often endorsed by government policies.

Environmental activism in the United States, coupled with institutional political support and the critical event of an oil spill that drew attention to environmental concerns, led to the establishment of an official day to celebrate – and advocate for – the environment. The extended life of the commemoration offers contemporary environmental activists the recurrent opportunity to renew, redefine, and assert their concerns.

Although environmental concerns have a very long history, the contemporary movement is often dated to the awakening to the dangers of air and water pollution, often tied to the publication of *Silent Spring* (Carson 1962), which was initially serialized in a major mainstream magazine (Meyer and Rohlinger 2012). Organizing against pollution took off during the 1960s, wrapped in concerns about public health, in many ways resurrecting and redefining the claims of the Progressive movement a half-century earlier.

In January 1969, just after Richard Nixon took the presidential oath of office, an oil well under a platform off the coast of Santa Barbara, California, blew out, pumping up to 100,000 barrels of oil into the ocean over more than a week, killing thousands of birds and aquatic animals, and visibly polluting the beaches. The oil spill provided both additional impetus and focus to the environmental movement, and committed politicians picked up on it. Senator Gaylord Nelson, of Wisconsin, set about pushing environmental concerns to the top of the political agenda, recruiting outside organizers to push for an Earth Day.

Dennis Hays, Nelson's key recruit, developed a national network initially located primarily in public schools and universities, to commemorate the oil spill. This emergent Earth Day Network, working closely with Congressional allies, developed an actionable legislative agenda to capitalize on the attention from the event. Two thousand colleges and universities and a much larger number of public schools celebrated the first Earth Day in 1970, engaging an estimated 20 million people (Nelson 1980; Rome 2003; Thulin 2019).

Broad and bipartisan support made environmental issues attractive to a Republican president (from California!) who had never expressed much interest in environmental issues in the past. In office, Nixon spoke about the importance of environmental issues, supported legislation regulating air and water quality, and created a new agency, the Environmental Protection Agency, which oversees such regulation and is charged with protecting public health and the environment (Rinde 2017).

The institutionalization of Earth Day, an annual occasion for environmental education and action, provided a ready structure for activists to use in advancing a range of claims over time. Its appeal extended beyond the United States, and it is now commemorated every April 22 in nearly 200 countries. The occasion itself doesn't define outcomes, but it provides a space for making claims and is a constant reminder of both problems and possibilities.

The Politics of Nuclear Power

The issues attendant to safe and sustainable energy production are more difficult and less adaptable to citizen concerns, and debates about nuclear energy have periodically emerged strongly and controversially across most Western democracies over the past half-century. Opposition to the growth of nuclear power developed along several distinct, but related lines of argument. First, nuclear power was far more expensive than existing sources of power, including both fossil fuels and alternative energy. Second, the production of fissionable material associated with nuclear power evoked connections to nuclear weaponry, and represented a threat to peace. Third, nuclear power plants, for reasons of economy and practicality, were frequently sited near bodies of water, commandeering large tracts of very attractive land. Fourth, the event of a nuclear accident could conceivably create massive environmental and health damage to surrounding areas. Reactor disasters at Chernobyl in 1986 and Fukushima in 2011 would give substance and image to such fears, spoiling farmland and spurring cancer clusters. Fifth, even the "safe" operation of nuclear plants, through the emission of radiation and the problem of storing nuclear waste, could create additional environmental, health, and security risks long into the future. Opponents of nuclear weapons advanced environmental, health, safety, and energy arguments in different mixes, depending upon the historical moment and the nature of the groups most committed to the campaigns. And they affected the broad range of social movement strategies for influence, ranging from civil disobedience at the sites of proposed nuclear plants to large demonstrations at those plants or national capitals, to testimony in public hearings to electoral campaigns.

Over the long haul, the most successful antinuclear campaign developed over decades in Germany. Antinuclear protests initially linked local residents in a wine-growing corner of Germany with student activists who mounted a series of demonstrations and occupation of a proposed plant in Wyhl in 1975. (At least some of those engaged were aware of a kin effort in the United States focused on a proposed plant at Seabrook, New Hampshire.) Protests spread to other potential nuclear sites, with different mixes of the same basic coalition: environmentalists and local residents. The Wyhl plant was never built, and the site ultimately became a nature preserve, but nuclear plants were established elsewhere in Germany.

The strong antinuclear movement, however, ensured that the process of building nuclear plants in Germany was more cumbersome and expensive than in other wealthy industrialized countries, and thus, less attractive to business and government. Due to the difficulty and expense of building plants there, nuclear power never comprised more than 20 percent of the power used in Germany.[12] In contrast, early in the twenty-first century, nuclear power generated 30–40 percent of power in Japan, about half of the power in Belgium, and upwards of 70 percent of the electricity in France. Activists' initial successes in Germany were not in stopping the development of nuclear power, but in constraining it.

Outside events, particularly reactor accidents in other countries, aided the development of the movement and its ultimate influence. The infrastructure of the antinuclear power movement provided a foundation for activism against nuclear weapons, growing in the wake of the Three Mile Island accident in the United States in 1979. Shortly thereafter, the environmental and peace movements grew into an environmentally-oriented political party, the Greens, which first gained seats in the European Parliament and then in state parliaments (Kitschelt 1989). Once the party had gained a threshold in German politics, it used its official status to promote environmental positions and to conduct oversight of German policies. The reactor accident at Chernobyl fed the antinuclear movement and the Green Party, as radiation from the accident, carried by the wind, contaminated game and soil in parts of Germany. By winning just a few seats in the Bundestag, the German parliament, Greens were able to publicize this damage, and to press for remediation. Although the Greens never gained 10 percent of the vote in federal elections, their presence kept the nuclear safety issue alive and visible. It wasn't necessarily the most salient issue, but when circumstances allowed, it was accessible to both activists and the public.

A Social Democratic alliance government with the Greens announced the intent to phase out nuclear power over time, beginning in 2000. Although the next government, a conservative alliance led by Chancellor Angela Merkel, intended to back away from that promise, events took control. In 2011, shortly after the Fukushima nuclear accident in Japan, Chancellor Merkel announced that Germany would phase out all nuclear power by 2022.[13]

Merkel's announcement was a victory for the antinuclear movement, but it was certainly not quick or obvious. The movement's efforts over decades put nuclear power under greater scrutiny than it was in other European countries, and helped build support for very tight safety standards. Activist efforts constrained the growth of nuclear power, reducing German dependence on it. When the Fukushima accident illustrated the activist case, there was already an institutional presence in German politics ready to offer the phase-out solution. Moreover, the efforts to limit nuclear power made it far more feasible for Germany to follow through on the phase-out than other nations more dependent upon nuclear power, like France or, more poignantly, Japan. The case of nuclear power in Germany is a story of movement influence, but not a simple one.

Although the long battle against nuclear energy seems to be moving to an outcome in Germany, political disputes about nuclear energy remain in most other rich countries. Contemporary concerns about climate change have helped make nuclear energy appear as an attractive alternative to fossil fuels: for all their environmental dangers, nuclear plants don't produce greenhouse gases. Even a shortened story of the antinuclear movement emphasizes how long and complicated the process of political change is. Even so, political disputes and contending movements on other issues can take even longer to resolve.

Abortion and Reproductive Rights

The abortion debate in the United States provides a particularly powerful illustration of the complications of a long timeline and sustained political engagement in shaping public policy. By the 1960s, safe abortions were available to American women who could pay to travel to countries where the procedure was available. Late in the 1960s, US states began considering the decriminalization of abortion, and a few legalized the medical procedure through contested political debates in state legislatures. Although social movement activists were involved in the debates, and in some places, in providing networks that helped individual women to obtain abortions, mass mobilization was unusual and limited. In 1973, the US Supreme Court, responding to a suit organized by an advocacy group in Texas, found a Constitutional right for a woman to seek abortion during the first two trimesters of a pregnancy, and recognized state interests in regulating the practice, particularly in the last trimester. Initially, what came to be a landmark decision in the case of *Roe v. Wade* was not particularly visible.[14]

But opinions on the practice and the law varied greatly, and did not split along party lines. While abortion rights groups looked to find new ways to advance a broader agenda, in short order the political initiative was captured by anti-abortion activists, who built broad organizations that extended beyond the Roman Catholic Church, and soon moved toward electoral politics. The court decision, *Roe v. Wade*, came in a period of political reform that focused on campaigns and elections, precipitated by the Watergate scandal. In the early 1970s, Congress passed a series of regulations that limited individual campaign contributions; in conjunction with electoral reforms that weakened party leadership, the reforms ushered in an era that emphasized the entrepreneurship of individual candidates in mobilizing constituencies and raising funds. Whereas under the old rules political parties sought to support candidates who were likely to win, and then to cooperate with the party leadership once in office, the new rules rewarded a different sort of aspirant for office. Rather than seek the direct endorsement of party bosses, candidates for Congress sought to raise money from passionate constituencies willing to help find hundreds of relatively small donations. The hopefuls also tried to find issues that would get people to turn out at the polls.

Abortion proved to be an ideal issue for motivating groups and individuals that the parties had previously neglected. In running for their parties' presidential nominations in 1976, Democrat Jimmy Carter and Republican Ronald Reagan found the passions of evangelicals to be a valuable asset. Carter, who won the Democratic Party nomination and the presidency, tried to find a middle position, supporting legislation that prevented Medicaid funding for abortion, and pledging to support the Supreme Court ruling. Reagan, having lost the Republican Party nomination in 1976, went deeper into the anti-abortion constituency, and organized his successful campaign for the presidency in 1980. Party regulars had previously seen Reagan as too old and too conservative to run nationally, but socially conservative activists at the grassroots pushed him to the fore of the Republican Party, and helped him win a landslide victory in the presidential election.

Abortion clinics also became a frontier in the battle for legal abortion. Anti-abortion activists augmented their electoral and protest efforts with protests in front of clinics. Mostly confrontational but nonviolent, anti-abortion crusaders worked to "counsel" women out of seeking abortions by yelling stylized details of the procedure and moral guidance. Not all efforts, however, were so peaceful. In the 1980s, a few people who saw abortion as murder attacked clinics with bombs. Later in the debate, enthusiasts of the anti-abortion cause posted names, addresses, and pictures of doctors who performed abortion. Zealots sometimes followed the cues by attacking doctors and killing them. At least 11 doctors have been killed since the early 1990s.[15]

These attacks didn't change policy, but they did affect what women's health clinics and abortion rights advocates thought they had to do.

As president, however, Reagan did relatively little to end legal access to abortion in the United States, constrained by the decisions of the Supreme Court; although he appointed conservative justices to the Supreme Court, not all of them supported overruling *Roe v. Wade*. Reagan's rhetoric, however, amplified by disruptive efforts by anti-abortion activists – including clinic bombings, made the issue more salient to supporters of abortion rights. Womens' rights activists moved legal abortion to the top of their agendas, and movements on both sides have dominated the political landscape for decades.

Partly a result of the institutional obstacles built into American politics, and partly because of the existence of powerful countermovements, policy has changed relatively little while the politics of abortion has become more and more partisan (Meyer and Staggenborg 1996). By the early 1980s, a serious aspirant for national office could not oppose legal abortion in the Democratic Party, nor support abortion rights within the Republican Party. By the following decade, a president could not ignore a potential judicial appointee's position on abortion, and both sides poured activists onto the streets, and money and supporters into institutional politics. Social movements made the issue more salient, but policy changes came far more slowly. In recent years, legislators in heavily Republican states have passed enhanced strictures on access to abortion, anticipating that new appointments to the Supreme Court would complete a majority that would allow them to stand. Over decades, activists on both sides of the issue have focused more intensively on Supreme Court appointments, with candidates for the presidency promising to deliver either the abolition (Republican candidates) or protection (Democratic candidates) of this Constitutional right. As president, Donald Trump was able to appoint three justices to the nine-member court, intensifying that focus for both supporters and opponents of abortion rights.

The abortion story in the United States illustrates the difficulty that social movements face in effecting influence on contested policies. In a democratic polity, whenever an organized force seems on the verge of effecting change, it is likely to mobilize a counterforce, often in movement form (Meyer and Staggenborg 1996) which will push in the other direction. It makes for messy and contested politics; in terms of policy, it makes for a kind of stalemate.[16] In the case of access to abortion in the United States, the battle has been fought around the margins for nearly 50 years. When abortion rights advocates enjoy institutional advantages, they push to extend access. Opponents fight to limit access by enforcing restrictions on clinics, doctors, and timelines. But the other side is always pushing back.

The Yellow Vest Protests

When activist campaigns make claims, no matter how passionately, they are still dependent upon responses from mainstream political institutions, which are likely to be partial at best. We can see the development of political responses in looking at a movement in France which is still developing. The yellow vest (*gilets jaunes*) protests in France have radically altered the nation's political dynamics, without coming close to satisfying the demands of the protesters. To understand the story, we need to start with the election of Emmanuel Macron in the spring of 2017. In an environment of intense political polarization, Macron had formed a new political party to represent a centrist, technocratic approach to policy. He handily defeated a nationalist candidate who ran on opposition to immigrants in the general election, and seemed to have afforded himself considerable room to maneuver in managing the economy. Upon taking power, Macron sought to *modernize* the economy to increase economic growth, cutting taxes and regulations on business. At the same time, to address climate change, he presided over increased taxes on fuel.

The first wave of opposition came from the French countryside, where a populist campaign against the cost of living and the cost of fuel developed. Initial stirrings of opposition came online, through a petition which quickly gathered hundreds of thousands of signatures, and organizers worked to make the movement visible in the streets – by blocking them. Donning yellow safety vests that all French motorists are required to keep in their cars, protesters surged on Paris in the fall of

2018, in an ongoing series of weekend protests. While the turnout at the demonstrations varied, generally decreasing over time, sometimes violent confrontations with police in the streets dominated the political news. Images of burning cars and tear gas spread over television and the Internet. When the movement didn't dissipate, President Macron began offering concessions. Without backing off on the tax cuts or fuel hikes, he announced an increase in the minimum wage, and promised to address and control immigration – a contested issue at the core of his opponent's political campaign. Initial concessions didn't stop the demonstrations.[17] It quickly became clear that the sustained demonstrations had accelerated the decline in Macron's popularity and stalled the neoliberal reforms he had intended to implement. Whether they will lead to the sorts of major changes in policy that those wearing the vests imagine remains unclear. Indeed, the composition of the coalition behind the protests, comprised mostly of the far left and far right, makes successful accommodation seem unlikely. Nonetheless, over the course of months, Macron continued to offer tax breaks to the people who seemed to be protesting, and the protests have become progressively smaller. At the same time, the financial cost of concessions is likely to constrain the options available to Macron in the future, and certainly to his successors. The story here is one of stimulus response, with the protesters creating a political problem for the government, and Macron responding incrementally to try to undermine the unity and urgency of his challengers. The outcomes of what is in this case an iterative process are impossible to predict in advance.

There is no question that the protests have affected public policy in France, but not by themselves. Moreover, absent a coherent program from either the protesters or the government, it's hard to assess the extent of what's possible or what's likely.

The French president has continued to try a combination of concessions, on benefits and taxes, with harsh policing in urban centers. The challenge for the protesters is to find a way to continue to mobilize in the face of this changing environment.

University Student Fees in the United Kingdom

Public universities started charging tuition fees in Great Britain in 1998, as a Labour government sought to reduce its spending. Initially, tuition was capped at £1,000 a year, and means-testing meant that less advantaged students paid less. Over time, however, subsequent governments sought to put more of the responsibility for paying for university education on students, so that government could pay less, and under the Higher Education Act 2004 fees rose to up to £3,000 a year. In 2010, a newly elected coalition government led by the Conservatives dramatically increased the cap on fees to £9,000, nearly tripling the previous cap.

Students took to the streets in a series of disruptive protests focused on London. More than 30,000 students turned out in London on November 10 of that year, with support from many other groups, including out-of-power parties and pensioners' groups. The National Union of Students (NUS), nominally the organizer of the march, was unable to control all of those participating, and against its opposition, a group of a few hundred students broke into the Conservative Party's headquarters, breaking windows, and attempting to occupy the site. Police kettled the crowd in front of the Millbank building, while occupiers threw eggs and shards of glass at them. Central London traffic was disrupted, and the NUS condemned the occupation. Somewhat smaller protests emerged in other British cities, but the occupation of Millbank overshadowed the grievances about tuition. Over the next several weeks, students staged strikes and marches across the country, sometimes clashing with police. In London particularly, police employed increasingly aggressive tactics to keep demonstrators from reaching their targets, leading to more clashes and more confrontation.

Conservative Party leaders focused on the violence at the demonstrations, rather than the issue of tuition hikes, emphasizing their commitment to maintaining order. Although the Welsh and Scottish parliaments implemented lower fees for their own students, the tuition hikes held, and institutionalized a pattern of routine fee hikes and more muted student protests. Although the student protests were effective in setting a political agenda, without the support of allies in government, it was difficult to make inroads in policy. Now, British universities charge university students more than in all but the United States (Olcese and Saunders 2014).

Summary

The stories about social movements and policy change complicate our understanding of how social movements work. Importantly, public policy is frequently the central core of what activists struggle to change – and sometimes they succeed. But social movements don't promote policy change on the time scale they want, and they rarely get all they ask for. Moreover, social movements are not alone in making claims on matters of policy. They are dependent upon allies, both inside and outside of government, whose efforts sometimes align with their own. Sometimes, activism can create perverse outcomes. By raising the salience of issues and threatening to effect change, movements can energize their opposition. In seeking to quell them, politicians often respond to those opponents rather than the initial instigators.

Most significantly, the time scale of change and the magnitude executed in democratic polities are complicated and unsteady. Although policy change seems to happen suddenly, this is rarely the case, and when we extend our historical analysis, we learn that even the overnight sensation is the product of decades of investment. To change a policy, activists need to fight to change the world – usually over a very long period of time.

Activists protest when they think it might help them get what they want – and when they think they can't get it any other way. Such decisions are sometimes strategic and well considered, and sometimes just a matter of habit. Organizers successfully mobilize movements when they can convince people that the issue at hand is urgent, that positive outcomes are possible, and that their efforts could make a difference.

At the same time, politicians often use such alternatives to capture or at least defuse social movements. The antinuclear weapons movement of the late 1950s and early 1960s did not end the arms race nor all nuclear testing. It did, however, lead to the Limited Test Ban Treaty, which ended atmospheric testing. First Eisenhower, then Kennedy, offered arms control proposals and talks with the Soviet Union, at least in part as a response to the movement. This peace movement established the framework for arms control in superpower relations, which subsequently spread to the entire international community.

The big story here is that social movements can have an influence on policy through a number of different mechanisms, all of which require interaction with mainstream political institutions. Social movement activism can change priorities, institutions, the decision-makers, and stories. The time scale of reform is much longer than we would initially think, and the stories that activists repeat with the intent of supporting their cause, routinely truncate the timeline. The tool of social movement activism is likely to work far better in some issue areas than others: when organizers challenge authorities who are unified on issues they think are important (often foreign and military policies, for example), they are going to have a more difficult time getting what they want – but that doesn't mean they don't matter. Activists can fight to stalemate, failing that, they can deter further unwanted moves in policy – as in the case of *Miss Saigon* casting actors in yellowface makeup. In looking at the 2003 war in Iraq, for example, a global coalition (Walgrave and Rucht 2010) was unable to deter the Bush administration from engaging in the war; the movement did, however, alter the targeting strategy of the administration to attempt to reduce civilian casualties (Arkin 2003). This modest and unacknowledged concession certainly wasn't what those who filled the streets were demanding, but that doesn't mean it was insignificant.

Social movements, by the popularity of their arguments, or more frequently, the strength of their support, can convince authorities to reexamine and possibly change their policy preferences. Movements can demand a litmus test for their support. Although movement activists promote specific policies – a nuclear freeze, an equal rights amendment, an end to legal abortion, or, more recently, a cap on malpractice awards – their demands are usually so absolute that they do not translate well into policy. (Placards and bumper stickers offer little space for nuanced debate.) Indeed, the clearest message that activists can generally send is absolute rejection: no to nuclear weapons, abortion, pesticides, or taxes. These admonitions rarely become policy, but by promoting their programs in stark moral terms, activists place the onus on others to offer alternative policies that are, depending on one's perspective, more moderate or more complex.

CHAPTER 4

Protest, Organizations, and Institutionalization

After a video depicting a Minneapolis police officer kneeling on George Floyd, a Black man in custody, for nearly ten minutes, killing him, protests against racialized police violence erupted across the United States. By all reports, many of the demonstrations were organized by novices: in Camden, New Jersey, Yolanda Deaver, whose beauty shop was shut down by the global coronavirus pandemic, was the moving force behind the local demonstration. She posted on Instagram, "the racist Police are killing our Black men," and announced a demonstration, which generated immediate response. The Camden police even wrote in to ask if its officers could join in support.[1]

In Red Hook, a neighborhood in Brooklyn, the prime mover was 22-year-old Na Dortch, who'd been to a few demonstrations in the past, but hadn't ever organized anything political before. He began by texting a friend, who agreed to help, and they reached out first to other friends. They produced a leaflet, created a new name for their new group (New BLQK Leaders), and announced a time and place. Police contacted him to get as much information as they could on the demonstration and its planned march route.[2] Deaver and Dortch were not outliers. Novice organizers put together the marches across Texas and in towns throughout New Jersey, and in neighborhoods all through New York City.[3]

The organizers weren't starting from scratch, exactly. Other organizers had worked hard in the past few years to make the issue of police violence broadly salient, and in publicizing organizing efforts, to suggest a sense of possibility. Additionally, the shut-downs from COVID-19 gave people the space to view those horrific videos and the freedom from daily responsibilities to think about how to fight injustice. And today's young people have developed a sophistication for using social media to get the word out; even then, all of the reports include a large component of old-fashioned person-to-person recruiting.

All of the demonstrations produced the kind of images we picture when we think of social movements, particularly people standing or marching in the streets, sometimes bumping up against counterdemonstrators or police or the military. They chant, hold signs, and make demands. But these visible and often dramatic efforts don't happen by themselves, nor are they all that social movements do. Rather, the visible push of a social movement protest is built on the purposeful efforts of people who work to make them happen. Organizers get permits, rent sound systems, post flyers and Internet memes, compile lists, and solicit speakers. They make the infrastructure of a social movement, and they keep working when the dramatic events are far less visible.

Organizers organize. They stage events, including protests, strikes, and civil disobedience actions. But they do more than that as well. Activist organizations file lawsuits, conduct and publish research that supports their positions, and they talk to legislators and campaign in elections. The groups that they create are often surprisingly resilient, surviving beyond the peak moments of a political movement (Wilson 1995; Zald and McCarthy 1987). Those organizations can provide the foundation for less contentious political action, action that may be very effective in influencing policy, long after the protests and disruptions are no longer visible. Leaving an organization in place is one outcome of a social movement – and it might be an important success. Sometimes, in seeking to respond to political insurgency, authorities make a place for social movements within government. At the national level, we see the creation of government departments concerned with labor, the environment, civil rights, or arms control. At the local level, we see the creation of civilian oversight boards for police, the environment, or schools. Government gets bigger, to be sure, but also potentially more responsive. Activists can find more stable positions a little closer to the levers of power that can afford the prospects for exercising political influence. In this chapter, we will look at the process of institutionalization, that is, building stable organizational structures outside or inside government through which to pursue – or manage – movement goals in a persistent, often routine, fashion.

It's a mistake to see social movements as a distinct form of political engagement that's separate from mainstream institutions or longstanding organizations. Although thinking about the eruption of political movements as a spontaneous coalescence of awareness, agency, and activism makes for a compelling story, it is not necessarily an accurate one. Organizations inspire, inform, and coordinate political activism, but beyond that, they often survive beyond the highlights of a social movement challenge, and continue to exert influence on both public policy and subsequent social movement activism. Importantly, some of those organizations operate more or less independently from the government, and sometimes build transnational ties. But organizations and institutions also develop within the state, providing an institutional presence to represent a set of views and constituencies.

In democratic states, protest movements are coordinated by established organizations that also need to find ways to support themselves as well as to advance their claims. Sometimes support can come from the government or political parties; sometimes it comes from interested parties with their own commitments and agendas. Formal organizations provide a foundation for continued protest and making claims, but – because they require activist energies and resources – they can also produce drag on the peak moments of mobilization. The establishment and maintenance of such organizations are one outcome of social movements, which defines part of institutionalization.

The other critical venue for institutionalization is within government. Social movements can build inroads into both the bureaucracy and mainstream politics to continue advancing their interests, often less visibly and more incrementally. In pluralist polities, governments often grow to address new concerns, and new bureaus, boards, and agencies reflect the effort to include new constituencies, develop new issues and problems, and explicitly recognize that government is taking on new responsibilities. Eighteenth-century governments didn't worry about the environment, and only at the end of the twentieth century did governments take up the problems of the Internet or of climate change.

Social movements can alter not only the substance of policy, but also how policy is made. It is not uncommon for governments to create new institutions such as departments and agencies in response to activists' demands. For example, President John F. Kennedy responded to the nuclear test ban movement by establishing the Arms Control and Disarmament Agency, which became a permanent voice and venue in the federal bureaucracy for arms control, speaking to a constituency first visible on the streets. Not too much longer afterward, in response to a burgeoning environmental movement, President Richard Nixon established the Environmental Protection Agency, a Cabinet-level agency charged with enforcing regulations and protecting the natural world. A glance at any organizational chart of government offices turns up numerous departments, boards, and commissions that trace their origins to popular mobilization, departments of ministries of labor, housing, and the environment, for example, and now, as mentioned in the previous chapter, climate change. Although these offices do not always support activist goals, their very existence represents a permanent institutional concern and a venue for making demands. Their establishment gives concerned people an obvious door to knock on when confronting a designated set of issues.

Social movements also spawn dedicated organizations that generally survive well after a movement's moment has passed. The environmental movement, for example, firmly established a "big ten" group of national organizations, including the Sierra Club (founded 1892) and the World Wildlife Fund (founded 1961), which survive primarily by raising money from self-defined environmentalists. It also gave rise to a number of transnational organizations that engage in protest, public education, and institutional politics, including Greenpeace (founded 1971). They cultivate donors by monitoring and publicizing government action and environmental conditions, lobbying elected officials and administrators, and occasionally mobilizing their supporters to do something more than mail in their annual membership renewals. Here too, the seemingly permanent establishment of nongovernmental organizations (NGOs) around the world, even if these groups often lose, fundamentally changed policymaking. Salaried officers of the organizations routinely screen high-level appointees to the judiciary and government bureaucracy and testify before legislatures. Mindful of this process, policymakers seek to preempt their arguments by modifying policy – or, at least, rhetoric.

The Organizational Dilemma and Institutionalization

Are organizations the achievement of powerful social movements or their end point? People who study social movements have been arguing about the impact of institutionalization for decades. Most notably, Frances Fox Piven and Richard Cloward, both experienced organizers for welfare rights, argued that organizations and institutionalization provide a drag on social movements, compromising their energy and integrity, without generating much in the way of benefits (Piven and Cloward 1977). Leaders of established organizations, they said, are more concerned with the survival of their group and the stability of a personal position than the shorter-term policy outcomes of a protest movement. This is, by the way, an old issue in social science. More than 100 years ago, a Swiss political scientist, Roberto Michels, concerned with organizational democracy, conducted a study of the German Social Democratic Party (SPD). This political party, he reasoned, explicitly concerned with democracy, would be the sort of organization most likely to practice internal democracy. Michels (1962 [1915]) found, however, that the leadership of the party developed interests and attitudes quite different from those of the rank and file, and internal democracy was essentially ineffectual. This "Iron Law of Oligarchy" is sometimes called the only law in political science.

Piven and Cloward's argument about social movements was based in a particular kind of movement, that is, one mobilizing on behalf of poor people. Their claim was that those people, poorly positioned to influence policy through any conventional means, had only disruption as a possible route to influence. In times of electoral disruption, they claimed, that disruption could provoke authorities to offer benefits to poor people in order to get them to stop protesting, and to reinforce existing social and political coalitions. But protest didn't automatically generate concessions. Officials could also repress those movements; it was impossible for activists to know in advance. In essence, it was advice to bang on an engine that wasn't operating properly: it might blow up, or it might start working ... for a while.

Thus, the advice from these longtime organizers was for activists to focus on creating disruption. They lionized organizations, like the Student Nonviolent Coordinating Committee (SNCC), that consistently focused on mobilization and disruption, rather than on building a strong institutional presence. Organizations that were concerned with their stability or ongoing relationships with elected officials or funders were likely to squander the unusual moments when social control broke down and people were in the streets. And, although Piven and Cloward wrote about movements of the poor, subsequent scholars have been perhaps too quick to apply their arguments to other kinds of movements.

But the story is more complicated. Suzanne Staggenborg (1988) took Piven and Cloward's ideas to explore the organization of the abortion rights movement. Staggenborg found that the organizational resources that leaders could command allowed them to monitor policy and events consistently, to respond opportunistically to changes in political alignments or critical events, to strategize, and to innovate. Sometimes, they even organized the protest events that we think of when we think of social movements. For reproductive rights, at least, Staggenborg found that the firm foundation provided by longstanding organizations was a resource for subsequent waves of mobilization. When we look at the outcomes of social movements, it therefore makes good sense to look at the organizations they create, and sometimes leave behind. Similarly, Marshall Ganz (2000), a veteran of the farmworkers' movement in the United States, argued that the history and victories of the United Farmworkers afforded its leader "strategic capacity" in subsequent campaigns to leverage a range of choices to effect influence.

Meanwhile, SNCC, which operated on a hyper-democratic model, struggled in trying to adapt to a changing political environment after the Voting Rights Act (Robnett 2002), which changed the opportunities the civil rights movement faced. Some activists pushed to work through the political system and run candidates for office, while others grew to distrust white leadership and pushed for a stronger Black nationalist perspective. The group fell apart, partly because there was no organized group with a vested interest in its survival. The activists went on to do other things, including both protest organizing and running for office, but the distinct contribution that SNCC offered to the broader civil rights movement disappeared.

The dissolution of an organization that prizes engagement over organizational survival is hardly unusual. Similarly structured groups that emphasize base democracies often disappear when peak mobilization passes. The Students for a Democratic Society (SDS) in the United States and the Sozialistische Deutsche Studentenbund (another SDS!) in West Germany, student movement groups in the 1960s, both dissolved early in the 1970s. Most notably, the grassroots groups that staged public occupations during the Great Recession, including the Indignados (15-M Movement) and Occupy in the United

States, also disappeared as organizations when the mobilization moment passed. They were not around to try to influence the shape of subsequent protest movements nor the policy debates that followed. There are advantages, as well as costs, to institutionalization.

It's reasonable to think about the influence of political organizations on the policy process or on subsequent social movements as contingent. Nothing is automatic. An established organization outside government may be able to exploit new opportunities, but opportunities are missed all of the time. Similarly, a government bureaucracy dedicated to any policy area – housing, income, or the environment – can provide steady institutional support for responsive policies. But political leadership can neuter or ignore that support. The point is that social movements can leave organizational structures in place after the moment of mobilization that affect both policies and movements for generations to come. We can see these organizations and institutions inside and outside of government.

The early part of the twentieth century was an age of organization. Suffrage advocates organized (Clemens 1997). Those women also pushed for activism on a range of other issues, particularly efforts against war and poverty. Labor organizers organized, building strong unions and gaining political representation in government. Racial justice and civil rights organizers organized, building resilient groups that could launch sustained challenges on matters of rights and policy. Farmers organized, building robust organizations that could press their interests in government, which expanded to accommodate those interests. Environmentalists organized, demanding government action to protect natural resources. We will look at some of these stories to see the ways in which purposeful organization of social movements affects both government bureaucracy and challenging movements.

Organized Labor, Recognized and Institutionalized

To start thinking about organizations as an accomplishment of social movement, it makes sense to start with organized labor. Dating back to the Marxism of the nineteenth century, analysts saw workers as the motive force for social change. The revolution that Marx predicted around the corner didn't arrive, at least not in the advanced industrialized nations where he saw it as inevitable. But the world he described was also radically different as a result of workers movements. In a way, it evokes the Biblical tale of Jonah we reviewed in chapter 2.

The point is that the warning of activism can promote change that makes a certain kind of activism less likely. Organized labor provides the most salient example.

Workers organized unions to bolster their bargaining power in the workplace, and their political influence in the state. Although union activism directed at employers is sometimes contrasted with that directed at politics, they really coexist in every consequential labor movement. Unions started to develop along with the rise of industrial capitalism in the most economically advanced states, but both business and governments initially opposed their existence. Organizing unions became possible with the restructuring of the workplace, in which people moved from the countryside to work in industrialized workplaces, notably factories. The factory floor put workers in touch with other workers, and cities made those workers neighbors as well. Proximity provided an opportunity for workers to recognize shared interests, and the chance to organize to make claims about wages and working conditions.

Initial battles were largely independent of the state, and this put workers at a huge disadvantage. Businesses could mobilize the forces of the state to suppress union activism. Over time, trade unions recognized the need to develop a political as well as a workplace bargaining strategy. By the end of the nineteenth century, trade unions could win recognition and a legitimate place in politics by linking economic leverage with political power. In most democratic states, organized labor developed as a major force in a left of center political party, often called "Labor." The party's threat to influence policy induced governments to offer some advantages, advantages that organizers used to leverage subsequent activism.

In America, the national government began collecting data on the well-being of workers at least partly in response to the efforts of organizing labor in the 1880s. In 1913, labor was established as a Cabinet-level department, one charged with monitoring and managing the state of America's workers. It would be decades before the agency started to affect that well-being by getting involved in collective bargaining.

Most notably, the political and economic turbulence of the 1930s led, in the United States, to the recognition and formalization of the place of organized labor in the political process. In 1935, the United States established the National Labor Relations Board, which monitored and regulated the process of workplace bargaining. Workers were given the right to try to organize unions, and a set of rules and routines for doing so, with a governmental body charged with overseeing the process. The organizational recognition of labor made it easier for workers to organize on their own behalf, while simultaneously routinizing the process of bargaining with employers and with government so that labor's claims-making would be less disruptive and less unpredictable.

The labor example illustrates two forms of institutionalization that reflect different, but complementary, ways in which movements matter. Mobilization of workers left in place formal bureaus within governments that are explicitly concerned with the well-being of working people. Those agencies collect data, evaluate policies, and monitor and often regulate relations between workers and employers. Labor unrest also left behind large bureaucratic unions that also represent the well-being of workers. They collect dues and fees from workers, and in exchange, negotiate contracts with employers. Those contracts contain agreements on wages and benefits, as well as rules and routines for work. The unions represent their workers in disputes with those employers. They often also support political parties and candidates whom their leaders believe will be more favorable to their interests when in office. This support can include formal endorsements, but also campaign contributions and the spirited support of union members.

Although you may see the unions demonstrating or organizing strikes, a large part of what they now do doesn't look exactly like movement work. At the same time, union leaders very much view their efforts in the context of representing labor's interests. But it is often less about workers generally, than about the particular members of each union. There is a clear interface between the formal organizations outside of government and those within, streamlining the process of making and evaluating policy – although this may come at the expense of a more vigorous advocacy and broader political engagement.

Movements Establish Organizations

Organizations provide an infrastructure for broad social movements, but those movements also create organizations that survive well beyond the initial flash of passionate activism that characterize a movement at its peak. Those organizations survive between peaks of broad activism, linking contemporary campaigns with those of the past (Taylor 1989). Organizations survive by building institutional routines and cultivating a consistent sense of support; this happens only by convincing funders, grassroots or institutional, inside or outside of government, that they represent some element of a movement's initial concerns. The work of sustaining an organization is generally less visible and much less dramatic than activism in the streets, but much of that activism would not take place without professionals paying attention to political opportunities, writing grants, staging events, and engaging in public education campaigns. We can see the development of movement organizations through the directed efforts of notable activists who built organizations for the campaigns of the moment that outlived both the campaigns and the organizer.

Jane Addams and the Politics of Peace and Justice

Born to a large, affluent, and influential family in 1860, Jane Addams developed a passion for social justice as a young woman. With scant professional opportunities open to young educated women like her, Addams committed to Chicago, and to what would later become known as social work. In 1889, she and Ellen Starr founded Hull House in Chicago's west side, the first settlement house in America, adapting a model they'd seen in England. They intended Hull House to provide services to a working-class, multi-ethnic neighborhood. But they also wanted it to provide a space for other women like them, mostly but not exclusively, white and advantaged, who were committed to activism and to social justice. In addition to creating a neighborhood kindergarten and day care, Hull House offered language, cooking, and arts instruction to women in the neighborhood. It was a center for arts, and provided a space for organizing campaigns for women's suffrage, against child labor, and for public parks and services more generally, and against segregating Chicago's public schools. In essence, the organizers tried to provide for working people the same sort of advantages they'd experienced. Moreover, an extraordinary range of socially engaged women passed through the place, including Florence Kelley, Julia Lathrop, Sophonisba Breckinridge, and Alice Hamilton. Addams also worked to bring attention to the efforts of anti-lynching crusader and journalist, Ida B. Wells (Michals 2017).

Hull House provided a center for services, a space for meetings, and a place for ambitious and socially committed women, mostly white women from advantaged backgrounds, to engage in meaningful social action. It was also a center for research on poverty; the settlement house sponsored studies of the neighborhood, reports on labor and housing conditions, and of public health, including the spread of infectious diseases. Addams herself taught night courses at the University of Chicago, and published prolifically in both popular and scholarly outlets,[4] but refused a regular academic appointment at the University, determined to emphasize social and political engagement instead. Hull house was also a platform – and a home – for Addams and, eventually, a much larger Progressive movement (Kretschmer and Meyer 2007). From her work and reputation at Hull House, Addams engaged in suffrage campaigns, efforts to reform policing, and campaigns for temperance – among many other issues. Hull House expanded to include a complex of nearby buildings, and functioned for decades after Addams's death, into the 1960s. Later designated a national landmark, it functions as a kind of museum for Addams's work and for the Progressive movement, situated on the University of Illinois-Chicago campus.

Jane Addams styled herself as a pragmatic pacifist, advancing the idea that in addition to the carnage of wars on the front lines, war and the preparations for war robbed communities of the resources necessary to create the conditions for full and fulfilling lives. She wrote and organized nationally and transnationally, serving as the leader of the Women's Peace Party in 1915, and then presided over international conferences intended to end war altogether – held both before and after World War I. She was a cofounder of the Women's International League for Peace and Freedom (WILPF),[5] officially chartered after World War I to prevent another war through concerted action of women around the world. When war came, activism continued – and continues. Embodying Addams's vision of linking social justice and anti-militarism, WILPF maintains chapters in dozens of countries, holds conferences, and has been engaged in antiwar, antinuclear, and anti-imperialist campaigns of all sorts since then. Its members have continued to organize during and between large pacifist and antiwar movements, proving to be a constant presence in activist coalitions, consistently able to educate and mobilize its members. Addams was the first American woman to win the Nobel Peace Prize in 1931, awarded in recognition of her efforts.

Addams's story is exceptional, but hardly unique. In addition to engagement in virtually countless social movement campaigns that influenced policy, she worked hard to build structures to support not only her activism, but that of others. To do so meant creating collaborations with others, and creating durable institutions with some flexibility to take on new issues. Importantly, effective organizations must contain and serve diverse interests and approaches to advancing the cause, adopting new issues and constituencies, and often including protest and more conventional politics (e.g.,

Brooker 2018; Fisher 2019; Kretschmer 2009, 2019; Reger and Staggenborg 2006).

W.E.B. Du Bois, the NAACP, and the Struggle for Racial Justice

Like Addams, W.E.B. Du Bois was a prolific writer, a committed activist, and an organizer skilled enough to build resilient organizations that would outlive him and comprise a critical force in a larger social movement that effectively promoted meaningful government action on civil rights. The first African American to earn a doctorate from Harvard University (in 1895), Du Bois wrote his dissertation on the slave trade. Although his thinking on many issues developed over time, he saw slavery and segregation as an essential component in American life, affecting race relations, politics, and political economy for generations after the Civil War.

At the same time as Du Bois produced a mountain of scholarship which included an unusually broad range of methods and analytical approaches, he committed himself to activism (Morris 2015). The scholarship commenced with description and analysis of the Black community in the United States, including a detailed case study of Philadelphia (Du Bois 1995 [1899]). Demonstrating at a block-by-block level the diversity within the Black population, the work showed the long shadow of discrimination and segregation on Black lives. In a later book, *The Souls of Black Folk* (2016 [1903]), written in a more poetic style, Du Bois identified the problem of "double consciousness," which referred to the idea that a Black man in the United States had to think about both his own perceptions, and how he was perceived as a Black man, such that he always had to see himself through the lens of how others regarded him.

As an activist, Du Bois began by organizing meetings to

discuss the problem of race, which soon began to make demands on matters of policy. In 1905, he was among a group of Black activists that met in Canada to form the Niagra movement, a campaign to end racial segregation and vociferously oppose a politics of accommodation they saw represented by Booker T. Washington. It garnered little influence, but some serious attention, notably from white progressives who were willing to embrace the cause. In 1909, a larger group, including Jane Addams and Ida B. Wells, came together to form the National Association for the Advancement of Colored People (NAACP), which offered a broad interracial, integration-oriented approach to politics.

In its early days, the organization deployed a range of approaches to engaging in politics, including traditional political campaigns (e.g., for integrating the officer corps of the military, against segregating the civil service), protests and marches (against the screening of *Birth of a Nation*, a film that romanticized the Ku Klux Klan), investigations (of riots and lynchings), and litigation. Du Bois himself was central, serving as Director of Publicity and Research for the organization, and editor of the NAACP journal, *The Crisis* for decades. In addition to explicitly political pieces, Du Bois waged a cultural campaign with the journal, publishing the work of many of the writers associated with the Harlem Renaissance. Du Bois was critical to the growth of the journal's circulation and the organization's membership in its first two decades. Growing cynical about the goal of racial integration, however, he left the organization in 1934, accepting an academic position at Atlanta University, and working for a kind of Black nationalism instead.

Fired by Atlanta University in 1943, deep into his seventies, Du Bois turned down other positions to return to the NAACP as Director of Special Research, and remained associated with the group until his death in 1963. He had disputes with other leaders about politics (he was a socialist and ardently opposed war) and a lack of support from NAACP allies when he was persecuted by the federal government for his leftist politics and when he (unsuccessfully) ran for US senator in 1950. Nonetheless, the organization was broad and diverse enough to endure internal conflicts and to lodge decades of challenges in American politics.

Likely best known is the litigation strategy employed by the NAACP Legal Defense Fund, long led by future Supreme Court Justice, Thurgood Marshall. The organization filed scores of lawsuits, campaigning against segregation, beginning with demanding that law schools and graduate schools consider applications from Black applicants, then cases involving residential segregation, and most famously, against racially segregated public schools (Kluger 1975).[6] Marshall argued *Brown v. Board of Education* in front of the Supreme Court in 1954, and a unanimous Court ruled that racial segregation, even if equal facilities for the races were provided, was unconstitutional. Although American public schools are no longer legally segregated, there is enormous racial sorting in education – and elsewhere – in American life, even nearly 70 years later. Nonetheless, the NAACP won a great legal victory, the result of many factors, including successful campaigns to desegregate other institutions, a sustained legal campaign, strong research and argument offered by a team of very accomplished lawyers, and a Cold War context in which mainstream political figures wanted to make progress on racial issues at home to counter Soviet propaganda (Dudziak 2000).

Both the Legal Defense Fund and the NAACP used the *Brown* decision as aspirational and as precedent to launch other legal and activist campaigns. The organization – and its members – were critical to the civil rights campaigns of the following decades. Rosa Parks, who famously refused to move to the back of a segregated bus in Montgomery, Alabama in the year after *Brown*, was chapter secretary of the local NAACP affiliate. After arrest, she was bailed out of jail by E.D. Nixon, who was the chapter's president. Leadership of the local chapter decided to turn the event into a campaign, and initiated a year-long boycott of the buses, while filing a lawsuit (Morris 1984; Theoharis 2018).

In 1960, four college freshmen at North Carolina Agricultural and Technical College, Joseph McNeil, Franklin McCain, Ezell Blair Jr., and David Richmond – all members of the NAACP's youth league – launched what became a nationwide sit-in campaign to desegregate public facilities, starting with lunch counters. Ella Baker, then Executive Secretary of the Southern Christian Leadership Conference, worked to organize a youth organization that would employ the sort of direct action tactics exemplified by the students. She organized the founding conference for the Student Nonviolent Coordinating Committee, and arranged for initial funding. Importantly, Baker had previously spent 15 years working for the NAACP, traveling across the country to help organize chapters. As a result, she was a very skilled and very well-connected organizer, who could help marshal necessary resources, including money, recruits, and publicity for the new group (Ransby 2003).

The NAACP has continued its efforts, taking up new issues and new constituencies in the ensuing decades. The group joined a broad coalition to oppose the US wars against Iraq, supported gay and lesbian rights, as well as immigrant rights. The organization fights for voting rights, and also pushes for economic equity and broad access to health care. The organization has survived for more than 100 years by adapting to new conditions, new problems, and the changing population.[7] The dense infrastructure it developed provides a ready resource to the movements it joins.

Movement Parties and Green Politics

The sharp separation between movement politics, organizing protests, and institutional politics, that is, pursuing power through conventional means of campaigns and elections, is always elusive. Social movements, like the individuals and organizations that animate them, often pursue both inside and outside strategies at the same time. One strategy, particularly visible in countries with proportional representation systems, is to form a party that grows out of the movement, directly putting advocates into parliament, and maybe government. This is the basic story behind the growth of Labor parties around the world more than 100 years ago. It's also the story of a progressive New Democratic Party in the western part of Canada (Schwartz 2002) and a French-speaking nationalist party in the eastern part of the same country (Hamilton and Pinard 1976). In all of these cases, growing social movements added competing for elective office to their tactical options. Forming a political party means establishing a potentially permanent presence on the political landscape, gaining access to routine media coverage, and potentially a share of policy-making power. It can also entail gaining salaries for party activists who win office, and subsidies to promote their messages. And it doesn't necessarily mean abandoning protest politics.

The most successful global movement that pursued a party strategy in the last part of the twentieth century carried environmental concerns into parliaments and politics around the world. Starting in the 1970s, Green parties emerged across developed countries, competing for office successfully in many of them, and even entering state governments.

Environmentalism, of course, has a history in many countries that extends as far back as the nineteenth century, but the party strategy didn't come to the fore until much later. The German case provides an excellent example of how and why.

In the wake of the student and youth movements of the 1960s, many activists moved from national to local politics, often addressing local environmental hazards, such as the construction of nuclear power plants or the expansion of airports. Locally organized citizen initiatives organized campaigns in what used to be West Germany, often funded by mainstream political parties, which included appeals to government, litigation, and protest, all infused with a bit of a counterculture orientation. Although most campaigns were unsuccessful, their presence changed the politics of development, and demonstrated the appeal of a left environmental perspective. They did, however, dramatically slow the development of nuclear power (Joppke 1993; Markham 2005).

Toward the end of the 1970s, as nuclear arms control talks between the United States and the Soviet Union faltered, the North Atlantic Treaty Organization (NATO) announced a new policy to link more strongly the fate of Western Europe to that of the United States, by deploying intermediate range nuclear missiles in five European countries. The so-called Euromissiles were extremely unpopular, provoking large protest movements, particularly strong in the countries scheduled to host the weapons, including Germany (Johnstone 1985). Linking constituencies and issues, environmental activists, calling themselves Greens, began to run for local office in some states. In January of 1980, local environmental groups and activists organized a founding conference, in which they organized a party that would compete for office at the federal level. The Greens were founded on principles of nonviolence, environmental justice, and base democracy (Frankland and Schoonmaker 1992; Kitschelt 1989).

In the 1980s, Greens established a presence at the federal level while simultaneously helping to organize protest campaigns on their core issues, sometimes winning election to state offices. In 1983, in a federal election that came at the height of the antinuclear movement, the Greens won more than 5 percent of the vote (the threshold for parliamentary representation), gaining 27 seats in the Bundestag, the West German parliament, and became part of the opposition to a conservative government. Although there were tensions in transitioning to professional politics,[8] the Greens successfully established themselves as a persistent third party, usually winning somewhere between 5 and 10 percent of the federal vote, and sometimes entered governing coalitions with other parties – on the left and right – at both the state and local level. Their presence ensured the routine representation of environmental concerns, slowing the development of nuclear power, and ultimately providing critical support for eventually committing to ending nuclear power in Germany – a clear victory, but a decision taken nearly 30 years after first entering parliament.

The Green movement adopted party structures in about 80 countries around the world, sometimes entering parliament, and sometimes serving as part of a coalition government. Their success was heavily affected by the electoral rules. In countries with proportional representation and a low threshold for representation, like Germany or Sweden, Green parties could survive nationally while polling less than 10 percent of the vote; in contrast, in countries with winner-take-all systems, like the United Kingdom, Greens are fortunate to gain a single seat in the parliament. Greens in the United States have yet to win representation in Congress.

The point is that the party strategy provides resources to the environmental movement, and sometimes the opportunity to influence policy.

Organizational Afterlives

Organizations stoke and coordinate mobilization, educating constituents and focusing action. These operations occur both inside social movements and inside the bureaucratic agencies of governments they seek to influence. Once established, they seek to sustain themselves, and that often means maintaining attention on the issues that originally animated them. These organizations matter over the long haul.

We can see the residue of social movements, as demonstrated by the conflicts about race in the past of the American South. Kenneth T. Andrews (2004) has conducted extensive studies on the legacy of civil rights activism in Mississippi. He found that the presence of activist organizations, generally NAACP chapters, in a county early in the 1960s was associated with successful pursuit of federal grants, higher Black voter turnout, and the election of Black officials later in the decade.

But it's not only civil rights activists who leave a legacy; their opponents do as well. Rory McVeigh and Kevin Estep (2019) examined the longer-term effects of the white supremacist Ku Klux Klan on politics in the South. Although the national profile and membership of the hate group has risen and fallen in response to political circumstances, law enforcement efforts, and organizing, local chapters spread an ideology that offered a default explanation for the disappointments and setbacks faced by white working-class people, particularly men. Even when Klan groups are less visible, they found, the counties in which they were active supplied disproportionate support for Republican candidates for office, most dramatically, Donald

Trump, who spoke a coded language of white nationalism which the Klan and other hate groups prospected.

In building organizations, inside and outside the state, social movement activists are working to coordinate their efforts in the near future, and investing in the future.

CHAPTER 5

Protest Movements, Culture, and Participants

The peace symbol,[1] the familiar circle bisected by a highly stylized tree, is ubiquitous in contemporary life. Although it's seen virtually everywhere, appropriated by all kinds of movements against war or weaponry and much else, its origins are far less known. The British Campaign for Nuclear Disarmament (CND) first used the symbol in its annual Aldermaston marches scheduled each Easter, beginning in 1958 (Kolsbun 2008). The marchers started in London, and covered 52 miles over several days on the way to the site of the British Atomic Weapons Research Establishment. Although the discernible influence on nuclear weapons policy was slight and slow, the campaign left a symbol in place that carried some of the movement's values.[2]

The design, by Gerald Holtom, who was also an activist concerned with the dangers of nuclear weaponry, super-imposed a simplified semaphore flag of an N over a D, surrounded by the circle; he cut off the flags. It turned out to be an extremely resilient design. The symbol appeared in the demonstrations against the Vietnam War in the 1960s, and globally reappears whenever there are protests against nuclear weapons or war. Sometimes, CND affiliates carry the symbol, but others have picked it up as well.

The symbol was so resilient and so transportable, that it sometimes appears as a mark of fashion, rather than any kind of politics. In the United States, a retailer of girl's clothing focusing on preteens sported the symbol as a logo, putting it on T-shirts, bags, and all kinds of sundries. The name of the retailer: Justice (Riley 2012).

Obviously, the committed antinuclear activists who marched against the arms race were not focused on one day influencing the fashion choices of preteen girls a continent away, but the movement of a symbol demonstrates the complicated way in which social movements can affect social change, particularly culture, values, and individual lives. It's reasonable to ask whether, divorced from its origins or intent, the peace symbol reflects any kind of change. But note that the CND sign was also deployed by peace movements globally in the years following the antinuclear campaign. Protesters against the Vietnam War, the invasion of Iraq, and far too many other military conflicts, displayed the old symbol on banners, placards, and T-shirts. The antinuclear campaign of the 1950s advanced a set of claims and values about war, peace, and justice; it was the cause for forming organizations and communities; it trained a set of activists who were available for political action in the moment, and for years afterward; and it contributed a set of symbols, like the peace sign, to a broader cultural movement that has become global. In this regard, it's like lots of other social movements. The symbol, explicitly designed as a shorthand for a set of claims and values, provided some sense of unity and identity within, first, CND, and then a broader peace movement, and then moved from a subculture into a much broader global culture, albeit with some redefinition in the process.

In this chapter we will examine the impact of social movement participation on the individuals who participate in them and on the broader culture. We'll begin by looking at the messy world of culture, which both influences and is influenced by social movements, and by the people who participate in them. Importantly, cultural change is not something wholly apart from political change. Changing values and opinions is a necessary component of effecting substantial policy reform. We'll then look at the longer-term influence of participation on an individual and a community.

Accessing and Assessing Culture

Culture is a soup that we consume and that we swim in. It includes symbols like the peace emblem designed to promote nuclear disarmament and the fashion climate that made it an attractive choice for adorning girls' T-shirts. Culture affects what we think is moral, just, and cool, our prejudices and our principles. Culture influences what we eat for breakfast, who we're likely to trust, and what we think about nuclear weapons. Cultural scripts and values vary across contexts, across groups and countries. And culture is not stagnant, as is readily demonstrated when you take a look at popular fashions in clothing or food from 50 years ago. Cultural norms move across the boundaries between countries over time, and between distinct subcultures and a broader set of national norms. Because culture is so all-encompassing, it's impossible to divorce it from the policy reform process.

But making sense of culture, much less the impact of social movements on culture writ large, is complicated by the sheer enormity and complexity of what goes in the cultural soup, as well as the back and forth between broader local and national cultures and movement subcultures. It's helpful to sort out a few elements of culture that are easier to observe to see change, which often occurs more quickly than changes in policy (Amenta and Polletta 2019; Earl 2004). We can think of culture as including products, practices, and values, each of which can be identified and tracked for influence. The people who are engaged in social movements carry cultural changes as well as political preferences.

Organizers draw from mainstream culture in order to mobilize constituencies and create a sense of a collective "we," a little different and separate from the political mainstream. The norms and values of the dominant culture are typically repeated and then adapted within a movement culture. Look, for example, at Woody Guthrie's labor anthem, "Union Maid," written to support organizing efforts and build solidarity among workers. Set to a familiar – and simple – melody, the song urges women to support the labor movement by finding and marrying union men, recycling gender norms in the service of labor solidarity (Lomax et al. 1967: 324–5). Beyond the content of the song, the song reflected an organizing tradition of folksingers armed with acoustic instruments leading sing-a-longs reciting social ills and announcing activist power (Roscigno and Danaher 2004; Roy 2010). The songs outlived the struggle of the moment, providing something of a recognizable cultural infrastructure for subsequent waves of activism. When union activism began to decline in the 1950s, blacklisted performers like Pete Seeger carried the songs from the labor movement to other audiences, including children at summer camps – who later ended up on the college campuses supporting a free speech movement in the 1960s – with a common musical vocabulary (Roy 2010). Cultural products provide connections within movements over time, and across movements, connecting waves of mobilization.

More recently, Aya Shoshan (2018) has compared egalitarian Occupy movements in Spain and Israel, finding the influence of other institutions on the internal workings of the movements. The Israeli activists, who shared an experience of mandatory military service, ran relatively quick meetings, and were quick to establish division of labor and military-like hierarchies of responsibility. In contrast, the Spanish activists adopted the norms of the alternative schools that many had attended, which afforded ample time and space for checking in and sharing personal as well as political concerns. The point is that while the somewhat similar movements operating in relatively affluent liberal democracies developed distinct styles of mobilization and organization, those styles reflected the cultures from which they emerged.

Social movements battle over cultural products because they think they matter. In the wake of the East European revolutions of 1989, activists worked to remove the memorials and monuments of the state Communist era. Statues of Lenin, Stalin, and Marx, along with the statues of local collaborators, were taken down, sometimes dramatically by mobs (Foote et al. 2000). Communist parties dissolved themselves and reconfigured under different names, and the names of public institutions were often renamed as well. Even in the post-Soviet Union, we saw cities renamed: Leningrad became St. Petersburg (again), and Stalingrad became Volgograd (for the first time), stripping the honorific from Communist heroes of the past.

When reformers in Poland gained control of the state after the fall of Communism, they commenced reconsidering not only the history of the Communist period, but also the much larger sweep of Polish history, recognizing that our understanding of the past affects what we think is possible or desirable for the future. In the 1990s, activists set about creating a Jewish museum of Polish history, recognizing the very large population of Jews in Poland prior to the Holocaust. In 2005, Poland established the museum in Warsaw (Gessen 2019). After the Law and Justice Party (PiS), a right-wing populist movement, gained majority control of the Polish parliament, however, they set about gaining control of the museums, investing the same aspirations in the cultivation of history – and of art, and culture more generally, that the reformers had (Donadio 2016; Marshall 2020). The government insisted on a history that was almost cartoonishly patriotic, one that didn't undermine any positive appraisals of the Polish people and state, and that didn't challenge audiences or make viewers uncomfortable.

In contemporary politics, battles play out over statues. In the United States, a broad movement against racialized police violence also challenged the display of more than 1,500 statues of Confederate politicians and military leaders from the Civil War. On its face, it seems like an odd, almost trivial demand, but it also seems odd that there would be a public display of the leaders of a failed insurgency displayed by the nation that won. A little history is in order: More than 100 years ago, a racist nationalist movement, which included the Ku Klux Klan, had set about promoting an alternative view of the Civil War, roughly 40–50 years after the war's conclusion. Defining the war as a noble "Lost Cause," they constructed monuments to the politicians and military leaders of the Confederacy. These monuments accompanied the institutionalization of a "Jim Crow" system of racial segregation (Southern Poverty Law Center 2020). The monuments were a tribute to white supremacy, a reminder of a racial order to all who passed by. Even when Jim Crow was legally dismantled, the monuments and their message remained.

The statues had been challenged many times, but attention returned to them during the emergence of a Black Lives Matter campaign in 2013. Although there are hundreds of statues, the battles over placement and commemoration were individual, site by site and monument by monument – and, usually, the statues remained in place. In 2017, just after the inauguration of Donald Trump as president, white nationalists planned a large rally in Charlottesville, Virginia, partly as a response to an effort to take down a statue commemorating Robert E. Lee, the commanding general of the Confederacy. The demonstration drew large numbers of counterdemonstrators, including clergy, pacifists, and self-identified "antifa" (antifascist) forces determined to confront racism aggressively. In the battles that emerged, a young woman was killed by a white nationalist who ran his car into a crowd of demonstrators. There were arrests, political conflicts, but the Lee statue remained (Signer 2020). Campaigns on college campuses brought additional attention to issues of racial justice, but statues – and names honoring historical racists – generally remained.

Just a few years later, however, in the midst of a global pandemic in 2020, the police killing of George Floyd by Minneapolis police underscored a larger pattern of violence and spurred an unprecedented series of demonstrations under the broad rubric, Black Lives Matter. Suddenly, local governments began taking down Confederate statues, renaming streets and buildings, and generally trying to redress a pattern of commemorations of white nationalism that had lasted more than a century. It's not that the 2020 demonstrations were better organized or that the earlier ones were failures. Rather, it was another instance of the long, slow process of social change. Activism in the years past had been part of the process of changing values such that the opposition to removing the statues began to erode. The battles over monuments and memorials are battles over public memory, and contests over the past are always about the future.

The statues, monuments, and museums are all cultural products, operating as both things in themselves and holders for a set of memories, meanings, and values. In and of themselves, they are less consequential than policies and practices, but they have effectively conveyed a message about the immediate world.

We can also see changes in values, sometimes tracked through public opinion polls. Although there is a classic liberal perception that people start with a good sense of their own interests and values, most people adapt their beliefs in response to their experiences, sometimes direct, and sometimes through the media they sample. Public opinion changes over time, in response to events and to political mobilization. Nowhere is this seen more dramatically than in the decades-long campaign for same-sex marriage.

By recognizing some unions, governments offer some status and privilege to couples who adhere to an accepted model. Although gay relationships of various sorts have existed for centuries, states have only granted official recognition to mixed-sex couples since the turn of the twenty-first century, when the Netherlands became the first country to recognize gay marriages. The policy change both reflected and promoted a global change in values that liberation movements had pushed for decades.

Gay and lesbian activism focused first on the recognition of gay people and a call for fair treatment from the state and society. Activism often appeared in pride marches, in which people publicly claimed a gay identity (Armstrong and Crage 2006). This was one element in a much larger campaign of "coming out," that is, acknowledging and claiming an often stigmatized identity. For the first activists, coming out was laden with risks: people were socially ostracized, lost employment opportunities, and suffered violence from police and from other people. As larger numbers of people came out, however, the risks diminished a little bit at a time, varying across countries, regions, and professions. Musicians, artists, and actors came out before athletes did, with politicians somewhere in between. As other people began to see a broader range of gay characters on television, on the playing field, in parliament, and at family picnics, public stigma began to erode.

In the United States, the campaign to legalize gay marriage came early in what was then called the gay liberation movement, when several same-sex couples appealed to state courts for a right to marry; they were unsuccessful, and a gay Minnesota couple's appeal to the United States Supreme Court was summarily rejected in 1972. Government response reflected a widespread prejudice against gay people. Evan Wolfson, then a law student, wrote a thesis outlining a civil rights case for gay marriage in the early 1980s.[3] Marriage equality became one issue among many for gay activists, whose concerns included police and thuggish violence, discrimination more generally, access to health care – particularly in the AIDS era, and military service. In conjunction with a new wave of lawsuits and appeals for marriage equality, activists staged demonstrations, commemorations, acts of civil disobedience, and artistic efforts. It became a little easier for gay people to claim their identity publicly, and some companies – mostly in competitive technology sectors – began to offer domestic benefits to their employees – a kind of workaround to the unavailability of marriage (Raeburn 2004). Every slight victory, in organizing, in visibility, in policy, and in recognition, made a next step easier to imagine and then to take. At the same time, the early – and modest – successes of the movement spurred a backlash, as conservative activists organized against gay rights. Mobilization on both sides of the issue increased the visibility of the claims, and effectively encouraged people to take sides (Fetner 2008). Conservative activists organized

campaigns for legislation and referenda that generally successfully banned same sex marriage (Soule 2014).

Initial victories on marriage rarely came from majorities.
More frequently, courts or ambitious mayors in states or local-
ities with stronger support for gay rights, found or declared a
right to marriage equality. Relatively quickly, public opinion
changed to support gay unions, moving in the United States
from 35 percent support in 2001 to 61 percent support in
2019.[4] This massive opinion change was the result of many
different, interrelated factors: policy change in some places,
an international movement, and greater visibility of gay and
lesbian people in a variety of different roles in artistic products
like films, music, and television. A broad, diverse, and international social movement was behind all of it. By the time the
United States Supreme Court considered the case of *Obergefell
v. Hodges* in 2015, marriage was available in some states and
many other countries, and far more broadly supported by the
public. The Supreme Court found that denying marriage to
gay couples violated the Constitution. It is clear that it was not
the words in the Constitution that had changed, but the social
and cultural world around them.

Over time, successful movements consolidate the cultural
values they advance. Four years after the Supreme Court
decision, a popular children's television show depicted a
same-sex wedding where the sex of the betrothed was not even
a plot point. The cartoon, *Arthur*, is a gentle depiction of the
children (all animals, including aardvarks, dogs, chimpanzees,
and cats) in a small town, and had been a fixture on public
television for more than 20 years. In an episode titled, "Mr.
Ratburn and the Special Someone," the very strict, demanding,
and caring third grade teacher – a rat, of course – tells the
children that he's getting married.

The appearance of another rat, a bossy female planning the

ceremony and reception, causes the kids to worry that their teacher isn't marrying someone nice. They're particularly concerned that he will take out his frustrations on his students with more onerous homework assignments. Ultimately, they're happy to learn that Mr. Ratburn's partner is someone nice, a male aardvark who makes chocolate. No Supreme Court cases are quoted, and the word "homogamy" doesn't come up. At end, the children are troubled only by how poorly the adults dance (Rao 2019).

The nonchalance about the Ratburn nuptial reflects and promotes changing social attitudes. Earlier episodes of related public television shows weren't shown in some parts of the country. In 2019, however, with a strong majority of Americans in support of same-sex unions, this wasn't a problem. To be sure, some religious conservatives used the show to rail about both deteriorating social norms and funding public television, but the criticisms were not echoed in more mainstream outlets, and there's no report that PBS refused to air the show anywhere. Culture and policy changes support each other.

Movements Change the People Who Make Them

Experience in a social movement, particularly if it's intense and extended, can mark a large turn in the trajectory of a life. The experience can make someone cynical about government or political opponents, hopeful and committed about allies, and competent in developing new skills for participating in social life. They learn about politics and public policy, make friends (and cultivate opponents), and take risks. Activists who've stayed up late talking politics and planning events, testified before a local zoning board, crowded in the streets with strangers in uncomfortable weather, sang folk songs in an affinity group while awaiting arrest, joked about slogans while painting signs, suffered ridicule and taunting from political opponents, or scattered to avoid tear gas, learned something about the world, their allies, and themselves. That knowledge can inform everything that follows.

We can't understand how movement participation affects participants until we recognize who is likely to participate in social movements in the first place. Generally, people who are willing to engage in social movements aren't exactly like those who don't, but they are not entirely different either. Participation, particularly over an extended period of time, accentuates the differences between activists and less engaged citizens (Corrigall-Brown 2011; Whalen and Flacks 1989). But movements differ in their concerns, their tactics, and the constituencies they're likely to reach.

We hear different stories about who participates in social movements. The cautionary tales told about the men who joined ultranationalist movements like the Nazis in the twentieth century emphasized disaffected individuals and alienation. Less educated, less engaged, these people sought social connection and direction. That premise animated criticisms of the activists of the 1960s, whose activism was likened to acting out. But empirical research found that the later activists were not only better educated than others in their generation, but also better psychologically adjusted, more deeply connected socially, and enjoyed better relationships with their parents (Keniston 1968).

People who are more likely to engage once in social movement participation are, of course, more likely to engage again. The initial participation reflects a disposition to engagement that is likely to persist. But movement participation itself has an impact. We know that people who have a stronger sense of self-efficacy, that is, a sense that they might make a difference, are more likely to participate in politics generally. Most often, such a sense of self comes with relative educational and economic advantage. For the most part, the people who engage in protest politics also engage in whatever conventional politics a democracy allows. It's not as if someone protests instead of say, voting; rather, people protest in addition to voting, calling legislators, and talking to friends about politics.

Being a part of a movement intensifies that sense of self, and it does more than that. Movement participation also educates those who engage on both public policies under contest and on the tactics of political engagement. It builds solidarity, that is, a sense of connection with others in a movement, both in the local groups that sponsor activity at the grassroots, and a sense of affiliation with more distant allies marching for the same cause (Fireman and Gamson 1979). Someone who begins to engage in a social movement goes to planning meetings, as well as demonstrations or events, cultivating membership in a larger community (Lichterman 1996; Munson 2009). She joins online groups and lists that provide information about issues and events. She attends potluck dinner parties and has side conversations with other activists about kids or movies or sports, as well as current events. The civic engagement of going to events means that the participant is more likely to be asked to join another cause later on (Rosenstone and Hansen 1993).

But the impact of a social movement on an individual depends upon what that movement wants and what it does. It's not a surprise that movements that demand more commitment are more likely to attract participants willing to make a large commitment. The signal study on long-term effects of social movements on participants is Doug McAdam's (1988) critical examination of the people who participated in

Freedom Summer, the 1964 civil rights education and voter registration project. The idea of the project was to engage relatively advantaged young people, primarily white students from elite universities in the North, in the civil rights struggle in Mississippi, the most contested area in the country. The theory underneath that strategy was that national attention would follow the young stars and force media and political responses. The theory worked, basically, but the young people's participation came with high risk. Shortly after arriving in Mississippi, three young activists, Mickey Schwerner, James Chaney, and Andrew Goodman, disappeared along with the car they were driving. The car turned up days later, with their beaten bodies in it.

The murder emphasized that this political campaign was, as McAdam put it, "high risk activism." Freedom Summer was clearly a campaign that demanded a lot from participants: the willingness to move to an unfamiliar site, to live away from old friends and family, and to risk their comfort and well-being, and even, as it turned out, their lives. McAdam tracked down a sample of people who had been accepted to participate in the volunteer project doing dangerous volunteer work in Mississippi during the height of the civil rights movement. Working through SNCC, volunteers ran Freedom schools and registered voters. They lived with those they organized with, and developed strong friendships and relationships based on engagement. Many years later, both the volunteers and the "no-shows," that is, those who were accepted but ended up not going to Mississippi, shared liberal views on matters of policy. But the volunteers were more likely to have engaged in subsequent political activism in a range of social movements on the left of the political spectrum. They were also more likely to have had peripatetic careers, slanted to teaching and other kinds of service, to earn less money than their cohort counterparts, and to have been divorced. Those who were most engaged were also most likely to maintain contact with their allies in the Mississippi project.

Most of this isn't so surprising: those who were willing to take great risks when young displayed a greater commitment when they were older. This commitment and attentiveness to the political movements of the time produced career interruptions, which created both professional and personal strains. Every choice to engage made the next engagement more likely. It's certainly possible that there were some important differences in character, background, or support not captured in surveys that led to the initial decision to participate, but it's also quite likely that the experience itself supported sustained social and political engagement. The volunteers saw that they could matter, and learned to take some satisfaction in helping to bend the arc of the moral universe. They also saw that they could stand up for what they believed in. It's not odd that these are all powerful lessons.

But all movements aren't the same. Moving from Boston or Berkeley to Biloxi to live for months is just fundamentally more intense than carrying a candle or placard at a march for a couple of hours on a summer day, or showing up at an organizational meeting or public hearing on a few odd evenings. Catherine Corrigall-Brown strategically sampled four different social movement organizations to discover how people were changed by their participation. Inductively, she lays out four possibilities: (a) an individual once recruited will stay recruited, engaged in the cause for the long haul; (b) an activist engaged will stay engaged, but not necessarily in the same group or for the same cause; (c) an individual can cycle in and out of political engagement; or (d) a one-time activist can decide to turn his attention elsewhere.

Corrigall-Brown conducted intensive interviews with people

who had participated in the United Farmworkers, a community group organized on zoning issues, a Catholic Workers house, and Concerned Women for America, a socially conservative group. These groups varied in their actions, their ideology, and the depth of their community. The neighborhood group met occasionally and focused on a limited set of local issues, while the Catholic Workers shared a home and meals as well as a cause in an effort to live the Gospel through pursuing social justice. It's not so surprising that the people who were engaged in groups that demanded more of them were more likely to be extensively engaged over time. Partly, this is a function of the initial commitment: people who are willing to move in with their movement allies have already demonstrated a greater commitment than someone who decides to show up at a meeting, but it's also a function of what happens within a group, and how the rest of the world deals with them.

What about hate groups and those Nazis mentioned earlier? Although there is far more research on more mainstream social movement groups, like those described above, a few scholars have gone into white nationalist groups to see the development of members' beliefs and identities (e.g., Blee 2002; Simi and Futtrell 2010; Simi et al. 2017). It's not as if activists develop their beliefs and then seek out the group that best represents them. Rather, initial recruitment can be based on a general frustration or a light social contact. Over time, however, the hate movement develops in those who join an integrated world and corresponding world view that is apart from mainstream culture and politics, with safe spaces for congregating, distinct and largely isolated sources of information, and preferred styles of gender roles, styles of dress, and reinforcing movement. Recruits become increasingly distanced from the political mainstream, and often face great difficulties in leaving the movement: their entire social world is nested within it, and they may be marked not only by stigmatized beliefs, but also physical signs, like tattoos, that make mainstream acceptance difficult.

The development of a total world view and an integrated community with distinct styles of conduct, preferred music, fashion, and sources of information, is not limited to groups we might find deplorable. Taylor and Whittier (1992) found that lesbian feminists developed distinct styles of dress and common musical tastes, solidifying a collective identity that extended well beyond the peak mobilization of the movement, carrying those styles and values into mainstream culture (Whittier 1995). Nepstad (2004) studied a group of radical Catholic peace and justice activists, and found that the development of a shared subculture and support network allowed individuals to stay engaged in social justice work, offering both material support (cooking, child care) as well as moral and ideological support. The structure developed in community allowed people to change their lives and keep them changed.

Let's sort out some of the factors that explain sustained commitment, and see why social movements can engender it. Movement participation is partly a function of belief. Movement activists who spend more time with their colleagues and engage on a range of issues are far more likely to develop an integrated and coherent sense of the issues. Really, many activists haven't even made up their mind on issues when they first turn out at an event. In studying anti-abortion activists, Ziad Munson found that participation in protest, including the meetings and trainings leading up to a protest, develop and deepen activists' commitment to both the issue and to their colleagues. They talk about the issues they care about, and deepen a common understanding, and even a vocabulary for action.

Commitment to issues comes along with a commitment

82

to others who share those beliefs. At some basic level, there is an element of time on task; that is, the amount of social connection, conversation, and concern that develops in concert with others. Groups that live together, share meals, child care, and social life require greater commitment, and then nurture that commitment. The social connections that activists make to others also afford them ongoing connections to other activists who will help recruit them to other efforts in the future. Those connections – social, intellectual, and emotional – build and solidify an identity as an activist, one who can come back out when needed or opportunity arises.

Understandably, although some individuals specialize in one set of issues, more commonly an activist identity affords the space to move across issues when opportunities or threats arise. It's not hard to understand how someone who protested against going to war on Iraq in 2003 would then protest against austerity policies in 2010, and then on behalf of immigrant rights in 2014. Although the issues change, the foundational identity underneath them would not. Someone who sees himself or herself as a purposeful and potentially influential actor is going to respond to the issue that they feel is most pressing or promising at the moment. Although some people pick an issue and stick with it throughout periods of intense and much less intense public attention, many others show an element of strategy or opportunism.

But the starting point is a sense of personal and political efficacy that comes from political engagement of any kind. Someone who takes on protest feels like she is entering into history, trying to bend the world to her moral sensibility. Such a take is ambitious, of course, but once taken, it's easier to imagine doing the same thing again. Protest can be socially and psychologically empowering. Franklin McCain, one of the four students at North Carolina Agricultural and Technical

College who started a sit-in campaign at a lunch counter in Greensboro, recalled years later, "Fifteen seconds after I sat on that stool, I had the most wonderful feeling. I had a feeling of liberation, restored manhood; I had a natural high. And I truly felt almost invincible" (quoted in Sitkoff 1981: 81). McCain remained engaged in the movement, and continued to serve on community boards throughout his life; he made his living as a research chemist. His three colleagues, Joseph McNeil, Jibreel Khazan (formerly Ezell Blair, Jr.), and David Richmond, also tried to work for social justice for the rest of their lives.[5] McNeil, a career Air Force officer who retired as a Major General, said that participating in the sit-in gave him a sense not only of power, but also responsibility, reporting more than 50 years later, "I walked away with an attitude that if our country is screwed up, don't give up. Unscrew it, but don't give up. Which, in retrospect, is pretty good for a bunch of teenagers."[6]

Activists can describe this as empowerment, while social psychologists may use the term, "self-efficacy," but the story is the same regardless. People who engage the world and try to make it better are likely to change themselves more profoundly. Their efforts, and the models they leave for others, make a difference over the very long haul. And culture and politics are never really all that separate. Social movements also change the people who participate in them, educating as well as mobilizing activists. They promote ongoing awareness and action that extends beyond the boundaries of one movement or campaign. Those who turn out at antiwar demonstrations today have often cut their activist teeth mobilizing against globalization, on behalf of labor, for animal rights or against welfare reform. By politicizing communities, connecting people, and promoting personal loyalties, social movements build the infrastructure not only of subsequent movements, but of a democratic civil society more generally.

It's important to report on the past in ways that recognize the role of activists, and the long process of promoting social change.

CHAPTER **6**

Claiming Credit

"Don't ever underestimate the power of pissed off teenagers," David Hogg wrote, after the Attorney General of New York State announced that she was filing a civil suit seeking the dissolution of the National Rifle Association (Gstalter 2020). Incorporated in New York, the NRA was subject to the state's regulation, and AG Leticia James charged that the organization and its top leadership failed to follow the law and had put the vast resources of the organization to corrupt purposes.[1] Hogg was one of the survivors of a high school shooting in Florida who then organized a campaign to promote gun safety regulations. The organization he cofounded, March for Our Lives, had filed a complaint with the New York Attorney General.

More than the formal complaint, however, March for Our Lives, by organizing protests, school walk-outs, lobbying campaigns, a national demonstration, and a voter registration campaign, had drawn additional attention to the problems associated with very easy access to firearms in America. The organization was hardly alone: March for Our Lives joined a network of other gun safety groups, and promoted policies that many others had already supported (Laschever and Meyer 2020). The organization had nothing to do with the governance and financing decisions of the NRA, nor with the state laws governing charitable organizations. AG James, newly elected to her position, had campaigned on the promise to be a more activist Attorney General, and was directly responsible for the decision to investigate the NRA, and then to initiate litigation. The "pissed off teens" Hogg lionized could be part of the story, by drawing attention to the problem, targeting the organization, and offering evidence of political benefits`for politicians acting just like Leticia James. But it's clearly a longer, more complicated story. Nonetheless, David Hogg was adamant about making sure that the teens he helped organize got some recognition. He claimed credit.[2]

The process of political change is so long and complicated, involving so many diverse actors, that the work of any one individual, group, or event can matter, but rarely by itself. There's a lot of editing involved in any story of significant social change, and David Hogg and March for Our Lives were wise in making sure it would be harder to edit them out. In this chapter, we're going to consider how our understanding of previous incidents of social protest and social change affect what we think is possible now. We're going to see that it's critical for activists to claim credit for their achievements, identifying the missing factors in simpler stories of social change.

Let's think, for example, about the story of America's Voting Rights Act.[3] Lyndon Johnson is the star of one compelling story about its passage in 1965. Politically skilled, LBJ gave a passionate speech to a full Congress, connecting civil rights and civil liberties domestically to a global crusade for democracy that included the war in Vietnam. "[I]t is all of us who must overcome the crippling legacy of bigotry and injustice. And we shall overcome." Johnson used all the tools of the presidency, including public rhetoric and private negotiations. By the end of the summer, he would sign the bill into law. All of this is true.

But there are other stories that are at least as true: Johnson's historic speech followed a series of dramatic marches led by civil rights activists in Selma, Alabama.[4] Courageous nonviolent crusaders, including future Congressman John Lewis, marched into brutal police beatings, drawing national attention, demonstrating their commitment and illustrating their cause. They set the political agenda for Johnson. This voting rights story centers around activist strategy, organization, and dedication. A slightly broader view recognizes that the Selma to Montgomery march built on more than a decade of similarly dramatic action that included sit-ins, marches, demonstrations, and organizing within the Democratic Party.

The fuller story is long and complicated, one in which social movement activists respond to and challenge political leaders, who are rarely the heroes in their stories. They promote changes in policy, politics, and rhetoric that, after years of hard work, sometimes seem to appear suddenly. The dynamics of change are complicated everywhere, but in America, where institutional obstacles are built into Constitutional design, virtually any reform requires extraordinary and persistent pressure. At least sometimes, that's a social movement specialty.

The stories of the ongoing campaigns about guns and about civil rights illustrate a range of political dynamics that reflect both essential elements of American politics, and the historical development of both American political institutions and the social movements that challenge them. In general, politicians disappoint the social movements that support them. Managing diverse political coalitions and an inventory of social problems, they are understandably reluctant to commit passionately to the issues that movements press, and often unable to deliver what activists want anyway. They must be forced, by political pressure and exigent circumstances, to take action even on issues they care deeply about.

Lyndon Johnson invested heavily in the Voting Rights

Act, after he had disappointed the civil rights movement by marginalizing the Mississippi Freedom Democratic Party at the 1964 Democratic convention. With his support for voting rights, Johnson promoted the transformation of what was once the solid Democratic South to the most reliable source of Republican voters in America. Despite Johnson's effective and politically costly commitment to civil rights, prominent activists, especially Martin Luther King, Jr., were unwilling to support his war in Vietnam in exchange. Although it's easy to see the moral logic of supporting both peace *and* justice, it's equally easy to see why Johnson saw ingratitude and betrayal.

Causality is always complicated, but politics is all about taking credit for achieving some desirable outcome; the stakes of doing so are particularly high for social protest movements. Popular narratives of social change assign some movements a critical role for promoting change, but ignore the influence of others. Gaining acceptance of a preferred narrative of influence is a neglected, but important, social movement achievement. Some movements and some activists are able to get at least a portion of the credit for promoting social change, while others are often ignored or even disparaged. It's worthwhile to figure out why. Movement activists and their competitors offer narratives of past influence to serve current political goals. In this way, the process of claiming credit is analogous to that of cultivating a reputation. In tightly controlled polities, both mythic and real, political authorities control mass media and the official historical record to present coherent, consistent, and self- and state-serving narratives that ascribe responsibility and blame; such narratives might be revised frequently during leadership shifts (think about the Ministry of Truth in George Orwell's *1984*). In actual democracies the process is more complicated; all versions of causality and responsibility can be contested. Politicians try to take credit for whatever popular outcomes they can, knowing that critics, journalists, and their opponents might take them to task for straining credulity. The stakes are high, however, and the relative openness of debate generally rewards the bold.

The stakes for successfully claiming credit are similarly high for social protest movements. The civil rights movement of the 1950s and 1960s, for example, plays a central role in virtually all narratives of race in contemporary politics, and is portrayed as a successful and heroic struggle for equality for African Americans, in consonance with values expressed by the Declaration of Independence. The establishment of a national day commemorating Martin Luther King, Jr., enacted under a Republican administration in the 1980s, marks the consolidation of the narrative's success. Of course, this isn't all. Virtually all of the Southern states in the United States now organize and promote "civil rights tourism," as does the National Park Service. The civil rights struggles of the 1950s and 1960s have become every bit as accepted a part of the heroic American story as the American Revolution, even promoted, and distorted by those who opposed the movement during its heyday. Even so, Martin Luther King, Jr. and Christian non-violence is given a primacy in the historical account that may marginalize the importance of other not quite allied racial justice activists who executed other strategies for promoting social change at the same time.

If the civil rights movement represents one end of the continuum of credit-claiming success, many other movements cluster at the opposite pole. Stories that protest is ineffective or counterproductive are common in public discourse. Curiously, often the people who lead and animate those movements of our time downplay the impact of their efforts. Christian Smith (1996) asked key activists involved in the 1980s movement against US intervention in Central America to evaluate their influence. Mostly, they were mercilessly self-critical, announcing that they fell well short of the goals they pursued, and were ready to blame the media, conservative political culture and/or political apathy, and themselves. After all, they worked so hard and wanted so much more. And this is a common story.

To take a more recent case, opponents of an American-led war against Iraq mobilized an unprecedented global campaign against military intervention, engaging millions of people in the full range of movement activities, from writing letters and emails to staging large demonstrations and civil disobedience actions (Walgrave and Rucht 2010). This movement changed the rhetoric and military strategy of the US, delayed the start of war, and engaged the United Nations (Arkin 2003), but these achievements seemed pale as tanks rolled across the desert. Still, a story that emphasizes only the defeats is not only partial, but also politically counterproductive. It provides no foundation for subsequent mobilization and reinforces a sense of futility among those who participated in the past as well as those who might march in the future.

Regardless of how dispassionate and well-informed scholars may assess the causes of movement influence, the popular story line about a movement's impact often does not line up with the scholarly consensus. The popular story line, however, is far more likely to affect what happens next; the stories people hear about the past influence how they view future possibilities and, most significantly, their prospective role in making it possible. Activists need to be concerned not only with changing the world, but with claiming credit for making a little progress in doing so. It's an uphill struggle, for a number of reasons that we'll discuss.

Social Movement Outcomes: You Can't Ever Get All You Want

The most obvious explanation for differing attributions of success is simple: some movements win more extensive responses more quickly than others; the actual accomplishments are at least partly relevant to the reputations that follow. But this is only part of the story. The civil rights movement changed the face of America, and the nature of racial politics to date. At the same time, so much of what activists demanded remains elusive, underscored far too dramatically by the campaigns against racialized police violence more than 50 years later. Widely articulated goals of equality and opportunity are belied by ongoing inequalities in education, employment, and elsewhere in American life. There is much the movement didn't win; but opponents, bystanders, and participants all recognize some accomplishments, even if viewing work to be done very differently.[5]

On the other hand, there are real accomplishments veterans of the Central America Solidarity movement could claim. Although the Sandinista government fell in Nicaragua, it did so from an election, not foreign military invasion that seemed possible in the early 1980s. Smith (1996) makes a compelling case that multinational peace politics, particularly efforts by the US government, were substantially influenced by the citizen movements of the 1980s. Although the outcomes were different from those activists sought, promoting procedural democracy and peace is hardly trivial. The absence of a movement narrative for what happened in Central America, however, left the Reagan administration uncontested in telling a story in which it ousted the Sandinistas – over the objections of a misguided and diffuse American left. In a story of movement containment of American military and foreign policy, incremental achievements could be seen as a foundation for subsequent efforts; in the story of Reagan triumphalism, such incremental achievements appear, at best, as pale consolation.

For virtually any social movement, there is an ample supply of actual events and conjecture available as raw material to allow partisans to brag about victories and mourn defeats. Challengers, opponents, and authorities construct competing stories in a contest of narrative, meaning, and politics. What's more, because social movements always struggle in at least somewhat adverse circumstances, representing minority viewpoints or constituencies, or majorities that are structurally disadvantaged in conventional politics, they are set up to lose more often than to win. This is the case for all sorts of movements, and the critical questions are where to set the bar for success, and how to determine who was influential in achieving what.

Beyond the difficulty of sorting out the influence of a large and diverse movement, assessing which movement elements or strategies were responsible for what outcomes is also an analytical and political challenge. To examine social movement influence, scholars have generally set the bar for success rather low, following William Gamson's (1990 [1975]) landmark study of challenging groups in the United States prior to World War II. Gamson assessed two distinct outcomes in regard to the state: a group can gain recognition as an actor; and/or a group can get some of its policy demands met. If the challenging group saw progress on any portion of any of its aims, the group was successful, even if it was not the only challenger advocating this reform; additionally, the time horizon for success ranged up to 15 years, even if the group had since disappeared, implicitly assuming that authorities might be responding to recently departed movements.

Activists, of course, who necessarily live in the politics of the moment, are unlikely to set the bar so low. Organizers recruit and mobilize by dramatically inflating their goals, urgency, and the prospects for success in the shorter term (Benford and Snow 2000; Gamson and Meyer 1996), and emphasize the potential influence of each new recruit's efforts (Benford 1993b). Meaningful change is always harder and takes longer than most people imagine when they first start pushing for it.

Subsequent attempts to assess the impact of social movements on public policy have generally offered less explicit comparison but provided more detail on particular policy issues, and offered different theories of how movements might exercise influence. Piven and Cloward (1977), for example, emphasized threat and disruption, arguing that authorities sometimes provide poor people easier access to social welfare benefits in order to quell disruptive protest. In contrast, writing on New Deal era pension and social welfare policies, Amenta (1998) argues that political movements gave institutional reformers cover and incentive to pursue the spending policies they already wanted, identifying mediation as the primary mechanism of influence. Looking at the protests against the war in Vietnam, scholars have argued that protests kept the issue of the war on the political agenda, constantly forcing elected officials to address the issue – but not mandating a particular policy choice; in this view, movements work primarily by agenda-setting (McAdam and Su 2002; Small 1988). Of course, these mechanisms can all be operating at once, and they vary across movements and over time. Nonetheless, how a movement exercises influence is likely to affect the ease with which authorities grant it credit. It seems far more likely for authorities to recognize the influence of moral suasion, new arguments, or evidence, on policy, than say, disruptive threat.

Claiming Influence in Politics and Culture

Even when movements get credit for enactment of a new policy that addresses their concerns, legislative and administrative processes guarantees compromises in execution – if not in goals. The nature of the legislative process in the United States essentially mandates both polemics outside government and compromise within institutions, such that most people involved are getting somewhat less than what they would want. At the same time, political pressures lead authorities to oversell any of the programs they propose, and any bits of legislation they had a hand in enacting (Edelman 1988). This means that even large and comprehensive reforms will offer less than at least some activists demanded and less than politicians promised. Disappointment is built into the process.

The political rhetoric of protest mobilization emphasizes urgency and moral certainty, focused on absolutes. It's a poor match for a political process that prizes compromise and produces incremental reforms. It's no surprise that most people engaged in the process are disappointed most of the time, and ambitious reformers are going to be quicker to see defeats than victories.

Although social movements make claims on matters of policy and advance reforms, movement influence can extend well beyond those changes in policy; there are often unclaimed, "spillover effects" (Meyer and Whittier 1994). The failure of the Equal Rights Amendment (ERA), which consumed a great deal of feminist effort during the 1970s, is a useful case in point. Despite the policy defeat, widespread cultural values and attitudes about women in politics and in the workforce changed dramatically (Mansbridge 1986). Oddly, then, we can imagine tales in which the movement failed to win ERA, and social and cultural changes resulted from other, undefined, factors. In short, it's easy to edit the movement out. When a movement extends its vision of an issue to a broader audience, its influence, and especially its capacity to claim influence, falters. Indeed, the more successful a movement is in promoting new norms and values, the more those values appear commonsensical and obvious. As a result, the paradox is that those activists find an even more difficult time in claiming credit for their influence, to no small degree because persons with no movement connections can claim ownership of movement values. People with no previous connection to the women's movement, for example, can claim to be feminists – or environmentalists or animal rights supporters or peace activists. In doing so, not only do they make explicit claims about their own identity, but also about the politics and identity of the larger movements.

As any movement is the product of a range of groups that cooperate, to varying degrees, for political gains, yet still differ among themselves (Meyer and Corrigall-Brown 2005; Rochon and Meyer 1997), the problem of identity and politics is particularly acute. In liberal democracies, the lines separating activists within a movement from other sympathizers are difficult to draw, and movements only weakly police their own boundaries (Benford 1993a). The label, "environmentalist," for example, defines few strict boundaries. One self-declared environmentalist may protest the production of carbon, calling for strict regulation, while another self-defined environmentalist can advocate building new roads to allow campers and hunters easier access to the wild.

As political and cultural circumstances change, individuals can focus on different beliefs, relationships, or characteristics to make claims on the basis of a different identity (see Mische 2003). A more congenial environment for women's rights, for example, might make it safer for some women to make claims on a gendered identity; it could also make the identity less problematic or salient for others. To summarize, the scholarly literature on the impact of social movements has identified numerous problems in assessing influence, including: (a) the diversity of efforts within and around a movement pressing for change; (b) numerous possible outcomes of mobilization, some of which are unlikely to be explicitly targeted by activists themselves; and (c) disputes about the mechanisms by which influence is effected. We need to add the story of movement influence. Most movements leave a trail of actions and statements that can provide the raw materials of a claim for credit, but the translation of such raw materials into a compelling and broadly resonant claim only sometimes takes place. For help in figuring out why, we can consider the research on reputation, social construction, and narratives.

Social Movements Cultivate a Reputation for Influence

Movements, organizations, and activists can work to develop a reputation for effectiveness, largely by making a compelling case for influence in making change. Here, we can take lessons from social science investigations of reputation in other areas, including the arts and mainstream politics. Lang and Lang (1988) show that an artist's posthumous reputation is only partly explained by the volume and quality of the artistic work. The artist's personal and professional networks, the quality of records left behind, and the persistence of posthumous promoters, who often operate with their own financial interest in mind, all influence reputation.

Employing a similar approach, Gary Alan Fine has examined the construction of the reputations of a range of political and cultural figures. In looking at Warren Harding's reputation, for example, Fine (1996) argues that the record was sufficiently extensive and complex to provide support for a story of great accomplishment – as well as the story of incompetence and corruption that came to dominate. Political entrepreneurs selected details of the record to construct a tale of Harding's failure in order to legitimate and promote their own agendas. The reputation they built lasted far longer than the agendas it was initially constructed to support.

Similarly, Fine (1999) contends that radical abolitionists tied their cause to John Brown's dramatic and violent crusade against slavery, constructing a martyr by editing and repackaging Brown's life and actions in ways that would resonate with broader cultural values. Vehemently opposed to the nonviolent approaches to social change offered by other abolitionists, Brown valorized action, staging dramatic raids in which he executed slave owners while trying to free enslaved people, most memorably leading a band of fewer than two dozen men in an attack on an armory in Harper's Ferry in West Virginia at the end of 1859. No enslaved people were freed, and the few armed abolitionists who survived, including Brown himself, were quickly tried and executed. One obvious take is that Brown and his men were unrealistic, underprepared and resourced, and clearly unsuccessful. On the other hand, the raid again underscored the instability of slavery as an institution to both supporters and opponents, and helped to stoke the conflict that erupted in Civil War in 1861.

Note that successfully building and maintaining a reputation may entail editing out a substantial portion of a figure's career and concerns. Bromberg and Fine (2002) examine singer Pete Seeger's development into an icon of American folk music over time, noting that Seeger's long membership in the Communist Party could easily have disqualified him from honors such as designation as a "living legend" by the Library of Congress and a lifetime achievement award from the Kennedy Center. These awards, however, along with a Grammy and the Harvard Arts Medal, came rather late in Seeger's career, decades after being blacklisted for Communist and antiwar activities. Outliving both enemies and his most controversial politics, however, Seeger saw a popular reputation built around political commitments to less problematic causes, particularly environmental issues, as he championed the construction of the Clearwater, a sloop that sailed the Hudson River in an effort to raise awareness about pollution.[6] It was one among many causes for the singer, but it gave reputation builders an easier way to find support. At the same time, his acceptance as a kind of icon reflects a kind of political cleansing that diluted the power of a rebellious image. Bromberg and Fine (2002: 1147) contend, "He is not dangerous, because he is not taken seriously. He is not fully heard, free to sing whatever he likes because this saintly old man can hardly be 'seriously' proposing rebellion. His reputation traps him." I'm not sure this is exactly right. Seeger was nearly 90 when he sang and played the banjo on the Washington mall at Barack Obama's inaugural festivities. He sang "This Land is Your Land," including the often excised verses that highlight economic privation and inequality, demanding political change. Even if one available picture of Seeger was, as Bromberg and Fine (2002) describe, as an affable grandfather, there was also space for offering radical – if not explicitly Communist – ideas.

But Bromberg and Fine (2002) are clearly onto something when they show that a similar process of cultivating acceptance for political heroes, including Abraham Lincoln and Martin Luther King, often means ignoring the more difficult and more radical politics those figures embraced (see also Schwartz 1996). Any figure who becomes a "consensus hero" comes to be of limited use to any cause. These studies of individual reputations can help us by identifying several important points for understanding the development of popular understandings about social movements and political influence. First, tales of influence, like reputations, are constructed from the raw material of events and actors. Second, the activists, historians, and politicians who try to promote their preferred under-standings of the past do so to support their current agendas. Third, the constructed reputations can be remarkably resilient and long-lived (see Schuman and Scott 1989), and can constrain as well as enable collective action. In organizing for the future, activists must make sense of the events of the past, explaining previous triumphs and defeats by constructing narratives that resonate with popular beliefs and shared values even as they challenge them.

Social Change Happens Slowly, Then Suddenly[7]

Political change often seems to come suddenly, after years of efforts that seemed like they failed. But when social movements matter, they do so in ways that are more complicated and time-consuming than a simple narrative can convey. Let's look at two cases of states in the American South deciding to alter the way they displayed the battle flag of the Confederacy – more than 150 years after the Confederacy was defeated.

The Confederate states fought under several flags, including the familiar "Stars and Bars" from 1861 to 1865, when their army surrendered to the Union forces at Appomattox, Virginia. After the period of Reconstruction ended, some Southern whites promoted a narrative of the Lost Cause, which found a nobility in their fight to preserve slavery. Toward the end of the nineteenth century, as the Ku Klux Klan was revived, Southern states began to display the Confederate flag, sometimes alongside the state flag, sometimes by itself.

The flag became more popular in the 1950s and 1960s, offered as a response to the civil rights movement. In South Carolina, for example, state legislators voted to display the Confederate flag over the state capitol in 1962, as the movement to end racial segregation was spreading across the South.

It's hardly surprising that the flag was a provocation to South Carolinians not enamored with the Confederacy, and from the mid-1990s onward, it was the subject of controversy, as reformers inside and outside government offered a range of responses ranging from striking the flag to adding a variety of displays that would contextualize it. Electoral politics in the state, however, made maintaining the status quo the easiest solution. In 2000, the National Collegiate Athletic Association (NCAA) announced that it would refuse to run championship competitions in the state as long as it displayed the flag.[8] The flag remained, a provocation and a problem, while the state suffered some financial and social losses.

In June of 2015, Bree Newsome, a Black woman, donned rock-climbing gear and scaled the 30-foot flagpole which displayed the Confederate flag outside the state capitol, spotted by a white ally, James Ian Tyson. Climbing, Newsome appeared more like the filmmaker and activist she was than a mountaineer, and she looked like she was battling her own fears as she grabbed the flag and brought it to the ground. She and Tyson were immediately arrested, and the flag was redisplayed within minutes. Newsome issued a statement outlining her goals, "We removed the flag today because we can't wait any longer. It's time for a new chapter where we are sincere about dismantling white supremacy and building toward true racial justice and equality" (Edwards 2015). It's worth noting that less than two weeks earlier, a young white supremacist had attended a Bible study session at a largely Black church in Charleston, the state capital, where he shot and killed nine parishioners. The killer's social media posts prominently displayed symbols of white supremacy, including the Confederate flag (Robles 2015).

Broad national discussion followed Newsome's climb. The Ku Klux Klan weighed in to support the restoration of the flag, holding a demonstration at the capitol, while business interests in South Carolina and around the country announced that the flag needed to be taken down.[9] Governor Nikki Haley, a conservative Republican who had earlier supported the flag's display as a symbol of Southern heritage, negotiated with state legislators to move the flag from display at the capitol to a museum.

It's too easy to make the mistake of attributing the flag's removal to the things that happened immediately before, giving too much credit to the Chamber of Commerce or to Governor Haley's ambitions and political skills; clearly, they were responding to the publicity and pressure that Bree Newsome's climb released. And it's not clear that Newsome would have made the climb – or gotten so much attention – had it not been for the egregious mass shooting that came before. We also need to remember that the debate about the flag had erupted periodically for the previous 20 years, with national organizations and businesses weighing in.

We can imagine many stories describing the decision to relocate the flag, emphasizing civil disobedience or business pressure or political ambitions. In real life, all of these factors mattered, over time. One could write a much longer summary of the issues and events that contributed to a relatively modest change in policy, but in the political debate, shorter stories will prevail, and they will matter. A story that centers Governor Haley's political acumen would edit out the importance of social and economic pressure that had built – and Bree Newsome's boldness and bravery. To be sure, Haley was adept at telling a new story about her own political shift, offering a newly public memory of growing up and experiencing feelings of discrimination as the daughter of Indian immigrants in explaining her change of mind. She earned national attention and accolades for her stance, and she certainly had no interest in talking about Bree Newsome's climb. Activists need to claim the space to tell their own stories, because it's much easier for politicians to ignore them after the fact.

After South Carolina's Confederate flag came down, the only one that remained in state display was in Mississippi's state flag,[10] which included the Stars and Bars, and dated from 1894, established roughly three decades after the Confederacy's defeat. As in South Carolina, Mississippi's flag had been the subject of increasing controversy during the first years of the twenty-first century. In 2020, when a wave of national demonstrations against racialized police violence swept the United States, racial justice activists in the state targeted the flag as well as other policies that would prove more complicated and difficult to change. Governor Tate Reeves, who had spent his political career dodging the issue of the flag, announced that he would be willing to sign a bill replacing the flag. Previously, he'd said the flag should only be changed through a state-wide referendum, on which he refused to take a position (Harrison 2020).

At the end of June 2020, each house of the state legislature passed a bill to strike the Confederate-inflected flag by establishing a special commission to consider new designs. Due to the timing of the legislative session, in order to pass the bill each house had to suspend its rules, requiring a two-thirds majority, and the margins for victory were tight. A small faction of senators agreed to support changing the flag if the state made a commitment to add the words, "In God We Trust," to the new design.

If we start the story in the summer of 2020, we can see that the demonstrations had a visible effect on agenda-setting, encouraging politicians to address an issue most had previously tried to ignore – although there was a faction of legislators who had already committed to changing the flag. Among the organizations that promoted replacing the flag were the Southeastern Conference, which governed top-level college sports; the NCAA, which threatened to ban championship competitions from the state if it did not change the flag; the leaders of the largest state universities and more than a dozen community colleges; the Mississippi Baptist Convention; and the massive retailer, Walmart, which announced that regardless of what the state government did, it would no longer display the existing flag. Putting the spotlight again on the flag issue, the university leaders, sports commissions, religious and commercial groups, all provided both support and incentives for legislators to take action. The demonstrations surely mattered, but not by themselves. Further, without legislative wrangling, leadership, and compromise, the bill would not have been passed and signed.

Even recognizing the complexities of the last few weeks of Mississippi's flag debate ignores far too much important work by activists and others. A fuller story might start with federal law enforcement officials protecting James Meredith, supported by the NAACP's legal defense fund, when he became the first Black student to register at the University of Mississippi in 1962 – over the opposition of the Governor. It would properly include the civil rights struggles in Mississippi that included SNCC's 1964 summer project, which established longstanding organizations that would continue to fight for local justice (Andrews 2004). It could also properly consider another controversy over the flag's display, when John Hawkins, president of the Black Student Union and the first Black cheerleader at the state's flagship university, refused to touch the state flag that the cheerleaders routinely waved. Hawkins had agreed to try out to be a cheerleader only because an activist student, Clara Bibbs, needed a partner in order to try out for the squad herself.

A fuller account would recognize more than a decade of bills proposed to replace the flag that failed in the state legislature, as well as the efforts of Governor Ronnie Musgrove, who appointed a special commission to design an alternative flag. Musgrove organized a state-wide referendum in which the commission's new design was pitted against the Confederate-inflected flag. By an overwhelming margin, Mississippi voters decided to keep the old flag.

A comprehensive story would also include the efforts of Laurin Stennis, granddaughter of the staunchly segregationist senator, John Stennis, working to atone for her ancestors by designing and promoting another new flag in 2014. The younger Stennis consulted with professional vexillologists, people who design flags, putting together a design that evoked Mississippi's pre-Confederate flag, a more attractive alternative than Musgrove's commission came up with. Stennis paid to manufacture her "Hospitality Flag," and gave it to a flag store to sell without taking any of the proceeds. She successfully pushed for her flag to provide a background for a vanity license plate, raising money for the state's civil rights museum.

And a full accounting of the process would certainly include Bree Newsome's climb in South Carolina in 2015, leaving Mississippi alone in still flying the Stars and Bars, and more visible and vulnerable as a result.

Again, the demonstrations for racial justice in Mississippi mattered, but they could only achieve the flag change because of all the work, seemingly not nearly as successful, other activists had done in pointing out the offense of the Confederate symbol, in promoting alternatives, and in building networks of activists and politicians. Even then, a changed flag is a slight response to the demands of those demonstrators, who were asking for wholesale changes in both policing and in a host of other policies on housing and health care as well. But changing the flag is a win, vindicating the efforts of decades of activists, and creating the conditions under which the next round of reforms is just a little bit more possible. The long history is complicated and contested, but demonstrates both the potential effectiveness of organizing and protesting, as well as the very long process of changing the world.

Constructing Causality and Telling Stories

The flag stories in South Carolina and Mississippi underscore how easy it is to construct alternative, but accurate, histories of particular political change. They also show how important it is for activists to claim and promote the influence they've been able to execute. In many ways, this recognition is nothing particularly new. Political figures of all sorts construct causal explanations. Although academics have long recognized the social construction of commonly understood histories (e.g., Best 1995; Holstein and Miller 2003; Spector and Kitsuse 2001), few have applied this insight to narratives of social movement influence. In order to engage and mobilize supporters, organizers need to show that their efforts might matter, and showing that they've mattered in the past is a helpful first step. Organizers can strategically craft stories about the past and about present challenges that make a case for their proposed reforms and for activism more generally (Stone 1997). Organizers are wise to stick with verifiable facts, but also to craft simple stories that offer an intelligible causal story.

As suggested above, there are more elements for potential stories about change than space to tell them, including efforts of an activist group, changes in a policy, changes in political conditions, and speeches and public statements. A convincing story will draw from these elements, heavily editing, and adding plot. But crafting a story is only part of the larger struggle in promoting it. The effective storyteller is mindful of distinct audiences, their values, expectations, and likely responses to different narratives, as well as the demands of different settings in which stories are offered. Daily newspapers, for example, offer less space than longer-form journalism, and thus respond better to shorter chains of causality and simpler claims. Ultimately, widely accepted stories combine an edited version of available elements, consonant with accepted facts, perhaps supplemented with fictions that resonate with longstanding national myths, widespread cultural beliefs, or familiar plots (Tilly 2003). As people compete to win support for their preferred story of influence, the factors that make one or another story predominate in politics are not limited to accuracy. The advocates' vigor and skill are critical to their narratives' acceptance, for, as Stone (1997: 202) notes

> There is always someone to tell a competing narrative, and getting others to believe one version of events rather than another is hardly automatic … A causal story is more likely to be successful if its proponents have visibility, access to media, and prominent positions; if it accords with widespread and deeply held cultural values; if it somehow captures and responds to a natural mood; and if its implicit prescription entails no radical redistribution of power or wealth.

Causal stories appear in both wholesale and retail forms, the former directed to broad audiences, the latter targeted to smaller distinct ones. Within social movements, activists reinforce their preferred stories through sermons, speeches, songs, and slogans. There is an inevitable tension in managing stories to win acceptance within a social movement community and to spread a message more broadly because social movements develop distinct internal cultures that distinguish them from mainstream society (Rochon 1998). Importantly, the more familiar a story is, and the better it fits with conventional political and moral values, the more likely it is to be accepted; of course, adhering to dominant story lines and values limits the kinds of demands you can make and tactics you can employ. Activists always face a difficult balancing act in trying to stretch, but not transgress, the boundaries of legitimacy.

Why Some Movement Stories Win

Many things affect movement activists' prospects for successfully claiming credit, including: the ambition of the movement's expressed goals; the survival of at least some of the organization's animating; the institutional positioning of allies or sympathetic participants; the relative costs and risks of claiming victory; and the nature of the constituency the represented. All affect the likelihood of credit claimers to get their version of the story out beyond the true believers to broader audiences.

Movement Goals
Movements always target for more than they ultimately get, and some movement factions nest the central demand of a campaign within a litany of much broader goals. Because all victories are partial – and because it takes forever to achieve them, it's important to figure out why some factions do better at claiming credit. Both very limited and very broad expressed

goals make victories harder to claim. Goals that don't affect all that many people are unlikely to interest all that many people. In recent years, activists have devoted a greater share of their efforts simply toward winning the rights to protest at specific places and in particular ways (della Porta 1999). That demonstrators may succeed in winning their desired space, or carry off the events they plan can be claimed as a victory for only a short time, and only among the already committed.

In evaluating the 2004 counter-inaugural protest he helped organize, for example, Brian Becker, national coordinator of Act Now to Stop War and End Racism (ANSWER), claimed, "We think this is a significant achievement for the antiwar movement. We have bleachers, a stage, a sound system, and we're right along the parade route. We feel we have succeeded" (Janofsky 2005). It's hard to imagine that many other opponents of President Bush's agendas felt so sanguine about their success as the president took the oath of office for a second term. While some activists may get tremendous satisfaction in, say, staging a large demonstration and hearing good speakers and music, such satisfaction isn't likely to spread beyond the faithful, nor is it likely to last. For the larger public and for most participants, the successful demonstration or protest event is also a means to some other end.

In the same way, educating activists and changing individual lives is important work, and certainly an outcome that social movements can claim, but it's hard to think that many people go out into the streets thinking primarily about changing individuals or establishing new organizations – except as a means to making larger gains. In contrast, groups seeking broader collective goods (Amenta and Young 1999; Cooper 1996) easily meet the challenge of significance, but face stronger competitors in claiming credit. Think about efforts to promote government action on climate change, for example.

The broad and extensive reforms needed to serve this end must engage people who are doing all kinds of different things, including conducting studies, campaigning for office, and protesting. Nothing that happens will feel like enough, and many people will be able to claim some share of the credit for any step forward.

Although a social movement may seek collective goods from the margins, as it approaches some policy impact, its claims will be taken up, albeit in some kind of diluted form, by more mainstream institutionally-oriented political actors. The general benefits of such policy reforms, be it cleaner air or more thoroughly labeled food packaging, will be claimed not only by the movement, but by more powerful institutional actors, with immediate credibility in mass media, permanent staffs to manage public relations, and perpetual campaigns in which they will have the opportunity to retell the story of their achievements. Because the benefit is diffuse, it is not only harder for movement actors to claim credit, but also less likely that some distinct constituency will feel the same stake in the goal's achievement. The cause of clean air, for example, might be taken up by anyone, and longtime activist groups should be wary about discrediting the efforts of its later converts, particularly if the newly recruited are better positioned to affect policy.

And any win is never really enough. Even for movements that can claim tangible victories, there's a problem with a finish line that keeps moving. When the modern environmental movement emerged in the 1960s, an initial focus on pesticides quickly generated real victories. Of course, environmentalists tried, and continue to try, to build upon such policy achievements and move further, pressing new "policy frontiers" (Gornick and Meyer 1998). As the movement succeeded in gaining some recognition and influence, participating organizations constantly sought new related issues on which to make claims (Rucht 1999), both to achieve their goals and to maintain their support. The work never done, organizers generally focus on the greatest threat or most salient current issue, leaving any past victories for others to claim.

Organizational Survival and the Politics of Coalitions
Like Coleridge's "Ancient Mariner" or Melville's Ishmael, someone must be around to tell the story and with a current motivation to promote that story. Organizations that do not focus on sustaining themselves may have substantial impact in the moment (Piven and Cloward 1977), but they are poorly positioned to take credit for their influence. Outliving the opponents and continuing visible action enhances the prospects of winning credit for the past – as we saw in the tale of Pete Seeger's installation as an American legend fully 40 years after the height of his popularity as a musician (Bromberg and Fine 2002). But activists, professional organizers, and groups move on to other issues and other organizations, often shifting the emphasis of their political concerns.

Many movements, like the citizen movements against nuclear power, or the global Occupy campaigns, were antagonistic to developing formal and permanent leadership structures (Dwyer 1983), and individual activists dropped in and out of participation. The antinuclear movement in the United States faded after the Three Mile Island accident in 1979, along with licenses for new nuclear power plants, a victory no one was around to claim (Jasper 1990; Joppke 1993). In Germany, many of its activists grew into a campaign for institutional power through Green politics. To be sure, supportive groups, like the Union of Concerned Scientists survived, but did so by turning to more salient issues such as nuclear weapons (Moore 1996). No group enjoyed the capacity and interest in issuing press releases, returning reporters' queries, or constantly correcting competitors' explanations for policy change.

In the United States, contemporary social movement politics are coalition politics, the product of organizations and individuals who affiliate in the service of particular campaigns and causes, but maintain their own visions of justice, repertoire of tactics, independent organizational needs, and distinct, yet often overlapping, constituencies (Meyer and Corrigall-Brown 2005; Rochon and Meyer 1997). Social movements succeed when the efforts of distinct organizations have a synergistic effect, even if some groups are short-lived. Their version of events, claims to effectiveness, and vision of what is to be done – in short, their story – disappears, particularly when other groups survive. Thus, in contemporary politics, the NAACP and, to a lesser extent, the SCLC (Southern Christian Leadership Council) are far better positioned to explain the influence of the civil rights movement than was SNCC, which imploded more than 30 years ago.

While SNCC's direct action campaigns were inspiring and influential, stories about more reformist politics predominate, with a focus on moral suasion more than political disruption. Similarly, the radical edge of the labor movement has its story told by academics far more than by organizers, and to much smaller audiences than its more mainstream allies. Because more moderate organizations are most likely to survive (Wilson 1995), popular stories about social movement influence tend to emphasize more institutional routes to effectiveness, downplaying the grassroots activity and mass mobilizations that animate movements.

The Risks of Victories
Declaring a victory and claiming credit for it brings risks to social movement activists. Celebrating victories can provoke

opponents into action (Meyer and Staggenborg 1996), while simultaneously and inadvertently encouraging complacency among supporters. For many interests, risk and threat rather than support from government generates mobilization of activism and financial contributions. In American abortion politics, for example, Supreme Court decisions are typically followed by press conferences in which groups on both sides of the issue declare defeat; activists want to heighten urgency, keep the faithful engaged, and solicit financial contributions. They need people to continue paying attention and offering time and money.

The abortion issue also illustrates the politics of compromise and partial policy resolutions. Although abortion has remained legal in the United States since 1973, movement organizations continually battle on a broad range of issues, ranging from explicit discussion of abortion to regulation of particular procedures to parental or spousal notification to the size of a buffer zone separating anti-abortion protesters from clinics; there are always potential threats.

Given the nature of social movement politics, stories of optimism or achievement are risky. Journalist Gregg Easterbrook (1995), a self-described liberal seeking to vindicate government action, argues that federal government action, prompted by the environmental movement, made huge progress in improving air and water quality. In his story, however, the environmentalists are whining winners. "Enviros won the last 20 years of political battles by a wide margin," Easterbrook (1995: 381, 383) writes, "but you'd never know it from their public statements ... As environmentalists have become effective lobbyists they have learned the negative tools of the trade: bluster, veiled threats, misrepresentation." The pressures of direct mail fundraising, he argues, lead environmentalists to employ hyperbole and distortion in order to continue to raise money.

From a contemporary standpoint, there are obvious problems with Easterbrook's critique. Newly recognized environmental problems, most notably climate change, can emerge strongly, and the achievements that he would have had environ-mentalists claim now seem pale and inadequate. Moreover, victories are often temporary, as most significant movements mobilize an opposition which may win sometimes as well.

More generally, however, a group that claims success risks forfeiting its capacity to mobilize, either to sustain networks and organizations and employment that it has developed, and also in terms of lodging subsequent claims. There are good reasons not to proclaim victory. Politically, acknowledging victory risks lessening urgency and ceding what is always a limited agenda space (Hilgartner and Bosk 1988) for issues to other causes and claimants; there is always more important work to be done. Organizationally, declaring a win risks embracing identification with more moderate allies and politics and forfeiting the urgency of their claims on supporters.

Paradoxically, a well-heeled group best positioned to get its claim of victory out risks the most in doing so. In the case of the civil rights movement, even as the public policies and social changes activists won were far less than the goals they articu-lated, activists did succeed in making it politically costly to attack the goals of inclusion – at least for a while. Opposition to civil rights was no longer articulated as a social good in polite society or mainstream politics. Such talk, if not belief, has been banished to the marginalized political netherworld of segregationist politics. Articulating support for the broad goals of racial integration and equality is a low-risk position, tied to no definite position in contemporary contested political debates. This was not always the case for advocates of civil rights for ethnic minorities, nor is it for those who express sympathy with gay and lesbian rights. Vanquishing the explicit opposition makes it easier to claim credit.

Marching into and through Institutions: Constituencies and Claimants

The relative positions and power of the people making claims have a great deal to do with what stories get out, and how they are received (Stone 1997). Movements that make inroads into established institutions, particularly winning elective office, promote individual people with both the stake and status to make claims about movement influence. To the extent that someone representing a social movement stands beside candidates for office, makes speeches in the legislature, and represents movement positions in policy debates, that person visibly demonstrates one element of movement influence. Increased capacity to make claims of influence, however, comes with constraints and somewhat different incentives.

The mostly absent debate about the end of the Cold War provides a disturbing illustration. Most peace movement organizations had begun to fade in the mid-1980s, as deployment of new missiles they vigorously opposed began and the arms control process was resurrected (Edwards and Marullo 1995). Opponents, often in government, were better positioned to interpret the restoration of arms control in the later 1980s and the fall of Communism in 1989. Pundits, politicians, and well-sponsored academics claimed that the threat of an eventual ballistic missile defense system, popularly known as "Star Wars", or just general toughness and spending during the 1980s, wore the Soviet Union down. Democratic allies of the peace movement in Congress claimed, instead, that 40 years of bipartisan containment policy achieved these ends. In short, politicians in both major political parties used the remarkable events of 1989 as grist for retelling old stories supporting their preferred policies and their political futures.

Evangelista (1999), using collections of Soviet documents that were available only after the end of the Cold War, makes a compelling argument that moderation from the West, particularly the United States, rather than hardline policies, produced and accelerated reform in the Soviet Union. Activists who made these arguments earlier (e.g., Cortright 1993; Meyer and Marullo 1992), however, got little attention. Neither academics nor activists enjoyed much capacity to promote alternative explanations for the end of the Cold War. Activists whose organizations had been crippled years before were poorly positioned to make claims of influence and credit, and indeed focused most of their attention on new, now more urgent or promising, issues. In effect, they were willing to accept the stories from those they believed had defeated them. At the same time, one-time allies of the movement ditched that affiliation in favor of others that appeared more fruitful; legislators who had eagerly portrayed themselves as peace activists in the early 1980s retrospectively donned the mantle of containment.

Policies cannot speak for themselves. When a movement is about the treatment of identifiable and distinct groups of people, for example, African Americans, women, gays and lesbians, individual careers can readily be seen as social movement successes. Appointment or election to government positions, or anointment by the mass media, enables them to claim credit for partial victories, even if those so advantaged are not hardcore movement activists, or represent a more moderate wing of the movement. Paradoxically, individuals who win elected office, even veterans of radical organizations, such as John Lewis from SNCC, or Tom Hayden from the Students for a Democratic Society, by virtue of their hard-won careers in mainstream politics, can't help but emphasize the importance of institutional politics. Winning access to such positions becomes both a movement triumph and the signal for a shift toward institutionally oriented politics.

Polletta (1998b) examined narratives of the civil rights movement employed by members of Congress on the floor of the House or Senate, and found that the stories were most likely to be told by African Americans, confined almost exclusively to commemorative occasions, and stressed an individual connection to Martin Luther King, Jr. – or his dream. She notes that "Speakers are clear that their own careers were made possible by the travails of an earlier generation of movement activists ... Their own careers become the next stage in a saga of African American struggle" (Polletta 1998c: 435). She notes an irony in the deployment of a movement narrative focusing on the action inside mainstream political institutions. Here, one-time activists gaining access to political institutions win the capacity to get a movement story out, but it is a story fixed in the past, emphasizing conventional politics for the future.

In contrast, individuals who win access through policy-focused movements have a more difficult time claiming credit for their movement; indeed, exercising influence within policymaking circles frequently entails disavowing movement connections. The peace activist who takes an appointment in the Arms Control and Disarmament Agency or the environmentalist who works for the Environmental Protection Agency, as examples, seem to disavow activist identification as part of the bargain, and citizen mobilization disappears as one of their explicit goals. Even when they claim connections with the movements they started with, activists in the street are liable to disavow them for excessive moderation. For some movements, winning access to political institutions essentially means slipping an identity, something people identified by characteristics beyond belief cannot easily do.

Middle-class movements organize on positions about salient issues, distinguish their participants from the larger world primarily on the basis of beliefs, although they may share norms of presentation, styles, and conversation. Indeed, seeking public support, they often emphasize how much like a non-mobilized and mainstream audience they are. When their ideas are accommodated, however, at most some portion of style or of belief is incorporated into governance. The connections between government employees seeking credibility and the movements that supported them seeking viability operate to attenuate connections between the margins and the mainstream. An elected official or bureaucrat presents ideas as her own, even if claiming identification with the movement at the same time.

Movements based on providing targeted advantages to an identifiable constituency are better positioned to claim credit than those that build support on the basis of belief. Skin color, gender, ethnicity, religion or even sexual orientation, are relatively "sticky" identities, while movements based on belief are far more "slippery." Sticky movements do a better job of claiming credit because their members have a harder time deserting them. Women in mainstream politics can now sometimes ignore the impact of the feminist movement (Sawyers and Meyer 1999), but African Americans who try to shed this identity have it thrust back upon them by mainstream politics and culture.

Why Claiming Credit Matters

The actual influence of a movement or any other actor, difficult to determine in any case, is only one factor determining the content of a story and the nature of the audiences who accept it. Nonetheless, the dominant narrative about the trajectory of a movement, or of the origins of a policy, becomes part of the culture in which movements arise (or not), legitimating certain kinds of claims, actors, and tactics, while undermining others. A story that emphasizes intentional and effective efforts by citizens legitimates social protest and simultaneously reinforces the political significance of interested actors outside government. In contrast, a story that emphasizes broad historical forces or the efforts only of committed individuals within government, works to delegitimize and demobilize potential citizen movements.

Similarly, as Polletta (1998a) notes, stories that emphasize accident, contingency, and spontaneity, belie the important work of organizing, portraying movements as almost magical. The old axiom that history belongs to the winners might properly by rephrased: those who win in the writing of history shape the future. A dominant story about the influence of a citizens' movement on politics and policy encourages extra-institutional mobilization on particular issues, provides a "demonstration effect" (Freeman 1983), and provides a resource for movements in the future. Even a story that tells of a movement's defeat, but offers an explanation of why and strategies for improvement, can also be a resource for subsequent mobilization (Voss 1998). In contrast, a dominant story that emphasizes the power of institutional actors to do what they want, for good or evil, robs incipient movements of a residuum of efficacy that makes sustained mobilization possible.

Organizers can use narratives of movements of the past to spur or support new efforts (Polletta 1998a). Narratives of past influence can maintain the enthusiasm of the faithful, mobilize new activists by providing a script for contemporary actions and make sense of current political challenges. That the civil rights movement is broadly accepted as a cause for significant improvements in the treatment of African Americans, both by the state and by individuals, has been a source of inspiration for other social movements – on the right as well as the left – providing a sense that the sometimes costly commitments people make in the service of a moral cause can be worthwhile. It has also spurred imitators in terms of both tactics and language. That demonstrations, marches, and civil disobedience were part of an effective repertoire of contention vindicates movement strategies – at least sometimes.

In contrast, that the sanctuary and nonintervention movements are viewed by those who initiated them as costly, and ultimately futile, has obvious bearing on the prospects for launching subsequent challenges on matters of foreign policy. In looking at the stories of influence told by social movement activists and their competitors, we can identify the implicit negotiations in constructing accepted narratives of influence. Perhaps the most successful case, that of the civil rights movement for African Americans, demonstrates both the extent and limits of success claimed. Although the movement is widely given credit for winning basic civil rights, its popular image emphasizes charismatic leadership, most notably in the eventual inclusion of Martin Luther King, Jr. in the pantheon of national heroes. An extended story, which includes decades of organizing that was less visible and the important influence of, at least, thousands of brave and committed activists at the grassroots is, in many ways, not only more accurate, but also more helpful.

The frequently told story of Rosa Parks' civil disobedience on a bus in Montgomery in December 1955 is decontextualized and depoliticized. Parks is remembered as a tired old lady, with rarely a mention of her connections to longstanding organizations like the NAACP and the Highlander Folk School's leadership programs. Ironically, her heroic reputation is based on editing out the training and organizational infrastructure that supported her heroism. Dramatic disobedient action, such as the sit-in movement which catapulted to national attention in Greensboro, North Carolina, in 1960, is treated similarly, as a spontaneous eruption (Polletta 1998a), although the sit-in was a well-established, and intensively organized, protest technique that had circulated throughout the South for nearly a decade (Morris 1984). In short, although the movement's influence is acknowledged, it is frequently defined as something inevitable or mystical, quite apart from the processes of contemporary politics, and surely beyond the aspirations of the citizens of today.

Even in a narrative of influence, the neglect of context and organization in favor of spontaneity or ambiguity in origins – what Taylor (1989) terms a myth of "immaculate conception" – undermines the prospects of subsequent mobilization, giving little clear direction to today's organizers. Told by established authorities, narratives of successful protests of the past, ranging from the Boston Tea Party to the March on Washington, have the ironic effect of reinforcing the primacy of institutional politics (Polletta 1998a, 1998b), and editing out the ongoing contentiousness of American politics (Meyer 2015).

Summary

Social change is difficult and time-consuming. The political world is complicated, and making any kind of meaningful change is difficult. Social movements *can* matter, to be sure, but not by themselves, and not necessarily in the ways organizers intend. Usually, even large victories relatively quickly represent so much less than many activists imagine at the outset. Further, the timeline along which change takes place is unpredictable and erratic. Although academics like historians work to get out a compelling story about the past, most of the stories of influence are told by people who have their own purposes in the present. Getting out a preferred story about the influence of movements in the past is meaningful and difficult; it requires sustained efforts by many allied people over time. Activists have to work to claim credit, and it's an ongoing struggle.

Claiming a victory can be a sword with multiple edges. In order to continue to organize and mobilize, activists need to maintain a sense of urgency along with a sense of potential influence. Claiming victories gracelessly, demanding more, is one strategy for doing so. Another is the development of a fortifying myth (Voss 1998), where a defeat on matters of policy is explained and coupled with a strategy for activism in the future (see, e.g., Boutcher 2011). Defeats can provide newly illustrated grievances, encouraging political engagement and often strategic and tactical innovation. Even in defeat, movements can activate and claim new partisans, and leave ideas on the political field that others can later pick up. Activists need to learn to view both defeats and victories as temporary and unstable, always demanding new work. Victories provoke opponents, and defeated opponents return and need to be engaged again and again.

Failing to claim credit, and to identify connections means that every new campaign has to invent itself from scratch, finding ways to create identities with people, convincing them of the unusual nature of a moment. Such efforts can win sporadic victories, and have the fruits of their labor claimed by others. Some participants will leave activism, feeling frustrated by the perceived futility of their work, and new organizations will constantly hold the primary responsibility for new mobilizations. By learning how to find and promote narratives of effective citizen protest and engaged activism in making the world better, we can help them educate, organize, and mobilize in the future.

Notes

Introduction

1 http://www.disruptj20.org/tag/press/ (accessed January 26, 2018).

2 Most of those arrested refused to cooperate with police or prosecutors, choosing to face trial rather than negotiate plea agreements. After a jury acquitted the first six defendants of all charges, the federal prosecutor dropped charges against most of the remaining defendants. See Ryan J. Reilly, "Justice Department Drops Felony Charges Against 129 Trump Inauguration Defendants but 59 other #J20 protesters will face trial." *The Huffington Post*, January 18, 2018. https://www.huffingtonpost.com/entry/j20-felony-charges_us_5a6122b4e4b074ce7a06d638 (accessed February 1, 2018).

3 Peta Australia, "Nearly Naked Peta Members to Take On Mercedes-Benz Fashion Festival for Refusing to Renounce Fur." https://www.peta.org.au/media/nearly-naked-peta-members-to-take-on-mercedes-benz-fashion-festival-for-refusing-to-renounce-fur/ (accessed November 13, 2020).

4 Greenpeace International, "Actress Lucy Lawless joins climate change survivor in protest against Arctic exploitation for Norwegian oil." July 21, 2017. https://www.greenpeace.org/international/press-release/7449/actress-lucy-lawless-joins-climate-change-survivor-in-protest-against-arctic-exploitation-for-norwegian-oil/ (accessed November 13, 2020).

5 Marc Santora and Anna Schaverien, "Anti-Brexit Protesters Descend on London as Parliament Debates." *The New York Times*, October 19, 2019.

6 Deeohn Ferris, "Environmental Justice: Moving Equity from Margins to Mainstream." *Nonprofit Quarterly*, August 15, 2019. https://nonprofitquarterly.org/

environmental-justice-moving-equity-from-margins-to-
mainstream/#:~:text=These%20are%3A%20Defenders%20of%20
Wildlife,Society%2C%20and%20World%20Wildlife%20Fund
(accessed November 13, 2020).

Chapter 1: Why Movements Emerge and How They Work

1 https://www.bostonteapartyship.com/museum (accessed February 6, 2018).
2 www.holocaustresearchproject.org/revolt/whiterose.html (accessed November 13, 2020).

Chapter 2: Protest, Revolution, and Regime Change

1 Dean Praetorius, 2011. "Mohamed ElBaradei: Egypt's Potential Future Leader?" *The Huffington Post*, May 25. https://www. huffingtonpost.com/2011/01/28/mohamed-elbaradei_n_815529. html (accessed February 21, 2018).
2 The text of the bill can be found at https://www.congress.gov/116/ bills/hres109/BILLS-116hres109ih.pdf (accessed November 14, 2020).
3 See, for example, the story of organizing Kurdish nationalist movements in Turkey (Kaválek and Mareš 2018).
4 This summary draws on Campbell (2016), Johnson and Schlemmer (1996), Lyman (2002), Masipa (2018) and Shapiro and Tebeau (2011).
5 The story of Indian independence, in which large-scale nonviolent action played a critical part, is also one in which the emergent international order and the onset of the Cold War was also critical – but that's not the story we tell here (Power 1969).
6 Howard Kaplan, 2014. "Apartheid on Trial: Mandela's Rivonia Speech from the Dock, Half a Century Later," *Social Education* 74(2): 63–67. https://www.americanbar.org/content/dam/aba/ images/public_education/ApartheidonTrial.pdf (accessed March 4, 2018). Also see http://www.sahistory.org.za/article/rivonia-trial-1963-1964 (accessed March 5, 2018).

7 The entirety of Mandela's speech can be found at https://www.
   sahistory.org.za/archive/court-transcript-statement-dock-nelson-
   mandela-pretoria-supreme-court-20-april-1964 (accessed March 5,
   2018).
8 Critical to undermining democratic elements of these revolutions
   has been an incremental resistance to substituting autocratic
   leadership for the rule of law. See Scheppele (2015).
9 Simon Johnson and Gary W. Loveman, 1995. "Starting Over:
   Poland After Communism," *Harvard Business Review*, March/
   April. https://hbr.org/1995/03/starting-over-poland-after-
   communism (accessed March 10, 2018).
10 See David Remnick's profile of Havel, "Letter from Prague: Exit
   Havel, The King Leaves the Castle." *The New Yorker*, February 17
   and 24, 2003. https://www.newyorker.com/magazine/2003/02/17/
   exit-havel (accessed March 11, 2018).
11 "Text of Havel's Speech to Congress," *The Washington Post*,
   February 22, 1990. https://www.washingtonpost.com/archive/
   politics/1990/02/22/text-of-havels-speech-to-congress/df98e177-
   778e-4c26-bd96-980089c4fcb2/?utm_term=.480eddd52a16
   (accessed March 11, 2018).
12 Jeri Laber, 1992. "Witch Hunt in Prague." *The New York Review
   of Books*, April 23. http://www.nybooks.com/articles/1992/04/23/
   witch-hunt-in-prague/ (accessed March 11, 2018).

CHAPTER 3: PROTEST AND POLICY

1 Details on the bill can be found at Maggie Astor, 2018. "Florida
   Gun Bill: What's in It and What Isn't." *The New York Times*,
   March 8. https://www.nytimes.com/2018/03/08/us/florida-gun-bill.
   html (accessed March 13, 2018).
2 Mike Spies, 2018. "The N.R.A. Lobbyist behind Florida's
   Pro-Gun Policies." *The New Yorker*, March 5, 2019. https://www.
   newyorker.com/magazine/2018/03/05/the-nra-lobbyist-behind-
   floridas-pro-gun-policies (accessed March 14, 2018).
3 A very helpful history of Australia's engagement with the politics
   of climate change can be found on a government website. See
   Anita Talberg, Simeon Hui, and Kate Loynes, 2016. "Australian
   Climate Change Policy to 2015: A Chronology." https://www.
   aph.gov.au/About_Parliament/Parliamentary_Departments/

Parliamentary_Library/pubs/rp/rp1516/Climate2015 (accessed November 14, 2020).

4 https://www.cnn.com/2018/01/24/us/larry-nassar-sentencing/index. html (accessed November 14, 2020).

5 https://news.stanford.edu/2016/04/25/stanford-climate-change-statement-board-trustees/ (accessed March 24, 2018).

6 https://www.cnn.com/2019/03/20/asia/new-zealand-christchurch-gun-ban-intl/index.html (accessed November 14, 2020).

7 A convenient overview of the draft and its opposition can be found at http://michiganintheworld.history.lsa.umich.edu/antivietnamwar/ exhibits/show/exhibit/draft_protests/the-military-draft-during-the- (accessed April 9, 2018).

8 Don Oberdorfer, 1978. "McGovern Backs Anti-Cambodia Action." *The Washington Post*, August 22. https:// www.washingtonpost.com/archive/politics/1978/08/22/ mcgovern-backs-anti-cambodia-action/ab290e4e-75ff-4275-a4a2-7517970cfbab/?utm_term=.b26c582edf9f (accessed November 14, 2020).

9 https://blog.humanesociety.org/2008/11/prop2-victory.html (accessed November 14, 2020).

10 Robin Manley, 2015. "Caged Resistance: California's Proposition 2 and Animal Welfare." *Brown Political Review*, February 22. http://www.brownpoliticalreview.org/2015/02/caged-resistance-californias-proposition-2-and-animal-welfare/ (accessed November 14, 2020).

11 Jason Lusk, 2015. "Effect of New California Laws on Egg Prices." Blog post. February 3. http://jaysonlusk.com/blog/2015/2/3/effect-of-new-california-laws-on-egg-prices (accessed November 14, 2020).

12 https://en.wikipedia.org/wiki/Nuclear_power_in_Germany (accessed November 14, 2020).

13 Caroline Jorant, 2011. "The Implications of Fukushima: The European Perspective." *Bulletin of the Atomic Scientists* 67(4): 14–17. See also https://www.thelocal.de/20160311/five-years-after-fukushima-germanys-energy-transition-still-faces-challenges

14 It's not surprising that a heated political battle spanning more than half a century has produced a massive literature, including polemical pieces, analyses of judicial decisions, and scholarly analyses of movement action and public policy. Staggenborg (1991) provides a very useful overview of the early development of this conflict.

15 The National Abortion Foundation maintains a listing of instances of violence against clinics and doctors providing legal abortions: https://prochoice.org/our-work/provider-security/ (accessed November 14, 2020).

16 Immigration politics traces a similar trajectory in the United States, albeit not quite as long-lived. Over the last two decades, however, immigrant rights and anti-immigrant movements have captured the major political parties and held each other in check, resulting in a political stalemate and largely incoherent and dysfunctional public policies. See Meyer and Reyes (2010).

17 https://www.npr.org/2018/12/10/675382720/french-president-macron-makes-concessions-to-yellow-vest-protesters
https://www.npr.org/2018/12/15/677015790/despite-concessions-macrons-struggles-with-yellow-vest-movement-deepen
https://www.thelocal.fr/20190206/macrons-10-billion-yellow-vest-concessions-hit-frances-finances-hard
http://www.ecns.cn/news/2019-04-28/detail-ifzhtktn3338656.shtml
(all accessed November 14, 2020).

Chapter 4: Protest, Organizations, and Institutionalization

1 Joseph Goldstein and Kevin Armstrong, 2020. "Could This City Hold the Key to the Future of Policing in America?" *The New York Times*, July 12.

2 The Red Hook story was reported by Dana Chivvis, 2020. "Grand Army," *This American Life*, Episode #708, *Here Again*, originally aired June 12. https://www.thisamericanlife.org/708/here-again

3 Jan Ransom and Annie Correal, 2020. "How the New York Protest Leaders Are Taking On the Establishment," *The New York Times*, June 11; Jessie Gomez, 2020. "Protest NJ: Residents Organize George Floyd Peaceful Protests for the First Time," *Morristown Daily Record*, June 4; Alexa Ura and Stacy Fernández, 2020. "In George Floyd-inspired Protests, Texas Organizers Find New Allies in Quest for Police Reforms," *The Texas Tribune*, June 10.

4 A good place to start into her writing is her memoir (Addams 2019 [1910]).

5 Women's International League for Peace and Freedom, https://
www.wilpf.org/
6 The strategic choice, to focus on education through litigation
rather than, for example, violence against Black people, was one
influenced by the availability of outside resources for one set of
issues and not the other. See Francis (2019).
7 https://www.naacp.org/
8 Particularly contentious was the initial aversion to leadership. At
first the Greens committed to rotate parliamentary seats among
members, but it wasn't long before parliamentary representatives,
citing their expertise and commitment gained by tenure in office,
were reluctant to rotate out, becoming professional politicians.

CHAPTER 5: PROTEST MOVEMENTS, CULTURE, AND PARTICIPANTS

1 https://www.logodesignlove.com/cnd-symbol (accessed November
16, 2020).
2 The marches didn't bring about nuclear disarmament, nor stop
Britain from developing its own nuclear arsenal. Eventually,
however, they led to support for the Limited Test Ban Treaty,
signed by Britain, the Soviet Union, and the United States in 1963.
CND survived that partial victory, and provided organizing and
infrastructure for subsequent peace and antinuclear campaigns. As
I write, CND is engaged in several activist campaigns, including an
effort to ban nuclear weapons by having the nations of the world
declare them illegal. https://cnduk.org/nuclear-ban-treaty-on-its-
way-the-countdown-is-on/ (accessed November 16, 2020).
3 Freedom to Marry, "How It Happened," http://www.
freedomtomarry.org/pages/how-it-happened
4 Pew Research Center, "Attitudes on Same-Sex Marriage," May 14,
2019. https://www.pewforum.org/fact-sheet/changing-attitudes-on-
gay-marriage/ (accessed November 16, 2020).
5 https://www.pbs.org/independentlens/februaryone/four.html
(accessed November 16, 2020).
6 https://www.smithsonianmag.com/smithsonian-institution/
lessons-worth-learning-moment-greensboro-four-sat-down-lunch-
counter-180974087/ (accessed November 16, 2020).

CHAPTER 6: CLAIMING CREDIT

1 https://ag.ny.gov/press-release/2020/attorney-general-james-files-lawsuit-dissolve-nra (accessed November 17, 2020). The NRA subsequently announced that it was filing for bankruptcy, and planned to move to Texas.

2 This chapter develops arguments I first made in Meyer (2006), and draws on that piece.

3 This section draws on Meyer (2019b) and Milkis and Tichenor (2018).

4 Ava DuVernay's wonderful 2014 film *Selma* provides a compelling account of voting rights that centers the activists in the streets, and portrays Johnson as a target and a reluctant reactor, rather than crusader, in the struggle for voting rights. The accuracy and fairness of his portrayal is at the center of a very useful debate about history. See Sorkin (2015).

5 It's also important to remember that there were people pushing for civil rights reforms who had no other connection to the movement – and this is also a common social movement story. In this case, experts in the foreign policy establishment during the Cold War wanted visible progress on civil rights to enhance America's appeal to would-be allies, and to counter propaganda about racial segregation advanced by the Soviet Union (Dudziak 2000).

6 https://usatoday30.usatoday.com/life/music/news/2009-01-18-inaug-concert_N.htm (accessed November 17, 2020).

7 I confess that this line is adapted from a line in Ernest Hemmingway's *The Sun Also Rises*. A character describes how he went bankrupt: "gradually, then suddenly."

8 In response to another wave of racial justice activism, the NCAA expanded the ban in 2020. https://apnews.com/article/bc2347ed8a69f52bc7b060b30661808c

9 https://www.scchamber.net/media-center/article/businesses-react-confederate-battle-flag%E2%80%99s-impending-removal (accessed November 17, 2020).

10 The account of the struggle over Mississippi's flag follows Radiolab (2020), "The Flag and the Fury," an extraordinary hour-long podcast.

References

Addams, Jane. 2019 [1910]. *Twenty Years at Hull House, with Autobiographical Notes*. Los Angeles, CA: Indo-European Publishing.

Alexander, Christopher. 2016. *Tunisia: From Stability to Revolution in the Maghreb*. London: Routledge.

Alimi, Eitan Y., and David S. Meyer. 2011. "Seasons of Change: Arab Spring and Political Opportunities." *Swiss Political Science Review* 17(4): 475–9.

Amenta, Edwin. 1998. *Bold Relief: Institutional Politics and the Origins of Modern American Social Policy*. Princeton, NJ: Princeton University Press.

Amenta, Edwin, Neal Caren, Elizabeth Chiarello, and Yang Su. 2010. "The Political Consequences of Social Movements." *Annual Review of Sociology* 36: 287–307.

Amenta, Edwin, Kathleen Dunleavy, and Mary Bernstein. 1994. "Stolen Thunder: Huey Long's Share our Wealth, Political Mediation, and the Second New Deal." *American Sociological Review* 59: 678–702.

Amenta, Edwin, and Francesca Polletta. 2019. "The Cultural Impacts of Social Movements." *Annual Review of Sociology* 45: 279–99.

Amenta, Edwin, and Michael P. Young. 1999. "Making an Impact: Conceptual and Methodological Implications of the Collective Goods Criterion." In Marco Giugni, Doug McAdam, and Charles Tilly, eds., *How Movements Matter:*

Theoretical and Comparative Studies on the Consequences of Social Movements. Minneapolis, MN: University of Minnesota Press, pp. 22–41.

Andrews, Kenneth T. 2004. *"Freedom is a Constant Struggle": The Mississippi Civil Rights Movement and Its Legacy*. Chicago, IL: University of Chicago Press.

Arkin, William M. 2003. "The Dividends of Delay." *Los Angeles Times*, February 23.

Armstrong, Elizabeth A., and Suzanna M. Crage. 2006. "Movements and Memory: The Making of the Stonewall Myth." *American Sociological Review* 71: 724–51.

Banaszak, Lee Ann. 2010. *The Women's Movement Inside and Outside the State*. New York: Cambridge University Press.

Baumgartner, Frank R., and Bryan D. Jones. 1993. *Agendas and Instability in American Politics*. Chicago, IL: University of Chicago Press.

Benford, Robert D. 1993a. "Frame Disputes within the Nuclear Disarmament Movement." *Social Forces* 71: 677–701.

Benford, Robert D. 1993b. "'You Could be the Hundredth Monkey': Collective Action Frames and Vocabularies of Motive within the Nuclear Disarmament Movement." *Sociological Quarterly* 34: 195–216.

Benford, Robert D., and David A. Snow. 2000. "Framing Processes and Social Movements: An Overview and Assessment." *Annual Review of Sociology* 26: 611–39.

Bennett, W. Lance, and Alexandra Segerberg. 2014. *The Logic of Connective Action: Digital Media and the Personalization of Contentious Politics*. New York: Cambridge University Press.

Bernstein, Iver. 1990. *The New York City Draft Riots: Their Significance for American Society and Politics in the Age of the Civil War*. New York: Oxford University Press.

Best, Joel, ed. 1995. *Images of Issues*, 2nd edn. Hawthorne, NY: Aldine de Gruyter.

Blee, Kathleen M. 2002. *Inside Organized Racism: Women in the Hate Movement*. Berkeley, CA: University of California Press.

Blee, Kathleen. 2012. *Making Democracy: How Activist Groups Form*. New York: Oxford University Press.

Boudreau, Vincent. 2004. *Resisting Dictatorship: Repression and Protest in Southeast Asia*. Cambridge: Cambridge University Press.

Boutcher, Steven A. 2011. "Mobilizing in the Shadow of the Law: Lesbian and Gay Rights in the Aftermath of Bowers v. Hardwick." *Research in Social Movements, Conflict, and Change* 31: 175–205.

Bracey, Glenn E., II. 2015. "Black Movements Need Black Theorizing: Exposing Implicit Whiteness in Political Process Theory," *Sociological Focus* 49(1): 11–27.

Bromberg, Minna, and Gary Alan Fine. 2002. "Resurrecting the Red: Pete Seeger and the Purification of Difficult Reputations." *American Sociological Review* 80: 1135–55.

Brooker, Megan E. 2018. "Indivisible: Invigorating and Redirecting the Grassroots." In D.S. Meyer and S. Tarrow, eds., *The Resistance: The Dawn of the Anti-Trump Opposition Movement*. New York: Oxford University Press, pp. 163–84.

Campbell, John. 2016. *Morning in South Africa*. Lanham, MD: Rowman & Littlefield.

Carson, Rachel. 1962. *Silent Spring*. New York: Houghton Mifflin.

Catsoulis, Jeannette. 2013. "Do Six-Ton Captives Dream of Freedom?" *The New York Times*, July 18. https://www.nytimes.com/2013/07/19/movies/blackfish-a-documentary-looks-critically-at-seaworld.html

Chenoweth, Erica, and Margherita Belgioioso. 2019. "The Physics of Dissent and the Effects of Movement Momentum." *Nature Human Behaviour* 3: 1088–95.

Chenoweth, Erica, and Maria Stephan. 2011. *Why Civil Resistance Works: The Strategic Logic of Nonviolent Conflict*. New York: Columbia University Press.

Clemens, Elisabeth S. 1997. *The People's Lobby: Organizational Innovation and the Rise of Interest Group Politics in the United States, 1890–1925*. Chicago, IL: University of Chicago Press.

Cooper, Alice H. 1996. "Public-Good Movements and the Dimensions of Political Process: Postwar German Peace Movements." *Comparative Political Studies* 29: 267–89.

Corrigall-Brown, Catherine. 2011. *Patterns of Protest: Trajectories of Participation in Social Movements*. Stanford, CA: Stanford University Press.

Cortright, David. 1993. *Peace Works: The Citizen's Role in Ending the Cold War*. Boulder, CO: Westview.

Davenport, Christian. 2007. *State Repression and the Domestic Democratic Peace*. New York: Cambridge University Press.

Davenport, Christian, Sarah A. Soule, and David A. Armstrong II. 2011. "Protesting While Black? The Differential Policing of American Activism, 1960 to 1990." *American Sociological Review* 76(1): 152–78.

Del Panta, Gianni. 2020. "Cross-Class and Cross-Ideological Convergences over Time: Insights from the Tunisian and Egyptian Revolutionary Uprisings." *Government and Opposition* 55(4): 634–52.

della Porta, Donatella. 1999. "Protest, Protesters, and Protest Policing: Public Discourse in Italy and Germany from the 1960s to the 1980s." In Marco Giugni, Doug McAdam, and Charles Tilly, eds., *How Movements Matter: Theoretical and Comparative Studies on the Consequences of Social*

Movements. Minneapolis, MN: University of Minnesota Press, pp. 66–96.

Djilas, Milovan. 1957. *The New Class: An Analysis of the Communist System*. New York: Harcourt Brace Jovanovich.

Donadio, Rachel. 2016. "A Museum Becomes a Battlefield over Poland's History." *The New York Times*, November 9.

Du Bois, W.E.B. 1995 [1899]. *The Philadelphia Negro: A Social Study*, introduction by Elijah Anderson. Philadelphia, PA: University of Pennsylvania Press.

Du Bois, W.E.B. 2016 [1903]. *The Souls of Black Folk*. Mineola, NY: Dover.

Dudziak, Mary L. 2000. *Cold War Civil Rights: Race and the Image of American Democracy*. Princeton, NJ: Princeton University Press.

Duverger, Maurice. 1954. *Political Parties: Their Organization and Activity in the Modern State*. New York: Wiley.

Dwyer, Lynn E. 1983. "Structure and Strategy in the Antinuclear Movement." In Jo Freeman, ed., *Social Movements of the Sixties and Seventies*. New York: Longman, pp. 148–61.

Earl, Jennifer. 2004. "The Cultural Consequences of Social Movements." In David A. Snow, Sarah A. Soule, and Hanspeter Kriesi, eds., *The Blackwell Companion to Social Movements*. Malden, MA: Blackwell, pp. 508–30.

Earl, Jennifer, and Katrina Kimport. 2011. *Digitally Enabled Social Change: Activism in the Internet Age*. Cambridge, MA: MIT Press.

Earl, Jennifer, Sarah Soule, and John D. McCarthy. 2003. "Protest Under Fire? Explaining the Policing of Protest." *American Sociological Review* 68: 581–606.

Easterbrook, Gregg. 1995. *A Moment on the Earth: The Coming Age of Environmental Optimism*. New York: Viking.

Edelman, Murray J. 1988. *Constructing the Political Spectacle.* Chicago, IL: University of Chicago Press.

Edwards, Bob, and Sam Marullo. 1995. "Organizational Mortality in a Declining Social Movement: The Demise of Peace Movement Organizations in the End of the Cold War Era." *American Sociological Review* 60: 908–27.

Edwards, Stassa. 2015. "Badass Bree Newsome Climbs S.C. Flagpole to Remove Confederate Flag," *Jezebel*, June 27. https://jezebel.com/badass-bree-newsome-climbs-s-c-flagpole-to-remove-conf-1714372554?utm_campaign=socialflow_jezebel_facebook&utm_source=jezebel_facebook&utm_medium=socialflow

Erikson, Robert S., and Laura Stoker. 2011. "Caught in the Draft: The Effects of Vietnam Draft Lottery Status on Political Attitudes." *American Political Science Review* 105(2): 221–37.

Evangelista, Matthew. 1999. *Unarmed Forces: The Transnational Movement to End the Cold War.* Ithaca, NY: Cornell University Press.

Fetner, Tina. 2008. *How the Religious Right Shaped Lesbian and Gay Activism.* Minneapolis, MN: University of Minnesota Press.

Fine, Gary Alan. 1996. "Reputational Entrepreneurs and the Memory of Incompetence: Melting Supporters, Partisan Warriors, and Images of President Harding." *American Journal of Sociology* 101: 1159–93.

Fine, Gary Alan. 1999. "John Brown's Body: Elites, Heroic Embodiment, and the Legitimation of Political Violence." *Social Problems* 46: 225–49.

Fireman, Bruce, and William A. Gamson. 1979. "Utilitarian Logic in the Resource Mobilization Perspective." In Mayer N. Zald and John D. McCarthy, eds., *The Dynamics of Social Movements.* Cambridge, MA: Winthrop, pp. 8–44.

Fisher, Dana R. 2019. *American Resistance: From the Women's March to the Blue Wave*. New York: Columbia University Press.

Foote, Kenneth E., Attila Tóth, and Anett Árvay. 2000. "Hungary after 1989: Inscribing a New Past on Place." *Geographical Review* 90(3): 301–34.

Francis, Megan Ming. 2019. "The Price of Civil Rights: Black Lives, White Funding, and Movement Capture," *Law and Social Inquiry* 53(1): 275–309.

Frankland, E. Gene, and Donald Schoonmaker. 1992. *Between Protest & Power: The Green Party in Germany*. Boulder, CO: Westview Press.

Freeman, Jo. 1983. "Introduction." In Jo Freeman, ed., *Social Movements of the Sixties and Seventies*. New York: Longman, pp. 1–7.

Gamson, William A. 1990 [1975]. *The Strategy of Social Protest*, 2nd edn. Belmont, CA: Wadsworth.

Gamson, William A., and David S. Meyer. 1996. "Framing Political Opportunity." In Doug McAdam, John D. McCarthy, and Mayer N. Zald, eds., *Comparative Perspectives on Social Movements: Political Opportunities, Mobilizing Structures, and Cultural Framings*. New York: Cambridge University Press, pp. 274–90.

Ganz, Marshall. 2000. "Resources and Resourcefulness: Strategic Capacity in the Unionization of California Agriculture, 1959–1966," *American Journal of Sociology* 105(4): 1003–62.

Garton Ash, Timothy. 1990. *The Magic Lantern: The Revolution of 1989 Witnessed in Warsaw, Budapest, Berlin, and Prague*. New York: Random House.

Gati, Charles. 2006. *Failed Illusions: Moscow, Washington, Budapest, and the 1956 Hungarian Revolt*. Stanford, CA: Stanford University Press.

Gessen, Masha. 2019. "Poland's Ruling Party Puts an Extraordinary Museum of Polish–Jewish History into Limbo." *The New Yorker*, September 23.

Giugni, Marco. 1998. "Was It Worth the Effort? The Outcomes and Consequences of Social Movements." *Annual Review of Sociology* 24: 371–93.

Goldberg, Denis. 2016. *A Life for Freedom: The Mission to End Racial Injustice in South Africa*. Lexington, KY: University Press of Kentucky.

Gornick, Janet C., and David S. Meyer. 1998. "Changing Political Opportunity: The Anti-Rape Movement and Public Policy." *Journal of Policy History* 10: 367–98.

Griswold, Wesley S. 1972. *The Night the Revolution Began: The Boston Tea Party, 1773*. Brattleboro, VT: S. Greene Press.

Gstalter, Morgan. 2020. "March For Our Lives Trolls NRA after NY Lawsuit: 'Sending Thoughts and Prayers.'" *The Hill*, August 6. https://thehill.com/blogs/blog-briefing-room/news/510880-march-for-our-lives-trolls-nra-after-new-york-lawsuit-sending

Hall, Richard L., and Frank Wayman. 1990. "Buying Time: Moneyed Interests and the Mobilization of Bias in Congressional Committees." *American Political Science Review* 84: 797–820.

Hamilton, Richard, and Maurice Pinard. 1976. "The Bases of Parti Quebecois Support in Recent Quebec Elections." *Canadian Journal of Political Science* 9(1): 3–26.

Harrison, Bobby. 2020. "Gov. Tate Reeves put himself in a no-win political position during state flag debate." *Mississippi Today*, July 5. https://mississippitoday.org/2020/07/05/gov-tate-reeves-put-himself-in-a-no-win-political-position-during-state-flag-debate/

Hasan, Hanaa. 2018. "Remembering Mohamed Bouazizi and

the Start of the Arab Spring." *Middle East Monitor*, December 17. https://www.middleeastmonitor.com/20181217-rememb ering-mohamed-bouazizi-and-the-start-of-the-arab-spring/

Havel, Vaclav. 1985. "The Power of the Powerless." In Havel et al. *The Power of the Powerless: Citizens against the State in Central Eastern Europe*. Armonk, NY: M.E. Sharpe, pp. 23–86.

Hicks, Alexander. 1999. *Social Democracy and Welfare Capitalism: A Century of Income Security Politics*. Ithaca, NY: Cornell University Press.

Hilgartner, Stephen, and Charles L. Bosk. 1988. "The Rise and Fall of Social Problems: A Public Arenas Model." *American Journal of Sociology* 94: 53–78.

Hill, Ronald Paul, Thomas Ainscough, Todd Shank, and Daryl Manullang. 2007. "Corporate Social Responsibility and Socially Responsible Investing: A Global Perspective." *Journal of Business Ethics* 70: 165–74.

Hirschman, Albert O. 1982. *Shifting Involvements: Private Interest and Public Action*. Princeton, NJ: Princeton University Press.

Holstein, James A., and Gale Miller. 2003. "Social Constructionism and Social Problems Work." In James A. Holstein and Gale Miller, eds., *Challenges and Choices: Constructionist Perspectives on Social Problems*. Hawthorne, NY: Aldine de Gruyter, pp. 70–91.

Jankofsky, Michael. 2005. "Demonstrators Revel in Opposition on Big Day for President." *The New York Times*, January 21.

Jasper, James M. 1990. *Nuclear Politics: Energy and the State in the United States, Sweden, and France*. Princeton, NJ: Princeton University Press.

Jepperson, Ronald L. 1991. "Institutions, Institutional Effects, and Institutionalism." In Walter Powell and Paul DiMaggio, eds., *The New Institutionalism in Organizational Analysis*. Chicago, IL: University of Chicago Press, pp. 143–53.

Johnson, R.W., and Lawrence Schlemmer, eds. 1996. *Launching Democracy in South Africa: The First Open Election, 1994*. New Haven, CT: Yale University Press.

Johnstone, Diana. 1985. *The Politics of the Euromissiles: Europe's Role in America's World*. New York: Schocken.

Joppke, Christian. 1993. *Mobilizing against Nuclear Energy: A Comparison of Germany and the United States*. Berkeley, CA: University of California Press.

Kaldor, Mary. 1998. *Democratization of Central and Eastern Europe*. London: Continuum Press.

Kaválek, Tomáš, and Miroslav Mareš. 2018. "PKK's Friends and Foes in the Middle East Since 1999." *Central European Journal of International and Security Studies* 12(2): 100–29.

Keck, Margaret E., and Kathryn Sikkink. 1988. *Activists beyond Borders: Advocacy Networks in International Politics*. Ithaca, NY: Cornell University Press.

Keniston, Kenneth. 1968. *Young Radicals*. New York: Harcourt, Brace and World.

King, Brayden. 2011. "The Tactical Disruptiveness of Movements: Sources of Market and Mediated Disruption in Corporate Boycotts." *Social Problems* 48: 491–517.

King, Brayden, and Sarah A. Soule. 2007. "Social Movements as Extra-Institutional Entrepreneurs: The Effect of Protest on Stock Price Returns." *Administrative Science Quarterly* 52(3): 413–42.

Kitschelt, Herbert P. 1989. *The Logics of Party Formation: Ecological Politics in Belgium and West Germany*. Ithaca, NY: Cornell University Press.

Kluger, Richard. 1975. *Simple Justice*. New York: Vintage.

Kolsbun, Ken. 2008. *Peace: The Biography of a Symbol*. Washington, DC: National Geographic.

Kretschmer, Kelsy. 2009. "Contested Loyalties: Dissident Identity Organizations, Institutions, and Social Movements." *Sociological Perspectives* 52(4): 433–54.

Kretschmer, Kelsy. 2019. *Fighting for NOW: Diversity and Discord in the National Organization for Women.* Minneapolis, MN: University of Minnesota Press.

Kretschmer, Kelsy, and David S. Meyer. 2007. "Platform Leadership: Cultivating Support for a Public Profile." *American Behavioral Scientist* 50(10): 1395–412.

Lang, Gladys Engel, and Kurt Lang. 1988. "Recognition and Renown: The Survival of Artistic Reputation." *American Journal of Sociology* 94: 79–109.

Laschever, Eulalie J., and David S. Meyer. 2021. "Growth and Decline of Opposing Movements: Gun Control and Gun Rights, 1945–2015." *Mobilization*, forthcoming.

Levy, Margaret, and Gillian Murphy. 2006. "Coalitions of Contention: The Case of the WTO Protests in Seattle." *Political Studies* 54: 651–70.

Lichterman, Paul. 1996. *The Search for Political Community: American Activists Reinventing Commitment.* New York: Cambridge University Press.

Lipsky, Michael. 1980. *Street Level Bureaucracy: Dilemmas of the Individual in Public Service.* New York: Russell Sage.

Lomax, Alan, Woody Guthrie, and Pete Seeger. 1967. *Hard Hitting Songs for Hard-Hit People.* New York: Oak Publications.

Luders, Joseph E. 2010. *The Civil Rights Movement and the Logic of Social Change.* New York: Cambridge University Press.

Lyman, Princeton N. 2002. *Partner to History: The U.S. Role in South Africa's Transition to Democracy.* Washington, DC: United States Institute of Peace.

Macdonald, Geoffrey, and Luke Waggoner. 2018. "Dashed

Hopes and Extremism in Tunisia." *Journal of Democracy* 29(1): 126–40.

Maier, Pauline. 1972. *From Resistance to Revolution: Colonial Radicals and the Development of American Opposition to Britain, 1765–1776*. New York: Knopf.

Maney, Gregory, Rachel Kutz-Flamenbaum, Deana A. Rohlinger, and Jeff Goodwin, eds. 2012. *Strategies for Social Change*. Minneapolis, MN: University of Minnesota Press.

Mansbridge, Jane. 1986. *Why We Lost the ERA*. Chicago, IL: University of Chicago Press.

Marable, Manning. 1974. "Death of the Quaker Slave Trade." *Quaker History* 63(1): 17–33.

Markham, William T. 2005. "Networking Local Environmental Groups in Germany: The Rise and Fall of the Federal Alliance of Citizens' Initiatives for Environmental Protection (BBU)." *Environmental Politics* 14(5): 667–85.

Marshall, Alex. 2020. "A Polish Museum Turns to the Right, and Artists Turn Away." *The New York Times*, January 8.

Masipa, Tshepo. 2018. "South Africa's Transition to Democracy and Democratic Consolidation: A Reflection on Socio-economic Challenges." *Journal of Public Affairs* 18(4): e1713.

Mason, David S. 1988. "Glasnost, Perestroika and Eastern Europe." *International Affairs* 64(3): 431–48.

Matthews, Nancy. 1994. *Confronting Rape: The Feminist Anti-Rape Movement and the State*. New York: Routledge.

Matthews, Robert O. 1990. "From Rhodesia to Zimbabwe: Prerequisites of a Settlement." *International Journal* 45(2): 292–333.

McAdam, Doug. 1982. *Political Process and the Origins of Black Insurgency*. Chicago, IL: University of Chicago Press.

McAdam, Doug. 1988. *Freedom Summer*. New York: Oxford University Press.

McAdam, Doug, and Yang Su. 2002. "The War at Home: Antiwar Protests and Congressional Voting, 1965 to 1973." *American Sociological Review* 67: 696–721.

McCarthy, John D., and Mayer N. Zald. 1977. "Resource Mobilization and Social Movements: A Partial Theory." *American Journal of Sociology* 82: 1212–41.

McDonnell, Mary Hunter, and Brayden King. 2013. "Keeping Up Appearances: Reputation Threat and Prosocial Responses to Social Movement Boycotts." *Administrative Science Quarterly* 58: 387–419.

McDonnell, Mary Hunter, Brayden King, and Sarah Soule. 2015. "A Dynamic Process Model of Private Politics: Activist Targeting and Corporate Receptivity to Social Challenges." *American Sociological Review* 80: 654–78.

McVeigh, Rory, and Kevin Estep. 2019. *The Politics of Losing: Trump, the Klan, and the Mainstreaming of Resentment.* New York: Columbia University Press.

Meyer, David S. 1990. *A Winter of Discontent: The Nuclear Freeze and American Politics.* New York: Praeger.

Meyer, David S. 1993. "Institutionalizing Dissent: The United States Structure of Political Opportunity and the End of the Nuclear Freeze Movement." *Sociological Forum* 8: 157–79.

Meyer, David S. 2004. "Protest and Political Opportunities." *Annual Review of Sociology* 30: 125–45.

Meyer, David S. 2006. "Claiming Credit: Stories of Movement Influence as Outcomes." *Mobilization* 11(3): 201–18.

Meyer, David S. 2014. *The Politics of Protest: Social Movements in America*, 2nd edn. New York: Oxford University Press.

Meyer, David S. 2019a. "How the Effectiveness of Non-violent Action is the Wrong Question for Activists, Academics, and Everyone Else." In Hank Johnston, ed., *Nonviolent Resistance and the State.* London: Routledge.

Meyer, David S. 2019b. "Review of Sidney M. Milkis and

Daniel J. Tichenor, *Rivalry and Reform: Presidents, Social Movements, and the Transformation of American Politics.*" *Perspectives on Politics* 17(4): 1187–8.

Meyer, David S., and Catherine Corrigall-Brown. 2005. "Coalitions and Political Context: U.S. Movements against Wars in Iraq." *Mobilization* 10(3): 327–44.

Meyer, David S., and Sam Marullo. 1992. "Grassroots Mobilization and International Change." *Research in Social Movements, Conflict and Change* 14: 99–147.

Meyer, David S., and Daisy Verduzco Reyes. 2010. "Social Movements and Contentious Politics." In Kevin Leicht and Craig Jenkins, eds., *Handbook of Politics, State, and Civil Society in a Global Perspective.* New York: Springer Science, pp. 217–33.

Meyer, David S., and Deana Rohlinger. 2012. "Big Books and Social Movements: A Myth of Ideas and Social Change." *Social Problems* 59(1): 136–53.

Meyer, David S., and Suzanne Staggenborg. 1996. "Movements, Countermovements, and the Structure of Political Opportunity." *American Journal of Sociology* 101: 1628–60.

Meyer, David S., and Sidney Tarrow, eds. 1998. *The Social Movement Society: Contentious Politics for a New Century.* Lanham, MD: Rowman & Littlefield.

Meyer, David S., and Nancy Whittier. 1994. "Social Movement Spillover." *Social Problems* 41: 277–98.

Michals, Debra. 2017. "Jane Addams." *National Women's History Museum.* https://www.womenshistory.org/educatio n-resources/biographies/jane-addams

Michels, Roberto. 1962 [1915]. *Political Parties.* New York: Collier.

Milkis, Sidney M., and Daniel J. Tichenor. 2018. *Rivalry and Reform: Presidents, Social Movements, and the*

Transformation of American Politics. Chicago, IL: University of Chicago Press.

Miller, Greg. 2012. "Judge Dismisses PETA's Constitutional Argument to Free SeaWorld Orcas." *Science News*, February 9. https://www.sciencemag.org/news/2012/02/judge-dismisses-petas-constitutional-argument-free-seaworld-orcas#:~:text=A%20federal%20judge%20in%20San, outlaws%20slavery%20and%20involuntary%20servitude

Mische, Ann. 2003. "Cross-talk in Movement: Reconceiving the Culture-Network Link." In Mario Diani and Doug McAdam, eds., *Social Movements and Networks: Relational Approaches to Collective Action*. Oxford: Oxford University Press, pp. 250–80.

Moore, Kelly. 1996. "Organizing Integrity: American Science and the Creation of Public Interest Organizations, 1955–1975." *American Journal of Sociology* 101: 1592–627.

Morris, Aldon D. 1984. *The Origins of the Civil Rights Movement: Black Communities Organizing for Change*. New York: Free Press.

Morris, Aldon D. 2015. *The Scholar Denied: W.E.B. Du Bois and the Birth of Modern Sociology*. Berkeley, CA: University of California Press.

Munson, Ziad. 2009. *The Making of Pro-Life Activists: How Social Movement Mobilization Works*. Chicago, IL: University of Chicago Press.

Nelson, Gaylord. 1980. "Earth Day '70: What It Meant." *EPA Journal*, April. https://archive.epa.gov/epa/aboutepa/earth-day-70-what-it-meant.html

Nepstad, Sharon Erickson. 2004. "Religion, Violence, and Peacemaking." *Journal for the Scientific Study of Religion* 43: 297–301.

Nuborn, Jud, and Annette Dumbach. 2007 [1986]. *Sophie*

Scholl and the White Rose, rev. and exp. edn. Oxford: Oneworld Publications.

Olcese, Cristiana, and Clare Saunders. 2014. "British Students in the Winter Protests: Still a New Social Movement?" In Sarah Pickard, ed., *Higher Education in the UK and the US: Converging University Models in a Global Academic World?* Leiden: Brill, pp. 250–71.

Oliver, Pamela A., Gerald Marwell, and Ruy Teixeira. 1985. "A Theory of Critical Mass: I. Interdependence, Group Heterogeneity, and the Production of Collective Action". *American Journal of Sociology* 91(3): 522–56.

Ost, David. 1990. *Solidarity and the Politics of Anti-Politics: Opposition and Reform in Poland since 1968*. Philadelphia, PA: Temple University Press.

Ost, David. 2006. *The Defeat of Solidarity: Anger and Politics in Postcommunist Europe*. Ithaca, NY: Cornell University Press.

Paine, Thomas. 2019 [1776]. *Common Sense*. https://billofrightsinstitute.org/wp-content/uploads/2019/08/CommonSense.pdf

Parsons, E.C.M., and Naomi A. Rose. 2018. "The Blackfish Effect: Corporate and Policy Change in the Face of Shifting Public Opinion on Captive Cetaceans." *Tourism in Marine Environments* 13(2–3): 73–83.

Paulson, Michael. 2017. "The Battle of 'Miss Saigon': Yellowface, Art and Opportunity." *The New York Times*, March 17.

Perkoski, Evan, and Erica Chenoweth. 2018. *Nonviolent Resistance and Prevention of Mass Killings during Popular Uprisings*. International Center on Nonviolent Conflict, Special Report Series, 2, May. https://www.nonviolent-conflict.org/wp-content/uploads/2017/07/

nonviolent-resistance-and-prevention-of-mass-killings-perkoski-chenoweth-2018-icnc.pdf

Piven, Frances Fox, and Richard A. Cloward. 1977. *Poor People's Movements: How They Succeed, Why They Fail.* New York: Vintage.

Polletta, Francesca. 1998a. "'It Was Like a Fever ...': Narrative and Identity in Social Protest." *Social Problems* 45: 137–59.

Polletta, Francesca. 1998b. "Legacies and Liabilities of an Insurgent Past: Remembering Martin Luther King on the House and Senate Floor." *Social Science History* 22(4): 479–512.

Polletta, Francesca. 1998c. "Contending Stories: Narrative in Social Movements." *Qualitative Sociology* 21: 419–46.

Power, Paul F. 1969. "Gandhi in South Africa." *The Journal of Modern African Studies* 7(3): 441–55.

Power, Samantha. 2002. *A Problem from Hell.* New York: Basic Books.

Radiolab. 2020. "The Flag and the Fury." July 12 (Shima Oliaee, producer). https://www.wnycstudios.org/podcasts/radiolab/articles/flag-and-fury

Raeburn, Nicole C. 2004. *Changing Corporate America from Inside Out.* Minneapolis, MN: University of Minnesota Press.

Ransby, Barbara. 2003. *Ella Baker and the Black Freedom Movement: A Radical Democratic Vision.* Chapel Hill, NC: University of North Carolina Press.

Rao, Sonia. 2019. "Mr. Ratburn Came Out as Gay and Got Married in the 'Arthur' Season Premiere." *The Washington Post,* May 14.

Reger, Jo, and Suzanne Staggenborg. 2006. "Patterns of Mobilization in Local Movement Organizations: Leadership and Strategy in Four National Organization for Women Chapters." *Sociological Perspectives* 49(3): 297–323.

Reynolds-Stenson, Heidi. 2017. "Protesting the Police: Police Brutality Claims as a Predictor of Police Repression of Protest." *Social Movement Studies* 17(1): 48–63.

Richards, Leonard L. 2002. *Shays's Rebellion: The American Revolution's Final Battle*. Philadelphia, PA: University of Pennsylvania Press.

Riley, Naomi Schaefer. 2012. "Clothes that make the ... 3-year-old." *New York Post*, August 25. https://nypost.com/2012/08/25/clothes-that-make-the-3-year-old/

Rinde, Meir. 2017. "Richard Nixon and the Rise of American Environmentalism." *Distillations*, June 2. https://www.sciencehistory.org/distillations/richard-nixon-and-the-rise-of-american-environmentalism

Robles, Frances. 2015. "Dylann Roof Photos and a Manifesto Are Posted on Website." *The New York Times*, June 20.

Robnett, Belinda. 2002. "External Events, Collective Identities, and Participation in Social Movement Organizations." In David S. Meyer, Belinda Robnett, and Nancy Whittier, eds., *Social Movements: Identity, Culture, and the State*. Oxford: Oxford University Press, pp. 266–85.

Rochon, Thomas R. 1998. *Culture Moves: Ideas, Activism, and Changing Values*. Princeton, NJ: Princeton University Press.

Rochon, Thomas R., and David S. Meyer, eds. 1997. *Coalitions and Political Movements: The Lessons of the Nuclear Freeze*. Boulder, CO: Lynne Rienner Publishers.

Rohlinger, Deana A. 2015. *Abortion Politics, Mass Media and Social Movements in America*. Cambridge: Cambridge University Press.

Rohlinger, Deana A. 2019. *New Media and Society*. New York: New York University Press.

Rome, Adam. 2003. "'Give Earth a Chance': The Environmental

Movement and the Sixties." *The Journal of American History* 90(2): 525–54.

Roscigno Vincent J., and William F. Danaher. 2004. *The Voice of Southern Labor: Radio, Music, and Textile Strikes, 1929–1934*. Minneapolis, MN: University of Minnesota Press.

Rosenstone, Stephen J., and John Mark Hansen. 1993. *Mobilization, Participation, and Democracy in America*. New York: Macmillan.

Roy, William G. 2010. *Reds, Whites, and Blues: Social Movements, Folk Music, and Race in the United States*. Princeton, NJ: Princeton University Press.

Rucht, Dieter. 1999. "The Impact of Environmental Movements in Western Societies." In Marco Giugni, Doug McAdam, and Charles Tilly, eds., *How Movements Matter: Theoretical and Comparative Studies on the Consequences of Social Movements*, Minneapolis, MN: University of Minnesota Press, pp. 204–24.

Sawyers, Traci M., and David S. Meyer. 1999. "Missed Opportunities: Social Movement Abeyance and Public Policy." *Social Problems* 46(2): 187–206.

Schattschneider, E.E. 1960. *The Semi-Sovereign People*. New York: Holt, Rinehart & Winston.

Scheppele, Kim Lane. 2015. "Understanding Hungary's Constitutional Revolution." In Armin von Bogdandy and Pál Sonnevend, eds., *Constitutional Crisis in the European Constitutional Area*. New York: Hart Publishing, pp. 111–24.

Schiff, Stacy. 2020. "The Boston Tea Party Was More Than That. It Was a Riot." *The New York Times*, August 13. https://www.nytimes.com/2020/08/13/opinion/protests-monuments-history.html

Schock, Kurt. 2004. *Unarmed Insurrections: People Power Movements in Nondemocracies*. Minneapolis, MN: University of Minnesota Press.

Schuman, Howard, and Jacqueline Scott. 1989. "Generations and Collective Memories." *American Sociological Review* 54: 359–81.

Schwartz, Barry. 1996. "Memory as a Cultural System: Abraham Lincoln in World War II." *American Sociological Review* 61: 908–27.

Schwartz, Mildred. 2002. "Factions and the Continuity of Political Challengers." In David S. Meyer, Nancy Whittier, and Belinda Robnett, eds., *Social Movements: Identity, Culture, and the State*. New York: Oxford University Press, pp. 157–70.

Shapiro, Ian, and Kareen Tebeau, eds. 2011. *After Apartheid: Reinventing South Africa?* Charlottesville, VA: University of Virginia Press.

Shoshan, Aya. 2018. "Habitus and Social Movements: How Militarism Affects Organizational Repertoires." *Social Movement Studies* 17(2): 144–58.

Siani-Davies, Peter. 2007. *The Romanian Revolution of December 1989*. Ithaca, NY: Cornell University Press.

Signer, Michael. 2020. *Cry Havoc: Charlottesville and American Democracy under Siege*. New York: Public Affairs.

Simi, Pete, Kathleen Blee, Matthew DeMichele, and Steven Windisch. 2017. "Addicted to Hate: Identity Residual among Former White Supremacists." *American Sociological Review* 82(6): 1167–87.

Simi, Pete, and Robert Futtrell. 2010. *American Swastika: Inside the White Power Movement's Hidden Spaces of Hate*. Lanham, MD: Rowman & Littlefield.

Sitkoff, Harvard. 1981. *The Struggle for Black Equality, 1954–1980*. New York: Hill and Wang.

Slaughter, Thomas P. 1986. *The Whiskey Rebellion: Frontier Epilogue to the American Revolution*. Oxford: Oxford University Press.

Small, Melvin. 1988. *Johnson, Nixon, and the Doves*. New Brunswick, NJ: Rutgers University Press.

Smith, Christian. 1996. *Resisting Reagan: The U.S. Central America Peace Movement*. Chicago, IL: University of Chicago Press.

Snow, David A., and Robert D. Benford. 1992. "Master Frames and Cycles of Protest." In Carol McClurg Mueller and Aldon D. Morris, eds., *Frontiers of Social Movement Theory*. New Haven, CT: Yale University Press, pp. 133–55.

Sorkin, Amy Davidson. 2015. "Why 'Selma' Is More Than Fair to L.B.J." *The New Yorker*, January 22.

Soule, Sarah A. 1997. "The Student Divestment Movement in the United States and Tactical Diffusion: The Shantytown Protest." *Social Forces* 75(3): 855–82.

Soule, Sarah A. 2014. "Going to the Chapel? Same-Sex Marriage Bans in the United States, 1973–2000." *Social Problems* 51(4): 453–77.

Southern Poverty Law Center. 2020. *Whose Heritage: Public Symbols of the Confederacy*. Montgomery, AL: SPLC. https://www.splcenter.org/sites/default/files/com_whose_heritage.pdf

Spector, Malcolm, and John I. Kitsuse. 2001. *Constructing Social Problems*. New Brunswick, NJ: Transaction Books.

Springborg, Robert. 2017. "The Rewards of Failure: Persisting Military Rule in Egypt." *British Journal of Middle Eastern Studies* 44(4): 478–96.

Staggenborg, Suzanne. 1988. "The Consequences of Professionalization and Formalization in the ProChoice Movement." *American Sociological Review* 53: 585–605.

Staggenborg, Suzanne. 1991. *The Pro-Choice Movement.* New York: Oxford University Press.

Stone, Deborah. 1997. *Policy Paradox: The Art of Political Decision Making.* New York: Norton.

Tarrow, Sidney. 2011. *Power in Movement*, 3rd edn. New York: Cambridge University Press.

Taylor, Verta A. 1989. "Social Movement Continuity: The Women's Movement in Abeyance." *American Sociological Review* 54: 761–75.

Taylor, Verta, and Nancy Whittier. 1992. "Collective Identity in Social Movement Communities." In Aldon D. Morris and Carol McClurg Mueller, eds., *Frontiers in Social Movement Theory.* New Haven, CT: Yale University Press, pp. 104–29.

Theoharis, Jeanne. 2018. *A More Beautiful and Terrible History: Beyond the Fables of the Civil Rights Movement.* Boston, MA: Beacon Press.

Thorne, Barrie. 1975. "Protest and the Problem of Credibility: Uses of Knowledge and Risk-Taking in the Draft Resistance Movement of the 1960's." *Social Problems* 23(2): 111–23.

Thulin, Lila. 2019. "How an Oil Spill 50 Years Ago Inspired the First Earth Day." *Smithsonian*, April 22. https://www.smithsonianmag.com/history/how-oil-spill-50-years-ago-inspired-first-earth-day-180972007/

Tilly, Charles. 1978. *From Mobilization to Revolution.* Reading, MA: Addison-Wesley.

Tilly, Charles. 2003. *Stories, Identities, and Political Change.* Lanham, MD: Rowman & Littlefield.

Tismaneanu, Vladimir. 2011. *Promises of 1968 Crisis, Illusion, and Utopia.* Budapest: Central European University Press.

Tucker, Robert C., ed. 1978. *The Marx-Engels Reader*, 2nd edn. New York: Norton.

Tufekci, Zeynep. 2017. *Twitter and Tear Gas: The Power*

and Fragility of Networked Protest. New Haven, CT: Yale University Press.

Voss, Kim. 1998. "Claim Making and the Framing of Defeats: The Interpretation of Losses by American British Labor Activists, 1886–1895." In Michael P. Hanagan, Leslie Page Moch, and Wayne te Brake, eds., *Challenging Authority: The Historical Study of Contentious Politics*. Minneapolis, MN: University of Minnesota Press, pp. 136–48.

Walgrave, Stefaan, and Dieter Rucht, eds. 2010. *The World Says No to War*. Minneapolis, MN: University of Minnesota Press.

Weed, Frank J. 1995. *Certainty of Justice: Reform in the Crime Victim Movement*. New York: Aldine de Gruyter.

Weinberger, Caspar W. 1990. *Fighting for Peace: Seven Critical Years in the Pentagon*. New York: Warner Books.

Whalen, Jack, and Richard Flacks. 1989. *Beyond the Barricades: The Sixties Generation Grows Up*. Philadelphia, PA: Temple University Press.

Whittier, Nancy. 1995. *Feminist Generations: The Persistence of the Radical Women's Movement*. Philadelphia, PA: Temple University Press.

Wills, Garry. 1978. *Inventing America: Jefferson's Declaration of Independence*. New York: Random House.

Wilson, James Q. 1995. *Political Organizations*, 2nd edn. Princeton, NJ: Princeton University Press.

Zald, Mayer N., and John D. McCarthy. 1987. *Social Movements in an Organizational Society*. New Brunswick, NJ: Transaction Books.

Zhao, Dingxin. 2001. *The Power of Tiananmen: State-Society Relations and the 1989 Beijing Student Movement*. Chicago, IL: University of Chicago Press.

Index